AUTHENTIC LEADERSHIP EFFECTIVENESS

for Individuals and Teams

ENDORSEMENTS

For those who struggle with the internal question of how to become a more effective leader and a fulfilled person at work and home, this book by Tineke Wulffers is a must-read. It does not dwell only on theory and academic examples but goes straight into real-life case studies and the structure of a programme that improves authentic leadership effectiveness. I personally enjoyed the case study of a journey embarked on by a leader, followed by his team. The business results and personal growth of everybody involved was amazing. It is clear that although the change took considerable time and resources, the payback from the improved business results was incredibly quick.

Jan Nothnagel, Plant Manager, SA Breweries

"Enough is enough" – a recent and by now famous quote from the UK Prime Minister on terrorism! In South Africa and elsewhere many have a similar sentiment about the state of current leadership in some of our organisations and countries. If you share that sentiment on leadership, this book by Dr Wulffers is a *"must-read"*. What really excited me are the personal benefits one can achieve through the Authentic Leadership journey. Getting to know and understand yourself better and becoming comfortable with yourself and the values you stand for, is a great foundation for any leader. Translating that personal comfort into improved results (as clearly demonstrated by Wulffers in her documented case studies) still requires good leadership, but the job is all but done. Once you understand the concept of leadership authenticity, the power of it lies in its simplicity and the excitement of the iterative journey of self-exploration, personal happiness, improved relationships and leadership, better business results and, most importantly, sustainability. This well documented coaching program of Wulffers offers a clear roadmap in achieving exactly that.

Willem Bosman, Brewery Operations Director – Mozambique and Malawi, Anheuser-Busch InBev SA/ NV (AB InBev)

This book takes one on a highly personal journey of confronting oneself as a leader to be truly authentic to the self, others, but most importantly, God. Reading it, I am reminded not only of my own personal leadership journey of growth, but I somehow found myself connecting even more with my truly authentic self. This is not a once-off literary read but a practical life tool that needs to be constantly revisited as we journey through life in our quest to be the best version of ourselves as we can truly be. The convenience of accessing such rich and helpful life tools in one book is the cherry on top for me. This is a must for any individual and collective leadership looking to unleash their inner selves, embrace their true purpose in their organisations and on this earth, and to live an enriched life!

Kgomotso Molobye, Managing Executive – Human Resources, Openserve

After reading this book, I realised that once you develop Authentic Leadership, everything seems to fall into place. The word *regulate* that was used as part of the process, has taken on a new meaning for me. I resonate with the values and morals of this journey. If you are willing to embark on this, you will be equipped with something great – a total shift in who you are. It made me realise that we can all become ineffective if we do not commit to change. I am now convinced that 'silver bullet' programmes, which are sometimes used in desperation to put a plaster over something that is not yet in place, do not work. Finally, Neo's story resonated with me, which made me realise that the impact of this journey is immense.

Hajira Fewster, Head of Human Resources, Sub Sahara Africa, Thomson Reuters

Tineke has produced a profound and timely work here. She has managed to beautifully, yet boldly articulate the dire leadership need we experience today. More than that, she has provided a way forward that reflects the kind of leadership she espouses. I found myself resonating deeply with her words, many times wanting to shout out, "That's what I've been trying to say for so long!" Years of deep reflection, thought, research and experience in working with leaders have allowed her to produce a masterpiece that needs to become a classic in the leadership library.

Mark Holtshousen, Master Executive Coach & Head of Global Career Management at MTN Group

From the start, this book punched me in the stomach and spoke to my heart. It is a bitter-sweet reminder that previous successes do not necessarily result in Authentic Leadership, and that the world desperately needs people, not just leaders, to embark on this journey. This journey is not, however, for the faint-hearted. It also will not fit all organisations because an organisation has to be truly willing to shift its mindset. Any organisation that is ready for true transformation should embark on this journey; just by committing to it, one would know that this organisation believes in the concepts derived from the greatest theorists and humanists. From my years of experience in understanding human behaviour, I can guarantee that those who do embark on the journey will, without a doubt, be more successful. Drawing information and understanding from these thought leaders, you end up with a knot in your stomach as you realise what it actually takes to be an authentic leader. If all people could take this journey, the world would be a better place.

Simone Vorster, Human Resource Strategist, Sub Sahara Africa, Thomson Reuters

Authentic Leadership Effectiveness for Individuals and Teams combines the best from academic literature with a practical approach as to how to develop this type of leadership effectiveness in real life. As HR professional, I enjoyed reading it, and I recommend this book to every coach, peer and leader who wants to make a difference and drive change from within. A brilliant piece of work!

Debbie Hameetman, Director: Human Resource Management for Manufacturing Europe, SABIC

Tineke brings a fresh, insightful perspective to how coaching can change lives in the workplace and beyond. Her years of experience in the coaching and leadership development field allow her to distil new ways of thinking and applying coaching. An essential read for those serious about transforming leadership and lives through coaching.

Lindsay Falkov, People Advisory Services – Executive Director, Ernst and Young LLP

Dr. Tineke Wulffers chose to write this book through the lens of a coach-practitioner. It is underpinned with relevant and robust theory and, at the same time, offers very practical and believable evidence that a programme designed to develop Authentic Leadership Effectiveness, works! I shall try to sum up the gems I discovered to enhance my own growth as well as that of my clients. Authentic leaders are spiritually informed beacons of hope who embrace truth and ethicality. They strive to be nobody but their best selves. The key to achieving this is a keen focus on character and substance, and not leadership style. Through heightened awareness and true introspection, leaders and teams of substance have reached a level of consciousness where they are motivated by a clarified (and in teams, co-created and agreed) purpose, values and contribution. They lead others with positive intent by inspiring trust and transparency, and in so doing, build effective leader-follower relations. The biggest learning for me personally from Tineke's work is how to display appropriate vulnerability and how to foster an environment where teams can do the same. I felt a strong sense of her true self being represented in her work and, just like a good novel, could not put it down, once I had started reading. What a blessing you have brought to the leadership-space!

Dr Salome van Coller-Peter, Head of MPhil in Management Coaching, University of Stellenbosch Business School, and author of the book Coaching Leadership Teams

In a time when so many are despondent about an apparent global void of high-calibre leaders, Tineke Wulffers' book on authentic leadership is a welcome call to both reflection and action. The text provides not only rich insights on the topic, but also serves as a helpful guide for coaches who seek to work with open-minded clients to build authentic leadership expertise.

Professor Nicola Kleyn, Dean: The University of Pretoria's Gordon Institute of Business Science

First published in 2017

ISBN: 978-1-86922-706-7 (Printed)
ISBN: 978-1-86922-707-4 (ePDF)

Published by KR Publishing
P O Box 3954
Randburg
2125
Republic of South Africa

Tel: (011) 706-6009
Fax: (011) 706-1127
E-mail: orders@knowres.co.za
Website: www.kr.co.za

Printed and bound: HartWood Digital Printing, 243 Alexandra Avenue, Halfway House, Midrand
Typesetting, layout and design: Cia Joubert, cia@knowres.co.za
Cover design: Marlene de Villiers, marlene@knowres.co.za
Editing and proofreading: Valda Strauss: valda@global.co.za
Project management: Cia Joubert, cia@knowres.co.za

AUTHENTIC LEADERSHIP EFFECTIVENESS

for Individuals and Teams

A Coaching Approach

by

Tineke Wulffers

kr
publishing

2017

ACKNOWLEDGMENTS

After 25 years in the IT software development industry, I chose in 2004 to change careers so that I could be psychologically more available to my young daughter at that time. My exploration of 'where to next?' led to my introduction to coaching, and more specifically, leadership coaching. However, wondering what more I needed to learn to enrich my coaching practice, in 2007, I enriched my coaching training and practice by embarking on a work-based learning Masters in Professional Coaching where I developed an interest in the development of authentic leadership, using a coaching approach. My Masters research was followed by some considerable work-based learning doctoral research on developing individual and team authentic leadership effectiveness, graduating in 2014 with a PhD in Personal and Professional Leadership. This book is the culmination of a fourteen-year journey that started in 2004. I could not have done so without the immense support and assistance from the following people, to whom I am deeply grateful.

- To all those leaders, both in South Africa and globally, whom I have had the pleasure to partner in their courageous journeys towards increased authentic leadership effectiveness. I hold you in such high esteem, as I have learnt and grown together with you!
- Specifically to those leaders that have allowed me to interview them about their experiences of their authentic leadership development journeys with me.
- To Dr Adrian Chan, one of the seminal researchers and authors on authentic leadership who influenced my work. Not only did he put time aside to write the foreword for me, but he also initially had the courage to look at my first draft of my book, with valuable feedback and guidance. How he managed to make sense of that first draft, still eludes me today!
- To Professor Nicola Kleyn, Dean of the Gordon Institute of Business Science, who allowed me to interview her on the leadership authenticity of Advocate Thuli Madonsela.
- To all those very busy leaders, who humbly and delightfully agreed to read my book, with the possibility of endorsing it. Request time from a busy leader, and they are likely to offer it!
- To Wilhelm Crous, Cia Joubert, and the publishing team at Knowledge Resources who have made it their business to disseminate the rich knowledge that we collectively have in South Africa. You are such a wonderful support and inspiration to researchers and authors!
- To Kathy Bennett, my dear friend and colleague. We have supported each other since 2006 whilst we travelled together on our academic and professional journeys. I am so blessed!
- To my housekeeper and friend, Anna Nkobele, who over the last 21 years has had unwavering faith in me, and who has always been there to support me. You're the best!

- To my beloved daughter, Hayley, who has walked this journey with me, and who has encouraged me to complete this work when I was ready to give it up for adoption. I love you!
- Finally, to Spirit, the Universe, the All-That-Is, I have marvelled at the support I received throughout this journey, often in extraordinary ways, sometimes with a bit of mischievous humour in the mix. All in all it confirms that I am on the journey that is destined for me.

DEDICATION

Leadership in general, be it that of a country, a political party, an organisation, or even at times academic or religious institution, is in crisis. The wellness of any system depends so much on the wellness of its leadership, and, as per the message in the poem *The Dash*, there is a new consciousness arising that we need to leave this world having provided a better legacy for our children.

The Dash

I read of a man who stood to speak
At the funeral of his friend.
He referred to the dates on her tombstone
from the Beginning ... to the End

He noted that first came the date of her birth and
Spoke of the second with tears,
But he said that what mattered most of all was the
Dash between those years.

For that dash represents all the time that she spent
Alive on earth,
And now only those who loved her
Know what that little line is worth

For it matters not, how much we own, the cars,
The house, the cash.
What matters is how we live and love
And how we spend our dash.

So think about this long and hard,
Are there things you'd like to change?
For you never know how much time is left.
(you could be at 'dash mid-range').

If we could just slow down enough to consider what's
True and what is real,
And always try to understand
The way other people feel.

And be less quick to anger,
And show appreciation more
And love the people in our lives
Like we've never loved before.

If we treat each other with respect, and more often
Wear a smile,
Remembering that this special dash
Might only last a little while

So, when your eulogy is being read
With your life's actions to rehash...
Would you be pleased with the things they have to say
About how you spent your dash?

– Anonymous –

I hereby dedicate the research shared in this book to a truly authentic leader, our beloved Tata Madiba – Nelson Mandela, who passed away at the age of 95 on 5th December 2013. When I read his published notes, and letters to loved ones during his 27 years in prison, now published in a book called *Conversations with Myself*, I realised that Madiba had found the secrets of the development of authentic leadership. This was despite the fact that in those days there were very few publications on authentic leadership, what it was, its impact, and criteria for developing such leadership. It felt to me that he could have written the books on such leadership, as the following letter from his Kroonstad Prison to his wife, dated 1 February 1975 illustrates[1].

...the cell is an ideal place to learn to know yourself, to search realistically and regularly the process of your own mind and feelings. In judging our progress as individuals, we tend to concentrate on external factors such as one's social position, influence and popularity, wealth and standard of education. These are, of course, important in measuring one's success in material matters and it is perfectly understandable if many people exert themselves mainly to achieve all these. But internal factors may be even more crucial in assessing one's development as a human being. Honesty, sincerity, simplicity, humility, pure generosity, absence of vanity, readiness to serve others – qualities which are within easy reach of every soul – are the foundation of one's spiritual life. Development in matters of this nature is inconceivable without serious introspection, without knowing yourself, your weaknesses and mistakes. At least, if for nothing else, the cell gives you the opportunity to look daily into your entire conduct, to overcome the bad and develop whatever is good in you. Regular meditation, say about 15 minutes a day before you turn in, can be very fruitful in this regard. You may find it difficult at first to pinpoint the negative features in your life, but the 10th attempt may yield rich rewards. Never forget that a saint is a sinner who keeps trying.

May his legacy live on; may future leadership take a leaf from his book and lead by an authentic leadership presence, like he did, being more true to self and leadership positions, with a moral and ethical underpinning, that considers the greater good of all!

CONTENTS

List of figures

FOREWORD BY DR ADRIAN CHAN

The world we live in today is one in which our traditional anchors of reality have been dislodged from their moorings. As leaders, we spend more time online in an electronically constructed alternate reality than in the real world. When interacting with those we lead, we would rather transact with them through an electronic medium that allows for a high degree of freedom for us to be who we really are not.

Indeed, what is the reality that leaders engage with these days? It used to be that leaders would seek to know the reality of the landscape so that they could lead with clarity. These days, it is now passé to operate based on truth and reality. Instead, leaders have become content with having different shades of truth and blatant lies conveniently passed off as half-truths, each asserting itself as all that is sufficient for the moment.

When a leader's notion of reality is shaped by shades of truths and half-truths, it may appear no longer necessary to be true to oneself. We become who we need to be in order to be well regarded by others in various social settings. We become who we need to be out of convenience, in order to get what we want from others. The high ideals, aspirations and drive to be the best that is expected of any leader, can become watered down to a level that is 'good enough for the moment' and nothing more.

Such is the new acceptable norm for leaders today. We are besieged on all sides and from within, to blend in, to conform, to compromise, and to lose the very elements that define our uniqueness and drive for better versions of ourselves.

It is against this backdrop that this book is timely. This book reminds us that we need to be authentic, to remain true to ourselves in the face of internal and external factors that may influence us to be otherwise. We need reminders that there is intrinsic value in being and behaving authentically – a value that is timeless and transcendent above the temporary social selves we take on in order to interact with the world and achieve material goals.

This book teaches us how to be authentic, first as human beings and then as leaders in our respective spheres of influence. We are all leaders blessed with our own unique spheres of influences, which we can abuse for temporary, self-indulgent benefits or use for the greater good of self and others. As leaders, we must not only be true to ourselves as human beings – we must aspire to be the best versions of ourselves for the sake of those that we lead and for the purpose for which we have been called to lead.

When we can lead with authenticity at the level of the best versions of ourselves, we point the way for others. We illuminate the way for others who have allowed their social self-constructs to fragment their sense of who they really are. We develop an inner resilience and wisdom to serve as a buffer and anchor against the tides of volatility, uncertainty, complexity and ambiguity that threaten to overwhelm our very sense of humanity.

I trust that in reading this book, you will undertake a personal journey of self-exploration, discovery and transformation. In order to experience the leadership we aspire to, there is so much that needs to be done and so little time in which to do it!

Adrian Chan, PhD
Leadership Resource Person
His Majesty's Secretariat
Kingdom of Bhutan

ABOUT THE AUTHOR

Tineke Wulffers divides her time between her practitioner and academic work. She is the director of the Moya Institute of Authentic Leadership Effectiveness. At times, her senior organisational leadership clients tell her that the organisational world can *squeeze the self out of the self*. In response, her passion is to facilitate the development of individual and team authentic leadership effectiveness for the greater good not only of themselves, but also their organisations and stakeholders. Her work allows leaders to enhance their leadership authenticity, inter-relational trust, and individual and team leadership effectiveness.

Tineke facilitates individual and team authentic leadership effectiveness and executive coaching journeys mainly at senior and executive organisational levels. She also trains leaders how to use coaching in their interactions with others. Her client list includes senior and executive leadership and management within organisations such as Adcock Ingram, EDCON, ABSA Bank, Absa Capital Bank, Standard Bank, FNB, Nedbank, Gold Fields, Cisco, AngloGold Ashanti, Johannesburg Water, Gauteng Provincial Government, Industrial Development Corporation, Sasol (Pty) Ltd, Anheuser-Busch InBev SA/NV (AB InBev), SABIC, Unicef, MTN and Vodacom. She works globally with leaders in South Africa, Europe, the Middle East, and the United States.

As an academic, she is affiliated with the University of Stellenbosch Business School (USB) and Wits Business School (WBS) in South Africa where she supervises and examines the work of post-graduate Masters and Doctoral students. She also lectures at various business schools, mostly on the topic of the development of authentic leadership effectiveness. She obtained her PhD in Personal and Professional Leadership in the Faculty of Management at the University of Johannesburg (SA) in 2014, and in 2009, she completed her Masters (cum laude) in Professional Coaching through Middlesex University (UK). She regularly writes academic articles on authentic leadership development, and she is a contributing author to a definitive book on leadership, entitled *Leadership – Perspectives from the Frontline*, published by Knowledge Resources in 2016.

Of Dutch parents but born in Port Elizabeth, South Africa, Tineke has both Dutch and South African nationality. She lives with her daughter in Johannesburg, South Africa, and is passionate about making a difference in the quality and calibre of leadership, both in South Africa and globally, in order to leave this world in a better place than she has found it. In her spare time, she loves hiking, mountainbiking, canoeing, listening to music, watching dance, reading, and travelling. For more information, visit: www.moyatf.co.za.

PREFACE

True leadership has always been more difficult to maintain in challenging times, but the unique stressors facing organisations throughout the world today call for renewed attention to what constitutes truly positive leadership. There is clearly a need for a better quality of leadership and higher leadership effectiveness, both at an individual and team level, and authentic leadership is often proposed to address these concerns. Much has been written about what authentic leadership (AL) is, and the positive effect of such leadership. Less is available on considerations towards the development of authentic leadership, and very little has been written about authentic leadership development interventions.

This book is aimed at various audiences. As the work is based both on academic and practitioner research, it might well be useful as a prescribed leadership and coaching book in business schools. On a more pragmatic level, it is targeted at organisational leadership development stakeholders, whether these are the leaders themselves, the leadership and organisational development departments, or leadership coaches.

The theoretical rationale underpinning this book is the notion that leadership authenticity builds trust, and that the development of inter-relational trust and trustworthiness builds and strengthens individual and team leadership effectiveness. As this work rests on the shoulders of giants in the research on AL, especially the earlier chapters in this book will specifically acknowledge these theoretical perspectives on the various aspects of AL, which will be combined with the author's own experiential understanding of these aspects.

This book aims to provide an outline of an effective individual and team authentic leadership effectiveness (ALE) programme, designed by the author, who herself is an ALE development facilitator. This will allow organisations to gain knowledge of an effective programme methodology, which is used daily, and has been evaluated in a doctoral study. The sense is that the development of authentic leadership requires a lifetime of experiences, and organisations do not always have the luxury of time for that to happen. An effective authentic leadership programme could considerably shorten the time required for the development of such positive and effective leadership, for the greater good of any organisation and its various stakeholders.

Overview

This book is divided up as follows.

Part I – Definition and Impact of Authentic Leadership – considers the need for authentic leadership, gives an overview of what is generally understood by authentic leadership. It also focuses on the impact of leadership authenticity on inter-relational trust, and on individual and team authentic leadership effectiveness.

Chapter 1 – Why the need for Authentic Leadership? – considers the need for authentic leadership by discussing the state of leadership today. An overview of the consequences of poor leadership is followed by introducing a better quality of leadership, with a brief introduction to leadership authenticity, the impact of leadership authenticity, development criteria for such leadership, and a consideration of leadership authenticity programmes to fast-track such developments. This chapter concludes with the rationale for better leadership and some well-known South African examples of authentic leadership.

Chapter 2 – Authentic Leadership Defined – gives a theoretical overview on authentic leadership. It introduces the concept of authenticity, and more specifically leadership authenticity, with specific consideration of a social cognitive view and processes involved in sustaining leadership authenticity. It concludes with some converging and diverging thoughts on leadership authenticity.

Chapter 3 – Applying Authentic Leadership – commences with the consequences of inauthentic moments during the leadership terms of well-known leaders. This is followed by interviews on the positive effect of authentic leadership moments on intrapersonal trust, followed by interpersonal trust between leaders and followers, and, as authentic leadership is a leadership by presence, authentic leaders may even have followers senior to them. The positive effect of leadership authenticity on individual leadership effectiveness is discussed, followed by an overview of the effect of authentic leadership on team leadership effectiveness, with specific focus on both lateral and vertical team leadership effectiveness. The discussion concludes with a consideration of the impact of authentic leadership on organisational outcomes and results.

Part II – Development of Authentic Leadership – forms the crux of this book. As the development of authentic leadership requires different considerations to what is mostly espoused in the field of leadership development, considerations and criteria for AL development and AL programmes are discussed. This is followed by a high-level and detailed overview of this specific individual and team ALE programme, which might well be a first. Finally, Part II concludes with a detailed, followed by three high-level case studies of the effects of the ALE programme under discussion.

Chapter 4 – Development of Authentic Leadership – discusses development levels towards the highest leadership effectiveness. It highlights the aspects that need to be included in such a development journey, followed by the importance of leader developmental readiness and commitment towards growing leadership authenticity. It considers how the development of political acumen can enhance authentic leadership, and how the development of such leadership can be measured.

Chapter 5 – Criteria for an AL Programme – commences with a discussion on the criteria for AL programmes in particular. The rationale for a coaching style of facilitation is discussed, followed by an outline of the various types of individual and team coaching modalities. It highlights the skills required across the board in individual and team coaching, and considers the role and importance of the presence of the authentic leadership coach, and more specifically the AL facilitator. It concludes with additional requirements, such as leader development readiness, and sustainability of the effects of AL development in a world that continually changes.

Chapter 6 – The Authentic Leadership Programme: High-level Underpinnings. Using a *stories approach*, very common in the development of leadership authenticity, it commences by sharing my profile as the developer and facilitator of this programme. It shares my thoughts and beliefs about the important considerations in the development of leadership authenticity, and links this to theoretical proposed guidelines. It outlines the conceptual framework that underpins this programme, and the coaching style used to facilitate this programme. It concludes with a systemic overview of the usual structure of an AL programme such as this one.

Chapter 7 – The Authentic Leadership Programme: A Detailed Overview. This chapter commences by outlining the structure of the overall programme. It continues by outlining the process model and the programme components used in each of the six steps in the development of the individual ALE, followed by the three steps in development of team ALE. In each step, it outlines the theoretical underpinnings, followed by feedback from the field. Finally, it highlights the tailorability of such a programme, together with considerations towards sustaining such outcomes in a world of uncertainty where the only thing that is constant is change.

Chapter 8 – Authentic Leadership Programme Effect: Detailed Case Study. This detailed case study focuses on my doctoral study, during which the direct programme effect on personal, interpersonal and organisational leadership authenticity, followed by the further effect on developing inter-relational trust, individual and team authentic leadership effectiveness, were evaluated.

Chapter 9 – Authentic Leadership Programme Effect: High-level Case Studies – reports on three case studies with a different focus on authentic leadership development in each case study. The first case study explores the story of an executive leader who, together with his leadership team, embarked on a journey of developing individual and team authentic leadership effectiveness, with a specific focus on the impact it had on their business results. The second case study explores whether authentic leadership and political acumen can co-exist. Finally, the third case study highlights views from the field on how individual and team authentic leadership can be sustained when all else constantly changes.

Part III – Well-known Examples of Leaders Through the Lens of Authentic Leadership – even though AL programmes have not really been available before, such leadership can be developed by means of introspection and commitment to further development during a lifetime of life experiences and work episodes.

Chapter 10 – Well-known Leaders Through the Lens of Authentic Leadership – reflects on what happens when personal and professional authentic leadership is lacking. This is followed by viewing through the lens of authentic leadership two well-known leadership examples, those being Helen Suzman, an erstwhile political opponent of the South African apartheid government, and Nelson Mandela, the first President of democratic South Africa, illustrating why they were such influential leaders.

Chapter 11 – A Final Word – considers the leadership lessons that emanate from these comparisons, followed by my personal reflections, as the author of this book.

ACRONYMNS

AL	Authentic leadership
ALD	Authentic leadership development
ALE	Authentic leadership effectiveness
ALEC	Authentic Leadership Effectiveness Charter
ALP	Authentic leadership programme
ANC	African National Congress
KBI	Key behavioural indicator
KPI	Key performance indicator
LDL	Leadership development level
MP	Member of Parliament
NEC	National executive council
POB	Positive organisational behaviour
POS	Positive organisational scholarship
RJ	Reflective journaling
SA	South Africa
VUCA	Volatile, uncertain, complex, ambiguous

PART I:

DEFINITION AND IMPACT OF AUTHENTIC LEADERSHIP

Chapter 1

WHY THE NEED FOR AUTHENTIC LEADERSHIP?

Not all leadership positions are filled by great and natural leaders, and similarly, one does not have to fill a leadership position in order to be experienced by self and others as a great leader. This implies that there is not always a direct relationship between leadership positions and leaders.

Martin Kalungu-Banda, in his book *Leading like Madiba*, reminds us that the "world is in dire need of great leaders, ones who inspire people not through words but by serving them; extraordinary leaders who attend to others and become beacons of hope"[2]. He further points out that this is required not only in the political contexts, but also in business organisations. Whereas people in organisations are often described as human resources, they are much more than that. They are not merely resources that are restricted to the work context, they are human beings, of different genders, races, religions, and ages, and what universally extraordinary leaders do, is to unite rather than polarise societies and nations. When extraordinary leaders become beacons of hope, they inspire others to be the best they can be as well. The word 'inspire' always reminds me of the word 'spiritual'; extraordinary leaders are driven by more than just their own egos; they are spiritually informed to consider the well-being of all those on whom they are able to have a positive effect. It becomes their life and leadership purpose, as was the case for Wangari Maathai in Kenya, and Nelson Mandela and still for Archbishop Desmond Tutu in South Africa, who all were recipients of the Nobel Peace Prize.

This chapter looks at the current state of leadership, and the consequences thereof. It considers the need for a better quality of leadership, and introduces the notion of AL. It briefly considers what AL is, the impact that such quality of leadership can have, and important criteria to consider when wishing to develop such leadership in organisations. Until recently, it appeared not to be possible to develop AL via a programme, but this has changed, and this book therefore focuses on how such leadership can be developed via an appropriate programme. Both Mandela and Tutu, well-known South African examples, are briefly viewed through the lens of AL, in order to give more meaning to this notion. This chapter concludes by inviting you to engage in an interactive leadership discussion on what the state of leadership is in your organisation and your country.

LEADERSHIP TODAY

True leadership has always been more difficult to maintain in challenging times, but the unique stressors facing organisations throughout the volatile, uncertain, complex, and ambiguous (VUCA) world today call for a renewed attention to what constitutes true and ethical leadership. These challenges have resulted in renewed focus on how our leaders can restore confidence, hope, and optimism. Leaders need to be agile and resilient, and be able to respond appropriately to catastrophic and extraordinary events. Leaders can also help those whom they serve in their search for meaning and connection by fostering new self-awareness. This requires that they genuinely relate to all stakeholders, whether these are employees, customers, suppliers, owners, and even communities. This is a big ask, as it requires that leaders need to be the change they wish to see, by developing own self-awareness and understanding what is meaningful to them.

I agree with Bill George, well-known author on AL, when he asserts that there is a need for leaders who lead with purpose, values, and integrity, who build enduring organisations, motivate their staff to provide superior customer service, and who create long-term value for shareholders. When problems surfaced at, for instance, Anderson, Tyco and Transmile, the extent of the leadership crisis within organisations became apparent, creating a widespread erosion of trust in business leaders. More recently, reputable international organisations such as Volkswagen who have admitted to cheating in emissions tests in their diesel cars in the US, received considerable press exposure[3] due to their extreme unethical behaviour. George[4] reminds us that what the world is searching for now is a way of leading that is based on character and substance rather than style of leadership, and integrity rather than image or position, in order to equip leaders to rebuild trust and to create compelling futures for themselves and their organisations.

We are continually reminded of the immensely negative impact of unethical leadership. We see it daily in the press, relating to both political and business dealings; we experience the heartache it creates for us in the organisations we work for; we fall foul of it when we buy goods and services from those who only have their own profit in mind. I facilitate leadership development at various financial institutions in South Africa and I have experienced a strong desire amongst my executive clients to work in a values-based leadership culture. A few years ago, international news headlines highlighted that there had been an extreme lack of integrity in the executive leadership of the parent company of one of our top five financial institutions[5]. This resulted in the immediate resignation of Bob Diamond, the CEO of that parent organisation, Barclays Bank, and even when having to report to the British parliament, he was accused of prevaricating whilst responding to the questions in Parliament[6]. The impact of such lack of integrity affected not only the parent company, but also my client organisation, illustrated as follows in a local online newspaper[7]:

Absa feels Barclays' pain

The woes at Absa's parent Barclays are also not helping. Barclays chief executive Bob Diamond resigned on Tuesday, followed a few hours later by the bank's chief operating officer, in a deepening scandal over the rigging of a key global interest rate ..."

In my role as AL development practitioner, I noted how this situation hurt those employees in our local financial institution who had served their employer for 10, 20 and, in some cases, even 40 years, many of whom were then retrenched in a cost-cutting exercise, through no wrong-doing of their own[8, 9]. Personal communication with one of the affected executive employees reminded me once again of the immense impact, not only on those employees and their self-worth, which in some instances has led to suicides and attempted suicides, but also on their families. Sadly, more recently, Barclays was once again in the press regarding the Libor rigging scandal[10].

The need for increased positive and moral leadership is not only in response to organisational scandals attributed to poor and unethical leadership. Due to the continual pressure often experienced at senior levels in organisations, many skilled and accomplished executives often feel that they are not good enough, which can have an adverse effect on their self-esteem at the expense of their careers and organisations, and, of course on those people who are unlucky enough to report to them. The more senior the leadership position in an organisation, the more leaders need to deliver through others. This means that they need to be able to inspire, influence and empower others to deliver to the best of their ability. It seems to me that so often leaders are promoted in more senior leadership positions due to their previous successes, which are based on their business or technical acumen rather than their leadership skills. Whilst they might have studied for years to prepare them for those previous technical successes, they are then expected to develop the requisite leadership skills by osmosis and shoulder enormous responsibilities to deliver through others, while they are not appropriately equipped to do so.

What tends to happen then is that they feel frustrated and disempowered as leaders. They start to fall back on what they do know, or might have experienced themselves in the past, which is to become autocrats and bullies in order to get others to deliver. This can lead to what is called role compression in those whom they lead, who then go below the radar in order to avoid the wrath of the leader. This may well result in the opposite of what the leader hoped to achieve, as he or she then becomes surrounded with team members who duck and dive and so achieve less than their role requires. Furthermore, those below them are often sent for further development, whilst they, very sadly, are unavailable for such journeys. I call this inappropriate invulnerability.

Whilst I have thus far referred mostly to individual leadership, it is also important to consider leadership teams and team leadership. Lencioni, founder and president of The Table Group, focuses on senior and executive team development and organisational health, and takes this further, stating that "it is not finance, not strategy, not technology, but teamwork that remains the *ultimate* competitive advantage, both because it is so powerful and so rare"[11]. This, therefore, is the difference between a smart organisation and a healthy organisation. Such teamwork can be developed only with a strong and positive leader at the helm, who can be both a role model and facilitate the process of developing effective teams, as will be illustrated in this book.

WHAT ARE THE CONSEQUENCES OF POOR LEADERSHIP?

Recent corporate scandals, such as the Barclays and Volkswagen scandals, have awakened our collective consciousness to the fact that self-interest, unchecked by ethical reasoning and obligation, can result in destructive greed. This greed destroys not only the lives of those leaders that are driven by it to ethical compromise (although these still too often walk away with golden handshakes), but ultimately it impacts on all stakeholders, as the outcomes trickle down organisational hierarchies, spilling over into communities and adversely impacting on the lives of unsuspecting families.

Heineman, General Electric's former Senior Vice President for Law and Public Affairs, took this a step further when he commented that bad and unethical organisational decision-making was the primary cause of the recent financial crisis and the subsequent global recession. He continued that the failure to fuse high performance with high integrity – to achieve the foundational goals of the modern corporation – has eroded trust in the free enterprise system and created a crisis in global capitalism[12].

In the case where a leader simply does not have the skills to inspire, influence and empower those they need to work with and deliver through, the consequences are that everyone works below the level required of them, which impacts on their performance and output. Trust then starts to diminish between leaders and those whom they lead, and leaders then either micromanage or, rather than delegate, start doing the work themselves. This then means that they themselves also start working at a level below what is expected of them.

Unless a way can be found to develop integrous and effective leadership within a reasonable time span, organisations like Anderson, Tyco, Transmile and more recently Volkswagen and Barclays, and even governments, will head the news in stories of corruption and achieving wealth at the expense of their citizens and even the world economy. In South Africa alone, one only has to *Google* to discover of just how many unethical actions and moments of inauthenticity, President Jacob Zuma, continues to be accused. For instance, there was no relational transparency about his rationale for firing highly respected and credible Ministers of Finance; Minister Nene at the end of 2015 and again, Minister Gordhan in 2017. Continual behaviour such as this has resulted in a loss of trust in him by his followers, whether within his cabinet or by the wider business and voter population. It has also had immense adverse financial effects on the South African economy, as the wider global community loses faith in the individual and collective leadership and future of the country.

In the case of the President of United States, Donald Trump, the jury was out soon after his election as to whether he was an authentic leader[13], and it highlights the difference between authenticity and leadership authenticity. Whilst Donald Trump could be regarded as authentic, he falls short of behaving as an authentic leader should. Whereas authenticity is being true to oneself, AL requires positive and ethical attributes such as integrity and truthfulness. Just as AL fosters authentic followers, sadly, the same can apply to inauthentic and unethical leadership, where, ultimately, systemic unethical behaviour becomes the norm.

ACHIEVING A BETTER QUALITY OF LEADERSHIP

The following discussion is divided into a brief introduction of what we know about leadership authenticity, the impact of leadership authenticity in general, and, specifically, on inter-relational trust and leadership effectiveness. It outlines important considerations in the development of leadership authenticity, and research done thus far on leadership authenticity programmes and the effectiveness of such programmes.

What is leadership authenticity?

> To be nobody-but-yourself – in a world which is doing its best, night and day, to make you everybody else – means to fight the hardest battle which any human being can fight; and never stop fighting[14].

This quote from Cummings confirms what a client of mine who is a senior manager at an international financial organisation, must have felt when she explained that, "the organisational world has the ability to squeeze the self out of the self". In his thesis, *Being and Nothingness*, the philosopher Jean Paul Sartre described *authenticity* as[15]:

> A personal search for meaning, arguing that mankind, having been confronted with the meaningless existence, embarks on a search for the true self. However, authenticity needs to be earned and emerges from its social context, under the guidance of one's own conscience.

Victor Frankl reminds us that at any moment, man must decide, for better or for worse, what will be the monument to his existence, or the legacy that he wishes to leave behind[16]. In my practitioner experience, there often comes a time where individuals start searching for who they really are, the purpose of their lives, and the legacy they wish to leave behind. This search for meaning ties in with how both Jean Paul Sartre and Victor Frankl relate to humanness and authenticity.

Whilst AL is a logical extension of the authentic self, it can also be regarded as the root construct of all positive leadership. Chan et al.[17] suggest that a leader who is authentic, therefore, can achieve more than one who is not. The extent to which the leader is authentic as a person directly affects the efficacy of his/her leadership of followers. Another view on authentic leadership by Avolio, Gardner, and Walumba is that [18]:

> Authentic leaders are leaders who: (a) know who they are, and what they *believe* in; (b) display transparency and consistency between their *values, ethical reasoning* and *actions*; (c) focus on developing *positive emotional states* such as confidence, optimism, hope, and resilience within themselves; (d) are widely known and respected for their *integrity*.

My own understanding of authentic leadership, simplistically explained, is that authentic leaders are leaders who know who they are and who are true to themselves. However, this begs the question of 'which self are we referring to?' This could partially be explained by Roberts, Dutton, Spreitzer, Heaphy and Quinn's reference to the reflective best-self, which refers to an individual's "cognitive representation of the qualities and characteristics displayed when at his or her best"[19]. Authentic leaders also need to be true to their leadership position, with a strong moral underpinning (which at times requires a good dose of moral courage), for the greater good of all. What exactly this means will be unpacked further.

The positive impact of authentic leadership

In my experience, authentic leadership is a leadership by *presence that transcends position.* This means that even the leaders of authentic leaders may become their followers, as those individuals recognise the abilities before them and allow themselves to be influenced by such leaders who may even be at a lower organisational level. Authentic leaders are experienced by their followers as true and natural leaders who have integrity, and who are ethical and trustworthy. They become empowering role models to followers as they lead in a manner that others recognise as authentic. Because they are able to embrace a strength-based vulnerability, they are willing to be more transparent, more open and self-disclose more, and in so doing, they evoke higher levels of follower trust. Followers then feel more comfortable to be authentic, embracing and enacting the positive values of authenticity. This has important implications for resultant outcomes and performance, suggesting that authenticity increases a leader's effectiveness.

As an authentic leader's ethical behaviour is infused into the organisational norms and relationships, the inter-relational trust between the leader and followers increases. The relational transparency further often leads to operational and organisational transparency. This has a further positive effect on behavioural and performance outcomes, as leaders and followers experience meaningful success, job satisfaction, organisational involvement, and commitment.

As inter-relational trust is an output of AL, individual and collective leadership authenticity are what is required to build the solid foundation of trust in any effective leadership team and organisation. The true measure of an effective team is whether it accomplishes the results that it sets out to achieve. In this respect, my insights on effective teams have aligned strongly with those of Patrick Lencioni who states that the foundation of any effective team is that each member is worthy of trust. Based on Lencioni's[20] observation on ineffective teams, insufficient attention to results is often due to an absence of trust, which leads to a fear of conflict and, therefore, a lack of commitment, which, in turn, results in avoidance of accountability. It therefore follows that the pyramid of strength in an effective leadership team is based on:

- a solid foundation of trust at the bottom of the pyramid, which leads to
- a freedom to have healthy disagreements, resulting in
- commitment to a course of action and
- a willingness to be accountable, which leads to
- achieving (and often exceeding) expected *results*.

One of my personal experiential learnings is that everything starts with self, including the development of trust. It is near impossible to trust unknown entities, and as one of my leader clients had shared with me recently, "Often, the most unknown entity is thyself." Therefore, before we can trust others, or be worthy of trust from others, we need to trust ourselves, and this becomes possible only once we have a deep understanding of ourselves, and a deep commitment towards developing towards our highest authentic selves.

How do we develop leadership authenticity?

AL can be regarded as the root construct of positive leadership[21], and it can also be equated to the highest level of leadership development levels (LDLs)[22]. It is therefore a very effective form of leadership. Eigel and Kuhnert[23] proposed five different levels of leadership effectiveness, which I will elaborate on in Chapter 4, and they pointed out that only a small percentage of leaders are able to operate at the highest level of leadership effectiveness.

Being able to lead self and others with awareness and authenticity often requires a journey of transformation where we need to explore the internal identity that drives us, and integrate all of life's experiences into a meaningful context so that we can understand how we have become who we are. In order to lead purposefully, we need to understand both our purpose and our hierarchy of values. The journey of developing leadership therefore is about getting to know our authentic self. It is about practising our values and principles, and understanding what motivates us so that we can lead purposefully and effectively. In my opinion, two considerations during this journey are:

1. The development of AL requires that we explore what is happening below the *emotional waterline*, which in the AL context I call the *emotional soil-line*. What I mean by this is that our behaviour, which can be noticed by others (above the soil-line), is informed by those aspects of ourselves that cannot be noticed by others, such as our beliefs, values, purpose (below the soil-line). This is often a very challenging journey, and very difficult to undertake on our own. It requires the skills of someone who will listen in a way that we truly feel heard, who asks those probing questions that ignite our minds and uncover blind spots, and who continually challenges us to move outside of our comfort zone, whilst supporting us when we do so.

2. New self-awareness does not automatically lead to change. It needs to be supported by self-regulation. Our existing ways are usually habitual, because of the way our neural pathways have been wired in our neurology. This most often requires a partnership

with an external experienced person to facilitate the rewiring of neural pathways from limiting to empowering habits. An effective leadership coach, for instance, could play such a role.

My work is aligned to thoughts by Chan et al.[24] who divided their research on AL development and the emergence of AL behaviour into 1) the intrapersonal processes, followed by 2) the effect of that on self, others, and outcomes. They illustrated a process model of the emergence of authentic behaviour, starting with self, and continued that every leader forms part of a bigger system, and that they interact, influence, and receive feedback from other members in their system.

Although Chan et al. in 2005 did not elaborate on the nature of the required leadership programme they did indicate that the process should ideally start with some kind of a leadership programme. Leadership authenticity development starts with self. Every leader's *followers* will observe and experience his or her behaviour, trying to make sense of it, particularly in terms of its authenticity. As AL inspires trust, the degree of perceived honesty, transparency, predictability and integrity will affect the quality of the leader-follower relationships. The leader will receive feedback from his or her followers, either formally or informally (this might require sensitive observation) that will indicate how authentically he/she comes across and where he/she might do things differently, thereby reinforcing the formation of an authentic culture within the organisation.

Leadership authenticity programmes

There has been a shift from traditional leadership theories to a focus on a new genre of leadership, such as AL, which focuses primarily on whom we are, and not only what we ought to do as leaders. This means that conventional leadership programmes, often of short duration and training-based, would be insufficient for the transformative nature of developing AL. The metric of time for development of AL is typically long, as it takes time for all AL characteristics to emerge, requiring life experiences and leadership episodes that provide development opportunities. This begs the question whether organisations can wait that long to have effective authentic leaders at the helm. It is all very well to have a theoretical understanding of leadership authenticity, and the positive impacts it can have; however, since so many organisations are still run today without a moral compass, an underpinning of AL, what is required is an understanding of how the development of such leadership can be fast-tracked. Avolio and Gardner[25] highlighted the complexity of AL development theory, and stated that they were not able to view AL development as a programme unless it were to be broadly labelled "life's program", meaning that the development had to emanate from the lessons offered by life, with possibly some training.

However, since 2008, my focus as an individual and team authentic leadership effectiveness (ALE) coach and facilitator has been to coach towards self-development of AL at senior and executive levels in organisations. I often find myself encouraging clients to remain authentically ethical, at times in blatantly inauthentic, unethical environments. I focus on the development of intrapersonal and interpersonal leadership skills whilst coaching *from the inside out* for an alignment of purpose, internal identity, values, beliefs, thoughts and feelings (emotional and mind states), and capabilities. Experience has shown me that all of these, together with vision, create meaning and drive authentic leadership behaviour. This book therefore focuses on a practitioner's perspective on developing AL.

SOME WELL-KNOWN SOUTH AFRICAN EXAMPLES OF AUTHENTIC LEADERSHIP

Three of the most well-known South African examples of authentic leaders are most probably Helen Suzman, who was one of the first White South Africans who fought apartheid from within the Parliament and who was nominated for the Nobel Peace Prize, Nelson Mandela, and Archbishop Desmond Tutu, both of whom were the recipients of the Nobel Peace Prize. Desmond Tutu, a retired South African Anglican cleric, is well known for his role in opposing apartheid in South Africa. As the head of the South African Council of Churches, Archbishop Tutu received the Nobel Peace Prize in 1984:

> ...not only as a gesture of support to him and to the South African Council of Churches of which he is leader, but also to all individuals and groups in South Africa who, with their concern for human dignity, fraternity and democracy, incite the admiration of the world[26].

Tutu's efforts contributed considerably to ending South African apartheid in 1994, when Nelson Mandela was elected as the first Black president of democratic South Africa. President Mandela appointed Tutu to head a Truth and Reconciliation Commission, tasked with investigating and reporting on the atrocities committed by both sides in the struggle during apartheid.

Much has been written about the leadership of Nelson Rolihlala Mandela, affectionately known as Tata Madiba, who together with President de Klerk, received the Nobel Peace Prize in 1993 *"for their work for the peaceful termination of the apartheid regime, and for laying the foundations for a new democratic South Africa"*. For me, Madiba is not only the most well known, but also one of best examples of what I understand to be an authentic leader. He was a leader who went beyond position, defined by the essence of his presence, and I always think of the three '*pr*'s that defined his leadership. Whether he was a *pr*esident or *pr*isoner, was irrelevant, as it was by his *pr*esence that he led everyone, friend and foe, to regard him as a leader. It is important to understand that authentic leaders are not perfect human beings. By his own admission, Mandela, in response to being described as a saint, said that he could not be regarded as a saint unless a saint was a sinner that kept trying to improve. He acknowledged that he had made mistakes, like all of us, but he always introspected and considered how not to repeat those mistakes.

We too can reflect on what has not gone as well as we would have liked and strive to do better in the future. Kalungu-Banda[27] states that "inspirational leadership makes all of us dig deep into the innermost parts of ourselves to find the very best that lies there and to make it available to ourselves and others". I once heard John Demartini explain the difference between inspiration and motivation. Inspiration by nature is intrinsic whereas motivation is extrinsic. Motivation is about motivating others to do what I want them to do, whereas in the case of inspiration others will decide whether they feel inspired by my presence and actions as a leader. In the case of Madiba, his authentic behaviour caused many people across the world to feel inspired by him. He truly displayed the behaviour that he wished to see in others in the world. He had a strong purpose and vision for a South Africa wherein no one race or group dominated another. For that purpose and vision, he was prepared to leave his family whom he loved and valued so much, to go to prison for 27 years. Although he was offered numerous opportunities to leave prison earlier than he did, he did not accept any of these offers until he was able to negotiate and manifest what he stood for and went to prison for. He lived and hoped to see his vision come true, knowing that for this purpose and vision, he was prepared to die, if need be. His espoused values were his enacted values, and his purpose was his highest value of all.

In my understanding of AL, Suzman, Tutu and Mandela have always endeavoured to be true to themselves and true to their leadership positions, with strong ethical underpinnings, for the greater good of all whom they served. For this, they needed considerable moral courage and strong moral compasses. They were not perfect; no one is, but they were always prepared to introspect and realign to their *True North* (*True North* being the essence of who they were and where they were heading in life), where and whenever necessary. Suzman and Mandela receive closer inspection through the lens of AL later in the book.

RATIONALE FOR BETTER LEADERSHIP

Meyer states that whilst "good leaders navigate through all weather; profound leadership occurs during a storm"[28]. True leadership is tested when an extreme crisis occurs within organisations or societies, such as we often witness on a day-to-day basis. I believe that it is this type of leadership, as referred to by Meyer, that is required in times of uncertainty in South Africa and internationally, and it is important to understand how this type of leadership can be developed.

When problems surfaced in various well-known international organisations, and the extent of the leadership crisis became apparent, this created a widespread erosion of trust in business leaders. However, this is not limited only to corporate organisations. In South Africa, the unethical behaviour of the president and some of his followers continually make headline news. For some time, the president of South Africa has been under the spotlight[29] over his excessive use of public funds for private gain. This includes expenditure on his private residence for himself and his family. Unfortunately, this type of behaviour trickles down to those who regard leaders as role models, leading to unethical behaviour permeating societies such leaders lead.

Interestingly though, in my AL development work, I experience many leadership clients who wish to develop the moral courage present in AL in order to allow them to respond to unethical challenges in an ethical manner. This requires a strong sense of self, a strong commitment to self, and a strong moral compass, as part of that *True North*. It furthermore requires 360° leadership, meaning that they are sometimes required to lead upwards as well, especially in state- and municipal-owned enterprises, which are continually exposed to unethical, politically connected requests for favours.

The underpinning theoretical rationale espoused in this book is the notion that leadership authenticity builds trust, and that the development of inter-relational trust and trustworthiness builds and strengthens individual and team authentic leadership effectiveness. More specifically, a practical contribution is envisaged for this book, as it outlines an empirical example of an individual and team leadership authenticity programme, and highlights its effectiveness, primarily in terms of the shift in the drivers of AL, specifically inter-relational trust as experienced by both my clients and those whose lives they affect inside and outside their organisations.

CONCLUSION

There is a dire need for ethical leaders who can inspire hope, particularly in our current volatile world of uncertainty and complexity. In the absence of appropriate leadership skills, leaders tend to become autocratic and operate below their true level of responsibility, creating uninspired and ineffective followers, thereby failing to achieve overall required outcomes. The journey to authenticity necessitates a specifically targeted programme, which develops both self-awareness and self-regulation of behaviour towards a *True North*.

YOUR PERSONAL REFLECTIONS: THE STATE OF LEADERSHIP

Consider the following:

1. Describe the quality of national leadership in your country. Are these leaders that you wish to follow? What do you believe about that?
2. Describe the quality of leadership in your organisation. Are these leaders you wish to follow? What do you believe about that?

Chapter 2

DEFINING AUTHENTIC LEADERSHIP

Whilst authors such as Robert Terry[30] had already attempted in the 1990s to define AL, it became a common focus as the urgency deepened in the early 2000s, following the corporate scandals attributed at that time to poor and unethical leadership. In addition, AL theory and practice received increased attention after the Gallup Leadership Institute (GLI) summit held in 2005 where numerous prominent researchers and authors contributed to a monographic and seminal book on leadership authenticity[31], which, in my opinion, has become the *bible* on leadership authenticity.

This overview elaborates further with theoretical perspectives of what leadership authenticity is. In order to have a better understanding of what leadership authenticity is, I unpack the concept of *authenticity*, not only in terms of what it is, but also in terms of what it is not. The processes of leadership authenticity are explored, commencing with the intrapersonal processes, which refer to the processes within the self. This is followed by the social cognitive processes, which are important in people leadership. I highlight how authenticity reflects in organisational leadership and explore whether AL and political acumen can co-exist. Finally, I share some converging and diverging thoughts on leadership authenticity, as this has been refined over the years, especially since 2005, to be more suitable to the requirements of leadership in the world of today.

WHAT IS AUTHENTICITY?

As already alluded to, a continual battle that we all fight in a world that would like to make us just like everyone else is to remain intrinsically who we really are. This applies especially in the organisational leadership context, which at times can "squeeze the self out of the self"; meaning that eventually, we are not even sure who we are anymore.

Authenticity is a term that is used in psychology as well as in sociology and existential philosophy, all of which define authenticity slightly differently. For the purpose of understanding leadership authenticity required in organisations today, authenticity is essentially the degree to which we are true to ourselves, despite external pressures, bearing in mind that we are in a material world where we encounter external forces and influences that might be very different from our own, our beliefs and values. This is exactly what the philosopher Sartre referred to when he said that there comes a point in one's life where one embarks on a search for the true self. I often notice that my clients find it hard to reflect who they really are whilst at work, and it can have an impact on their effectiveness if they do not feel comfortable in their own skin.

Often I find that my leader clients, although successful, reach a point where they become aware of a need for more meaning and wanting to make a difference, so that they can be of service for the greater good for all. This aligns with the thoughts of Victor Frankl, the father of logotherapy (the focus on the meaning of human existence), that, "at any moment, man must decide, for better or for worse, what will be the monument of his existence"[32]. In the context of authentic leadership, this is an extremely important distinction, as leaders might appear to be true to themselves, but not necessarily for the greater good of those whom they ought to serve in their leadership position.

Whilst there are many perspectives about what authenticity is, it is best understood not only by what it is, but also by what it is not. For instance, whilst sincerity can be regarded one of the cornerstones of authenticity in organisations, authenticity is not about sincerity, impression management, or self-monitoring. Whereas sincerity encompasses a lack of pretence, with a feeling of congruence in one's relationships and interactions with others, authenticity, on the other hand, is a self-referential state of being. This is an important distinction; authenticity is about regulating one's behaviour with one's true self. This means knowing and staying true to one's internal compass comprising one's purpose and values, even when there is no one else present.

Impression management usually occurs when an inauthentic person aligns his or her behaviour to what they believe is expected of them, rather than being aligned to an internal compass that keeps one true to self. Impression management could be described as a strategic presentation of self, which can change, depending on external influences, with the intention of influencing and evoking a desired response from others. Impression management might also be the result of a lack of self-awareness of who the self really is, whereas the authentic person will ensure that the impression created is consistent with the true self.

Recently a client of mine, who had developed AL during our programme together, told me that his organisation had a new CEO. As they had recently undergone restructuring, resulting in retrenchments from the most senior levels down, he anticipated that everyone in senior levels would be clamouring to be noticed by the new CEO. His leadership outcome was to explore what he could do to create a favourable impression on the CEO. I reminded him that he was already extremely effective and a great asset to his organisation, and we explored what he had recently learnt about himself during his AL developing journey. He was reminded of his purpose in the organisation, and his vision for the organisation. My client realised that he did not need to do anything extraordinary to create an impression on the incoming CEO, as in time, it was bound to happen all by itself. All he needed to do was to continue his self-regulation so that his behaviour consistently reflected his ALE. Ultimately, this would be much easier than developing strategies for impression management.

There therefore appears to be an inverse link between degree of authenticity and degree of self-monitoring. High self-monitoring is often exercised by those who are less authentic, who are reported to have multiple selves, which are not necessarily who they truly are, and who display different behaviours according to what is perceived to be appropriate for the situation. On the other hand, high self-regulators will refer inwards for guidance in terms of how to behave appropriately whilst remaining authentic and true to themselves.

Authenticity, therefore, is internally referenced, meaning looking inwards at oneself, allowing oneself to be guided by an internal compass; it includes both self-awareness and a commitment to align one's internal identity, purpose and values, irrespective of the situation, whereas inauthenticity is more externally or socially referenced. This does not mean, however, that an authentic person does not take cognisance of his or her environment, especially when in a position of leadership, nor does it mean that leaders who are high self-monitors, and therefore not regarded as authentic, are necessarily ineffective leaders.

UNDERSTANDING LEADERSHIP AUTHENTICITY

AL is an emerging theory of leadership. It has received increased focus from 2005 onwards, mainly due to cases of inauthentic leadership at that time, particularly as highlighted in the press, which sharpened the outcry for a new standard of integrity and public accountability in leadership. AL, based on the tenets of positive psychology, has emerged as one response to the call for higher standards of character and integrity in leadership, as it seeks to find a way to move organisations, communities, and societies forward by focusing on what is right for the greater good.

To a large extent, my thoughts are aligned with the theoretical framework for AL, proposed by Chan et al.[33], who both supported and extended the thoughts posed by Sartre's authenticity theory (to be true to ourselves), and extending this to leadership authenticity, as follows. It is important to divide AL development and the emergence of AL behaviour into 1) the intrapersonal (self-leadership) processes, followed by 2) the effect of that on self, others, and outcomes. This development process should ideally start with a leadership programme, which would begin with the authentic development of oneself. As followers observe and evaluate the authenticity in leaders' behaviours, this affects trust and relationships between leaders and followers, either positively or negatively. As the leader receives diagnostic feedback through the follower feedback loop, this serves to inform him or her, and so reinforce the evolution of a more AL organisational culture. The major sub-processes of leadership authenticity include:

1. Leaders' self-clarity and understanding of their internal selves, meaning to develop a deep awareness of self, of who they are, followed by;
2. A commitment to regulate the self by, for instance, ensuring that there is congruence between *who* they believe they are, their life and leadership purpose, the values that they espouse, what they believe about self and others, and their behaviours.
3. This then allows their behaviours to become an expression of their internal selves, which others can observe. As every leader forms part of a bigger system in which they interact, influence, and receive feedback, they are continually informed as to their perceived AL and effectiveness.

Kernis[34], one of the initial thought leaders on AL, proposed four basic dimensions of AL, those being awareness, unbiased (balanced) processing, relational transparency, and action (behaviour). Although AL development requires the presence of self- and social awareness, reflected in behaviour, it is the remaining two dimensions, starting with unbiased, also called balanced, processing, that require further discussion. In my experiential understanding, this has to do with thinking about, and processing all that happens, in a balanced way. Nothing and no one is all bad or all good, nor is any situation ever completely hopeless, or guaranteed to be without any challenges. Once we can accept this, and think and process accordingly, it becomes liberating, as we no longer hold on to either positive or negative fantasies. Relational transparency is also important as it helps others to be on the same page as us, and as this sometimes requires courage, it has the ability to create trust between others and ourselves. All of these add to developing authentic leaders that others wish to follow.

Especially from 2005 onwards, there has been a focus on expanding the requirements of AL to include a moral component. Whilst self-awareness and self-regulation are core components of the development and maintenance of leadership authenticity, we need to include further desirable qualities, such as moral/ethical considerations, and a continual focus on further development of self and others. In my experience, it is this moral component, combined with the ability to manage and further develop positive psychological states of mind and emotions for the greater good of all, which allows leaders to become true leaders, firstly of self, and thereafter of others.

I have learnt from my clients that *moral courage* is required when the *ethically correct* choice needs to be made even if the consequences for that leader could be undesirable. Having the moral courage to do what is right allows them to live with themselves and sleep better at night. Having this understanding of what is morally good, displaying moral courage, and holding oneself accountable for staying aligned with this understanding ultimately lead to *psychological ownership,* meaning that we take responsibility for what we think and feel, say and do. Once these aspects reflect in the leader's behaviour, it often flows over into that of the followers as well, which indicates that the opposite of the saying that *the fish rots from the head,* can also apply. In short, authentic leaders are moral agents who take ownership of, and responsibility for the end results of their actions and, if appropriate, for the actions of their followers.

The notion of *positive psychological capital,* now regarded as an underpinning of AL, was initiated at the turn of the century by a new movement called *positive psychology.* Led by Martin Seligman, the then president of the *American Psychological Association (APA),* they wanted to redirect the focus of psychology away from the singular emphasis on healing mental illnesses and pathology to the more actualising approach of taking individuals from good to great[35]. Rather than just aiming to fix what is wrong in people, positive psychology follows a strengths-based approach; it is out of this movement that two related movements, *positive organisational scholarship,* and *positive organisational behaviour* evolved, which focused on positivity and a strength-based approach to management and leadership in the workplace. Positive organisational behaviour includes four psychological states, those being self-efficacy/confidence, hope, optimism, and resilience, and together these are referred to as positive psychological capital.

Positive psychological capital in leadership authenticity offers the internal resources that allow challenging events to trigger heightened self-awareness and self-regulatory behaviours as part of the process of positive self-development. This in turn has a direct impact on leadership effectiveness, trust, and follower/team effectiveness, as will be reflected in the case studies outlined in this book. There is a relationship between: 1) self-efficacy, described as the confidence in one's ability to execute a specific course of action; 2) hope, which allows leaders to achieve their goals; 3) optimism, which allows the leader to frame events in a helpful way; and 4) resilience, the capacity to bounce back from adversity, uncertainty, or failure. These equip the leader to achieve desirable outcomes such as job satisfaction, organisational commitment and organisational effectiveness in a VUCA environment of today. It is important to note though that whilst the four psychological states of confidence, hope, optimism, and resilience are very important, these are not necessarily sufficient to reflect and sustain leadership authenticity. In my experience, further states such as (self-) accountability/ownership, (self) belief, (self-) commitment, consistency, courage, (self-) honesty, trust in self and others, truthfulness, and respect all contribute considerably to leadership authenticity.

Authentic leaders operate from a set of values that focuses on doing what they perceive to be right for those whom they lead. Because they are value-centred, these leaders seek to reduce any existing gaps between their espoused and their enacted values. They often make the development of others a priority. By being true to their own values, and acting in ways that are consistent with those values, authentic leaders develop their followers into leaders as well.

However, with the aforementioned description of ideal AL, it is extremely important to remember that authentic leaders are also only human, and therefore do need to allow themselves to be vulnerable in non-defensive recognition of their own strengths, as well as their weaknesses. This ability in itself then becomes a strength, allowing for further development. Authentic leaders have to be aware of their vulnerabilities and weaknesses, and be transparent enough to allow discussions of these areas with others. Not only does this allow for further self-development, it also allows followers to identify more readily with leaders, resulting in more positive and influential relationships between leaders and followers. However, a word of caution: this vulnerability, which is called *balanced vulnerability*, should be appropriate in the context in which it is displayed. A specific example of stepping into the psychological state of vulnerability is by sharing life stories – both the positive and the challenging aspects – which enhances transparency that usually increases followers' trust in their leaders. This allows authentic leaders to go first, whether in committing to an action or recognising areas in which they need further development. This is useful when leading teams, or taking the lead even when there is great personal risk in doing so. By going first, leaders model a hopeful confidence in the future.

I do also frame the concept of balanced vulnerability as *appropriate vulnerability*, as most psychological states can be used appropriately or inappropriately. Just as one has appropriate versus inappropriate vulnerability, the same can be said for invulnerability. *Inappropriate invulnerability* could occur, for instance, when an organisational leader suggests that those who report to the leader are not performing and that they require assistance, whilst all along the problem lies with the leader. As an AL practitioner, I have experienced very senior organisational leaders in positions of power who are very undermining towards those they lead, leading to role compression, and ultimately underperformance in their teams. Such leaders are often not available to receive feedback on how their leadership is experienced, and they refuse to acknowledge that they themselves have development gaps.

In one example that I personally experienced, although this leader gave his blessing for me to continue work with his team, he was personally unavailable for further development, and he was heard to say that he did not wish to be *psychologically unpacked*. I call this inappropriate invulnerability, which is the opposite of appropriate strength-based vulnerability. I continued my work with those direct reports who had experienced his undermining leadership so that they could develop AL and be effective within their own context as leaders, *despite* rather than *because of* his leadership style. Since an authentic leader is a leader by presence that transcends position, I often remind my clients that their stakeholders extend beyond their manager; that together with their managers they need to serve their teams, seniors, and their organisation and its stakeholders as a whole. I then introduce the concepts, not usually known in verb format, which I refer to as *to ordinate* rather than *to subordinate* or *super ordinate*. In the case of ordinating, we interact respectfully with one another and treat each other as equals. I often find that, when leaders fear their super ordinating bullying seniors – those seniors back down immediately when the leaders on the AL journey learn to ordinate in their interaction with those seniors. They then become leaders to their seniors with examples of effective leadership behaviour that cannot be ignored.

Authentic leadership can be summarised as a logical extension of the authentic self, and can be considered a foundation of positive leadership[36]. They are leaders who know who they are and what they *believe* in; who display transparency and consistency between their *values*, ethical reasoning and actions; who focus on developing *positive emotional states* such as confidence, optimism, hope, and resilience within themselves; and who are widely known and respected for their *integrity*[37]. Not only are they are deeply aware of how they think and behave and aware of the context within which they operate with a positive regard for their followers, they are also perceived by others as being aware of their own and others' values/ moral perspectives, knowledge and strengths. This can further build follower confidence through increasing their followers' self-efficacy.

In terms of developing leadership authenticity, it is important to understand both the functioning and emergence of leadership authenticity within the organisational systems in which leaders operate. Next, you will find a more in-depth look at AL, which outlines a social cognitive view, followed by the social cognitive processes of AL, strongly influenced by research done by Chan et al.[38] and corroborated by my own practitioner experience.

A social cognitive view of leadership authenticity

From a social cognitive perspective, leadership authenticity has two key features: 1) self-knowledge of our core inner self, which happens below the invisible soil-line unavailable to others and, 2) the need for us to present our core self through our behaviour, which happens above the soil-line, for others to experience. Self-knowledge is gained through the act of developing self-awareness, and the dynamic process of applying self-awareness describes the process of introspection that requires that individuals continually question and re-assess their self-identities, values, beliefs, strengths, and weaknesses. We also need to bear in mind a third social cognitive variable: environmental influence. Whilst it might be easier to be authentic when all is well, leaders more often face challenges in remaining authentic to themselves and their roles as leaders when facing additional situational leadership challenges. This is what was meant when Meyer stated that, whilst "good leaders navigate through all weather, profound leadership occurs during a storm"[39]. Profound leadership is tested when profound crises occur.

An important consideration therefore, more fully explored when considering the development of leadership authenticity, is that authenticity varies along a continuum – from complete inauthenticity to full authenticity – determined by the extent to which leaders remain true, especially to their core purpose, internal identity, values, and beliefs. I always encourage my clients never to think of themselves as having achieved full authenticity as it might diminish their need for further development and growth. We can always reach higher levels of authentic growth and effectiveness. Higher levels of authenticity are not static states; rather these states best allow us to increase effectiveness through further growth.

Social cognitive processes of leadership authenticity

At this point, I would like to introduce the notion of what I call an *internal AL Compass*. In academic literature, this is referred to as our schematic self-system, also called a self-schema, which includes one's purpose and vision, one's values and ethics, beliefs, self-identity, attributes and skills, and emotions. This concept could be compared to that of a worldview, which is usually described as the way in which each of us constructs and responds to our view of ourselves and of the world in which we live. This view could either empower or limit our effectiveness. Spinelli[40] added an intermediate level by proposing at least three primary systemic sub-structures, those being *self-construct*, *other-construct*, and *world-construct*. He added that an individual has a sum of beliefs, values, views, attitudes, meanings, assumptions, and conclusions, together with associated behaviours, feelings, and emotions, which are maintained regarding our:

- self-construct – how do I view myself;
- other-construct – how do I view others, be they specific others or others in general; and
- world-construct – how do I view the the world, be it in terms of its living or non-living components.

A strongly developed congruent internal AL Compass is what we require to stay *True North*. When referring to the concept of being true to ourselves, or wishing to develop authenticity, and more specifically leadership authenticity, it is important to be aware of the elements included in our internal AL Compass. Furthermore, we need to commit to self-regulating those internal AL Compass elements that allow our AL to reflect in our behaviour. This will be further elaborated upon during discussion on AL development (ALD).

Leadership authenticity processes therefore include: 1) self-clarity regarding one's internal AL Compass, which could include purpose and goals, identity, values, beliefs, and psychological attributes; and 2) and the ability and commitment to regulate one's behavioural self to be true to the AL Compass elements, even during challenging leadership episodes. Increasing that self-clarity requires continuous self-reflection or introspection. This is an on-going rather than a static process, as life is dynamic and brings new leadership episodes and life events that test and further develop leadership authenticity. Understanding one's purpose, self-identity, values, beliefs, and psychological states requires not only continuous self-reflection and introspection, it also requires that we consult and request feedback from others.

Developing self-knowledge through self-awareness is the first step, but developing and sustaining leadership authenticity also requires self-regulation, so that leaders' behaviours become an expression of their core values, identity, beliefs, emotions, and goals. In my experience when facilitating the development of AL, an increased self-awareness and understanding of these elements, unaccompanied by self-regulation, can result in impacts ranging from a lack of growth towards increased authenticity, to a false sense of authenticity and self-growth. I usually warn my clients that only once awareness of the various aspects and dimensions of the core self has been deepened, can and does the real work of self-regulations start by continually aligning behaviour to one's AL Compass.

The following discussion outlines aspects such as the cognitive structure of the authentic self as reflected in the internal AL Compass, and the multi-dimensionality and cognitive functioning of the internal AL Compass. I discuss the importance of understanding and processing at a meta-, or higher level, and the functioning of the personal and interpersonal feedback loops.

Cognitive structure of the authentic self: It is important to reflect continuously on the core *self* and accompanying behaviour, in response to the daily interactions, which our environment provides us, so that we can refine our internal AL Compass. Chan et al. referred to the *phenomenological* self as "a person's awareness, arising out of interactions with his environment, of his own beliefs, values, attitudes, the links between them, and their implications for his behaviour"[41]. This provides a framework for asking existential questions, such as: 'What is my purpose, and what are my goals?'; 'Who am I really?'; 'What are my core values that I need to adhere to?'; 'What do I believe about self and others?'; 'What emotions drive my behaviour?'; 'How are these limiting or empowering me?' Once we have a sense of these elements that make up our internal AL Compass, we can ask 'How strong is the golden thread that runs through all of these?'

Finally, from a development perspective there needs to be a temporal dimension to the self-concept, where a leader identifies not only a view of the *current self*, but also of the *possible self*. Your current internal AL Compass, therefore, will reflect a culmination of all your experiences to date. Your *possible self-system* can evolve by refining your current internal AL Compass, so that it can continue to support who you could become, at an increasingly higher level of authenticity. This provides a strong motivation for continuous improvement, and your ongoing development towards even fuller authenticity.

Multi-dimensionality and cognitive functioning of the *internal AL Compass*: Our self-system, as reflected in our internal compass, is not one-dimensional; it is complex, interconnected, and multidimensional. As human beings, we do not operate in one context only; for instance, we operate both at work and at home, and might well be leaders in both contexts. We could therefore have various *working* internal compasses, according to the roles, situations, and environments within which we need to operate, and these working internal compasses all need to be subsets of our main internal AL Compass. An authentic leader whose leadership therefore spans many social contexts is motivated to choose and regulate responses and behaviours consistent with his/her working internal compass, depending on the specific context. He or she is able to manage the on-going tension between who he/she really is and the social demands of each role.

For instance, I often explain to my clients that I dress very differently when going to client meetings compared to when I am not at work. Yet I always dress authentically, whilst being mindful of the context in which I expect myself to be at any one time. In the same way, I do not behave the same whilst on holiday as in my professional context. In my professional context, I am very conscious of time, and mindful of being on time, and when I am on holiday, time often becomes inconsequential. I reflect on how best to be effective whilst being true to whom I really am.

Although the internal AL Compass is not one-dimensional, and indeed consists of the various working internal compasses that the leader can draw from in various situations, it is important to note that, for a truly authentic leader, the working internal compass always remains a subset of his/her *main internal AL Compass*, and therefore a part of the true self. The leader knows and understands which working internal compass to draw from in response to the requirements of the situation at hand. However, the values associated with the main internal AL Compass of the authentic self are usually also present in the activation of each of the working internal compasses, which produces a strong commitment to self during leadership episodes.

It is therefore important to note that these working internal compasses, via the core internal AL Compass, can cross-pollinate. For instance, when facilitating the development of leadership authenticity with my organisational leaders, I usually do not insist that this development should start with the work context. At times, a leader experiences burning issues outside of work, so I allow the leader to guide me in terms of the contexts in which he or she wishes to start the journey of developing AL. I noticed that, once this authenticity has been achieved in one context, the self-information developed is stored in the leader's episodic and semantic memory, and becomes available for retrieval and use in all of the contexts in which the leader operates.

Understanding and processing at a higher level: Authentic leaders think about their thinking, and this is what I mean about understanding and processing at a higher level. This helps them to assess and make sense of information relating to the self, and allows them to adjust the reasoning that will inform their responses. Thereafter they can select and activate their working internal compasses in order to achieve their intended outcomes whilst remaining true to themselves.

This links to the philosophies of authors such as Victor Frankl and Stephen Covey. A well-known saying by Frankl, first penned during his years as a prisoner in Nazi camps, was that the quality of life is determined not so much by what happens to us, but rather by how we choose to respond to those events[42]. Covey[43] elaborated by referring to the processes such as thinking and feeling that inform responses in attempting to achieve outcomes, which result in either empowering or limiting responses. He introduced the concept of the *circle of concern*, being the environment as it is, versus the *circle of influence*, which is the way we choose to think, both of ourselves and of *what is*. Therefore, if we decide what is and is not within our circle of influence, we avoid expending energy on things over which we ultimately have no control. Our circle of influence will expand or contract within the circle of concern, depending on the way we regulate our sense of self and our responses in trying to achieve intended outcomes, whilst remaining true to ourselves within any environment or situation. I encourage my clients to move from problem- to possibility-thinking.

Functions of the systemic feedback loop: The role of systemic feedback in the emergence of leadership authenticity is two-fold. Initially, as we lead, the cues we receive from our environment will activate certain of our working internal compasses. We will then respond to this information by repeating or dispensing with the behaviours we demonstrated. This will again elicit cues and feedback, which will serve as a control function, verifying the level of perceived authenticity of our leadership. Over time, we will increasingly display our authentically effective self, whilst receiving ongoing verification feedback.

LEADERSHIP AUTHENTICITY AND POLITICAL ACUMEN: CAN THEY CO-EXIST?

Organisational politics is often present and very relevant in most organisations, yet it still appears to be under-researched in the field of AL. Few people feel neutral about the presence of politics in organisations. There is a saying that the taller the tree, the more it catches the wind, and the same applies in organisations. The more senior leaders are in organisations, the more they need to navigate the politics that exist in these organisations. So whilst the presence of politics is a given, it is the meaning given to political skills, or acumen, that needs to be examined in the context of authentic leadership, as these skills can be used either for self-serving or altruistic intent, for destructive or benevolent purposes, in an authentic or a manipulative manner. It is important to remember that leaders lead in a social context. It is therefore not always enough for authentic leaders simply to be true to their values and beliefs, if those do not assist them in generating trust with their followers, and increasing their effectiveness as leaders. Political skills, if used appropriately, can help authentic leaders to increase their AL effectiveness.

Political skills can be defined as: "The ability to effectively understand others at work and to use such knowledge to influence others to act in ways that enhance one's personal and/or organisational objectives"[44]. When not combined with leadership authenticity, leaders might combine social astuteness with different behaviours to suit the situational demands, by means of self-monitoring and feigned sincerity, for their own self-interest. When combined with AL, leader political skill provides the social ingenuity, behavioural flexibility and adaptability necessary to empower, influence and inspire followers, and thereby to meet the expectations of the organisation.

I define authentic leadership as being true to self, true to one's leadership position, with a strong moral underpinning, for the greater good of all. The answer to whether incorporating political acumen in one's everyday behaviour will take away or add to one's authentic leadership will help determine whether these two constructs can co-exist. In Chapter 4, I share some thoughts on how political acumen can be developed in alignment with AL.

Leadership authenticity: Converging and diverging thoughts

At the GLI summit on AL, held in 2004 in the wake of the ethical organisational scandals at that time, there was a was a growing recognition of[45]:

- the importance of integrity, character, and genuine trustworthy leader-follower relationships in developing effective leadership;
- the importance of positive psychological states, and positive behaviour; and
- the need for a strength-based approach to individual and organisational development.

More specifically, there was a convergence of opinion that leadership authenticity is not purely intrapersonal and self-referential, as in the case of an authentic individual. In the case of leadership, it involves interpersonal influence between leaders and followers, which can happen only once there is integrity and inter-relational trust.

Secondly, rather than judging a person as authentic or inauthentic, as already mentioned, the authenticity of leaders should be viewed as existing on a continuum, the development of which requires enhancing both self-awareness and self-regulation. These processes need to be seen in the light of what outcomes the leader is tasked with achieving, what behaviours will be required, and what necessary underpinnings are required to support appropriate behaviour.

More specifically, in terms of AL, it is important to remember that the moral component, which requires relational transparency, needs to be present. Furthermore, AL requires emotional intelligence, hope, optimism, and both passion and compassion[46]. This then has a positive impact on the relationship between leaders and followers, which becomes especially important in extreme and exceptional circumstances.

However, not all of the thought leaders at that time necessarily agreed on all the themes that define AL. While there was some agreement that leadership authenticity needs to include a moral component which, one might argue, can be enhanced by positive psychological capital such as optimism, confidence, hope, and resilience, not all thought leaders agreed that the moral component should automatically be included in the construct of leadership authenticity.

Understanding our internal identity, and understanding what is important to us in terms of our values, are important antecedents to developing resilience. It is the positive psychological capital of resilience that enables leaders to be agile, to adapt, to bounce back, and to flourish in times of uncertainty and adversity. These qualities might well explain the increased focus on leadership authenticity in response to the unethical corporate scandals that emerged at that time. However, others[47, 48] argued that a leader could be authentic and true to self without reaching a high level of moral development or adhering to high ethical standards.

The main difference between the two divergent approaches regarding the inclusion of a moral component in authenticity seems to lie in differing definitions of leadership authenticity. Whilst the narrower approach might wish to remain true to the original concept of authenticity, which is to be true to the self, the broader approach could be regarded as a more recent pragmatic approach. It takes into account what might be required from an authentic individual to be true to a leadership role, not only as a leader of self, but also of others, within corporate and political organisations. However, in the light of the moral dilemmas that leadership is presented with today, I believe that the moral element in authentic leadership is non-negotiable. Without this moral component, one could otherwise argue that leaders, perhaps like Trump and Zuma, are strong examples of AL.

Furthermore, the broader, pragmatic stance also includes strong underpinnings of positive psychology, which holds that all individuals have goodness and strengths that they need to be aware of, and to which they need to align their behaviour, so that they can have a positive impact, specifically on followers, for the greater good of all. My underpinnings of AL are aligned this broader and more pragmatic stance on leadership authenticity.

CONCLUSION

This chapter commenced with an outline of the principal theoretical perspectives on what leadership authenticity is, enriched by my own experiences as an AL practitioner. In order to have a better understanding of what leadership authenticity is, I unpacked the concept of *authenticity*, not only in terms of what it is, but also in terms of what it is not. The processes of leadership authenticity were explored, commencing with the intrapersonal processes, followed by the social cognitive processes. I reflected on whether leadership authenticity and political acumen can co-exist, and finally, I shared some converging and diverging thoughts on leadership authenticity, and indicated how I align myself with the more pragmatic stance on AL, summarised as follows.

- Authenticity is the degree to which we are aware of who we are and are true to ourselves, in spite of external pressures. Authentic Leadership is based on the extension of the authentic self and becomes a foundation of positive leadership.
- Leaders are observed by followers who evaluate leadership behaviour according to its authenticity, which thereby inspires trust or generates distrust. Leaders can, through a process of self-awareness, unbiased processing and relational transparency, use the feedback from followers to become ever more authentic.
- Authentic leadership is underpinned by the notion of positive psychological capital. It requires an internal AL Compass that is value-centred and includes recognition of both individual strengths and weaknesses, and enactment of espoused behaviour.
- Authentic leadership, which includes the positive psychological state of moral courage, is considered as an answer to the moral dilemmas that we often witness in the organisational world of today.

YOUR PERSONAL REFLECTIONS: HOW AUTHENTIC A LEADER ARE YOU?

Consider the following:

1. Knowing what you know now, how well do you show up as an authentic leader?
2. What AL qualities would you like to develop further?

GROUP DISCUSSION: AUTHENTIC LEADERSHIP IN YOUR ORGANISATION

Consider the following:

1. Knowing what you know now, what AL qualities are required in your organisational leadership?
2. How well does the leadership in your organisation align with the required AL qualities?

Chapter 3

APPLYING AUTHENTIC LEADERSHIP

Whilst authentic leadership may look and sound very interesting in theory, it is in its application that it needs to prove its worth. This chapter intends to do just that.

AL has been described as the root construct of all positive forms of leadership, and of itself has also been proven to be very effective as a form of leadership. Are leaders, even those who have worked through a comprehensive AL programme, necessarily 100% authentic at all times? Are leaders who have not thought about authenticity in their roles necessarily inauthentic? Leaders are also only human and developing and practising positive leadership is always a journey. Lesser authentic leaders may still have authentic moments, and the reverse is also true. It is prudent to be mindful of the fact that AL is not about impression management; rather, an authentic leader self-regulates behaviour to be congruent towards the leader's best self. Followers will decide whether they perceive their leaders to be authentic as leaders. Furthermore, followers will decide whether they can trust a leader. It is the iterative process of AL growth, already described, that ultimately has an impact on the organisational outcomes that need to be achieved.

At this point, it is important to distinguish between leaders and followers in the conventional hierarchical sense versus the AL sense. As authentic leaders lead by a presence that can transcend their position, their leadership can have a 360° influence. Authentic leaders can lead even their leaders, or those with whom they might have a dotted line relationship, whom they need to influence all the same. This therefore means that authentic followers are all of those with whom they are in contact, even those senior to them, whether in hierarchical terms, age or experience.

This chapter commences with a closer look at examples of the consequences of inauthentic moments in prominent international leaders, the effect that these moments have had on subsequent perceptions of their followers, on the outcomes that they were mandated to achieve, and on further consequences beyond their mandate. The review then continues by exploring the effect of AL on inter-relational trust between leaders and followers, on individual leadership effectiveness, and on lateral (peer) and vertical (teams below and sometimes even above) team leadership effectiveness. Finally, it concludes with the potential effect of AL on organisational outcomes. This is very important, as the primary focus of the majority of organisations is to meet or exceed their organisational targets.

WHAT WE HAVE TO LOSE WITHOUT LEADERSHIP AUTHENTICITY

To illustrate the consequences of moments of inauthentic leadership, I researched two global organisational leaders. I considered their inauthentic moments and the consequences of these. I chose the examples of CEO Bob Diamond in the Barclays scandals and CEO Martin Winterkorn in the Volkswagen scandal, to illustrate the consequences of inauthentic moments. In each of the two examples, I outline these inauthentic moments and how they have been viewed by the public, followed by my own reflections of the consequences of a lack of authentic leadership behaviour at that moment in time.

Example 1 refers to Bob Diamond whilst he was the CEO of Barclays Bank. In the article 'Barclays – a lesson in leadership'[49], Stephen Archer considers the role of the leaders in the fall-out of the Barclays Libor scandal. The following are some excerpts from his article.

> *The banking community has been viewed as villains ever since Northern Rock was the first to have the wheels come off in 2007 – nearly five years ago. The Bank of England has also become tainted by the latest scandal. A few less mentioned facts on Barclays; firstly, the $450 million (£290 million) fine: $93 million of this was by the FSA – the rest was by US regulators....*
>
> *Barclays chief executive Bob Diamond, his COO and the chairman, have resigned but will the removal of the head cure poor behaviour amongst the other 140,000 employees? Judging by the repetitiveness of bank management errors, it seems that the lessons are either not being learned or not learned fast enough. No matter what the failure..., the root cause is the failure of leadership. But how can we say it is leadership when a) Diamond had achieved significant financial results for Barclays and b) it was not him personally that fixed the rates? It appears that he was an effective leader, he got things done and huge numbers of people were marshalled to achieve good results for the bank. But Diamond is what we call an EBL – an effective but bad leader... Generally, only effective leaders make it to the top but because of narcissism, insecurities or other personal flaws they are often really bad leaders...*
>
> *But what defines a 'good' rather than an 'effective' leader? The problem we have is that generally leaders are only measured on effectiveness and results. How they got the results and the price of what may be unacceptable or unworthy practice is very rarely evaluated. Bad leaders usually preside over, create or tolerate a bad culture. What is culture? It is 'the way we do things around here'. Leaders may set the culture by their explicit instruction, tolerance and the sorts of things they reward. In so doing the leaders set the cultural tone.*
>
> *Good culture in turn is a reflection of good values that are brought to life day after day. It cannot be lip service or an act. It has to be authentic. When Diamond was hired, was he hired for his previous achievements or his values? Clearly, we need talent: skills for the business and the softer skills of leadership and the methods of recruitment as directed by boards will have to be expanded to gain far deeper insight into people. This means governing boards must also assess the values and culture that is going to deliver the best results for the business.*

Example 2 of an inauthentic moment refers to Martin Winterkorn whilst he was the CEO of Volkswagen, a well-known brand in the motor vehicle industry. In the article "VW's emissions scandal: a test of authentic leadership?"[50], Claire Gallagher considers the role of leadership in the fall-out from the VW's emissions scandal. The following are some excerpts from her article, commencing with a comment from a disappointed member of the public.

Member of public: *I'm so disappointed to hear about the Volkswagen emissions scandal. Don't get me wrong, I'm no "petrol head", nor am I the owner of a Volkswagen car. I'm a mum, a dedicated consumer and self-confessed optimist. So when I hear that Volkswagen has deliberately misled us over emissions I feel terribly let down. I simply expected more from such a well-respected brand.*

So, what did they actually do?: *Following an investigation from the US Environment Protection Agency (EPA), VW has admitted to intentionally rigging emissions tests in diesel-powered cars. It appears that software was programmed to switch engines to a cleaner mode during official emissions testing. After testing, the software switches off and the same cars were found to emit as much as 40 times the legal amount of pollution. VW have now stopped selling diesel models in the US (representing a quarter of their sales). The share price plummeted 20 per cent within 24 hours of the news breaking; they potentially face fines of up to $18 billion, criminal charges for their executives and are likely to be beset by a number of class action lawsuits in the US. An investigation into their European emissions testing has just started and who knows what that may reveal. Is it possible that the car industry is just as flawed as the financial services industry?*

Team VW: *Certainly the damage to the Volkswagen brand is immense, but what of the damage to their people, the 592,586 staff who turn up to work every day? As production of diesel cars is on hold, the implications for VW workers are potentially devastating. CEO Martin Winterkorn has already stood down, but sitting on a €14.9 million pay package, this should be easier to bear than plant workers facing salary cuts or possible redundancies. Winterkorn issued an apology and ordered an external investigation into the matter. "The board of management takes these findings very seriously," he said. "I personally am deeply sorry that we have broken the trust of our customers and the public." Disappointingly no mention of his employees, those who may bear the brunt of this fiasco and who'll have to painstakingly rebuild VW from the inside out...*

Requirement for authentic leadership: *So how will VW measure the internal fall-out of this scandal and what will they do to recover? VW needs leaders who will come clean, acknowledging what went wrong and determined to make amends. They need to create a culture that is focused on everyone doing their best every day and doing the right thing, where everyone is aware of and invested in protecting the VW brand and reputation. They need to rebuild pride and trust in their organisation, from the inside out. I want to hear stories from employees about how VW are putting things right, stories that demonstrate how their leaders are contrite and steadily rebuilding confidence. I'd like to see the executives, who have enjoyed the privileges of leadership, now lead by example.*

These examples illustrate leaders who lacked values-driven leadership. Whilst effective leadership might be equated to what extent results are achieved, morally effective leadership is about *how* those results are achieved. The Barclays example illustrates that the culture of an organisation is informed by what leaders explicitly instruct, tolerate or reward, and in this case, the "wrong" values were rewarded. Leaders need to be positive examples to followers of what is expected in terms of their behaviours. This needs to be considered when a leader is hired, so that the values that an organisation espouses become their enacted values. Only then can we expect authentically effective leadership that will deliver the best results for the business on a sustainable basis.

Sadly, this is not always the case and individuals are hired for a variety of reasons that seldom include a realistic assessment of personal values. When leadership was inauthentic, as illustrated in the VW's emission scandal, it negatively affected the trust of the ordinary person in the street who always regarded VW as a brand of integrity. It also had huge financial repercussions as the VW sales plummeted, and further costs were required to pay for fines and lawsuits. This resulted in a knock-on effect on VW employees who were not only emotionally but also financially affected by the impact of the inauthentic choices that were allowed by their CEO. Yet the CEO did not accept sufficient ownership in the part he and his leadership team had played in this unethical behaviour within their organisation, and instead walked away with a golden handshake.

The afore-mentioned examples illustrate that effective and good leadership are not necessarily the same thing. The difference lies in how a leader achieves effectiveness; for instance, were intended results achieved through ethical or unethical means, or else were these results achieved at the expense of others? In these illustrated moments, the leaders failed as authentic leaders as they did not take psychological ownership or responsibility for their choices and behaviours, nor did they reflect moral considerations or balanced processing in their behaviours. These leaders did not reflect relational transparency regarding their agendas, and as a result, their followers, whether those were employees, clients, or voters, no longer trusted them or considered them to be a fit as leaders. It is for this reason that I refer to authentic leadership effectiveness (ALE) where I refer to a leader being effective by being true to self, true to the leadership position, with a strong moral underpinning, for the greater good of all whom they need to serve. When this does not happen, the consequences can be considerable.

WHAT WE HAVE TO GAIN FROM AUTHENTIC LEADERSHIP

In illustrating the positive effects of authentic moments, I once again considered well-known international leaders, both in the corporate and political fields, and delved into some of their published authentic moments. Whilst I do consider well-known political leaders through the lens of AL in a later chapter, in this instance, I chose to interview three corporate leaders with whom I had a personal AL development relationship and whom I had not seen for at least a year. In the interests of anonymity, I changed their names. The first leader, Neo, previously at a senior and now at an executive level, had allowed me to partner her in her journey towards increasing her AL presence. Her environment was challenging since she reported to an autocratic organisational leader in whose presence she would always lose her confidence. Misha and Noma, the second and third leaders, both previously in specialist positions and reluctant to lead, had since been promoted to senior leadership levels. In their new positions, they needed to work on increasing their AL presence in order to effectively lead their teams and deliver effectively through others.

I decided on adopting a slightly different perspective when I approached Professor Nicola Kleyn (identified as Prof Nicola), the Dean of the Gordon Institute of Business Science (GIBS), a leading Business School in South Africa. I asked her to share her perception as a follower of Advocate Thuli Madonsela (identified as Adv Thuli) as an authentic leader. Adv Thuli led the office of the Public Protector of South Africa until October 2016, a role that had been most challenging and in the public face, due to the unethical behaviour of the SA president and his followers. Following were the first two questions I had asked each of the three leaders.

Question 1: Please describe your current leadership position, and your responsibilities whilst in this position.

> *Neo: I have been the Vice President (VP) of human resources for an international mining organisation since Sept 2014. I am the HR function leader for this mining organisation, and accountable for ensuring that the human resources and public affairs strategies for the organisation are implemented. The mining division is represented in various provinces, and is the beginning of the value chain of the organisation. The department has about 160 people across the mining division and I service a total employee portfolio of around 8000 people.*
>
> *Misha: I am currently based at a financial institution in a management position, although I don't necessarily manage the same people on a day-to-day basis. I manage people on a project-by-project [dotted line] basis.*
>
> *Noma: I form part of a large national South African organisation in a turnaround phase. The role has 14 people reporting into it, it looks over multi-billion South African Rand portfolio. I'd never managed a Profit & Loss before and I thought I would do so badly. As I was thinking about whether to apply for this role or not, I asked myself a question, "what would **Confident, Inspirational Noma** (my internal identity) do?", and the answer was that she would apply for this role. In the end, I got the role, and I've just been so amazed at how I've been able to be successful in this role. It is a much bigger responsibility. I manage a portfolio of over R5bn. I manage a team of 14 people whereas before I only had a team of one person. The role has a lot of visibility to the CEO, so every month I have to present the progress that we are making. We have very aggressive performance targets that we need to achieve, and so far we've managed to achieve those targets. It's been a very big shift from where I was before to where I am now.*

Question 2: Describe a moment where you experienced yourself being a truly authentic leader. What about this moment allowed you to regard this as an authentic moment?

> *Neo: Before I took up this position, the previous culture was that as a VP I could not interact with people on the shop floor, and I never understood it. HR Consultants were not even allowed to look me in the eye and greet, and I would bump into them, and hug them. It was weird and you could see that they were extremely uncomfortable, but apparently that's one of the things that*

they appreciate now about working for this particular department. I changed how they were used to being treated, how they were being engaged, and I was just me being myself. That was a huge moment, which shifted the dynamics in the department. For the department that used to be called Human Remains, it livened up.

Misha: *I am a creative thinker, and as a result, our organisation has adopted some of my ideas, and have recently introduced these into very exciting pilot projects. I am currently on three of these projects across the organisation where I am part of a team, and in some I am leading the team as well. Managing dotted line relationships is extremely challenging because you don't have the authority like in the solid line positions, and you are dealing with different teams all of the time. So you have those challenges associated in dealing with different individuals. I had previously chosen not to manage people because I had always thought of people as most difficult to work with; but then I realised that regardless of whether I want to manage people or not, one must be able to work with people and through people to do what needs to get done.*

I think an authentic leader is a leader who can lead anyone regardless of position and skill. That has allowed me also to lead my manager who is both administrative and strategic. I have noticed that she now gives me a lot of freedom to do whatever I have to do, to present and move with my ideas. That has allowed me to lead her in managing me, and that is when the team dynamics work much better. When you are authentic, people trust you and trust your word, and in order for them to trust your word, you have to be authentic about everything. What guides my authentic moments, are my experiences, my value system, my work ethics, and my relationships with people. If I'm going to say something, they must know that I truly believe in it, and I want to engage on it. I would like to sleep well at night knowing that I did a good job wherever I could, within my responsibilities, and that I've done the best that I could possibly have done, because of the work ethics and values I hold dear.

Noma: *One example was when I was actually leading upwards with my current manager whilst discussing a project where we had to get work done. His approach is quite aggressive and upfront, and his approach was "let's just do it; people will follow and it will be fine". My whole leadership purpose is inspiring others and myself to do the right thing, and in that moment. I pushed back and said, "this isn't the right thing to do; if you force people to do something they might follow in the beginning, but if they've not bought into it, eventually they're going to lose interest and we're not going to be successful". I had to have my first tough conversation with him around an approach where we take people along the way, equip them, and get their buy-in. It was very scary because I had just started working for him. I did not want him to get the impression that I was lazy or didn't want to achieve results because I was pushing back on the process, but I actually had the strength to say this is not the right way to do it. We followed my approach and we got much better results and much better buy-in, and we were successful in the project.*

The examples of ongoing authentic moments indicate that these leaders lead beyond their positions, by means of their presence. They do not hesitate to lead upwards as well. These leaders have internal AL Compasses that remind them of who they are. As we will see later on in the interviews, they are keenly aware of their internal identities and their leadership purposes. They are informed by the values they hold dear, and the fact that they are all surrounded by other human beings with whom they collectively need to serve a greater purpose. This helps them to get their own egos out of the way, and allows them both to listen to others, and to be listened to by others. They have also learnt to have the moral courage to have crucial conversations that allow them to achieve much better buy-in, and as a further benefit, much better results. When one is authentic, others will trust you, and in order for others to continue to trust you, you need to remain consistently authentic.

From a follower perspective, my first question to Prof Nicola was to describe in detail a moment, or moments, where she had experienced Adv Thuli as being a truly authentic leader, in her capacity as the head of the Office of the Public Protector of South Africa.

Prof Nicola: I'm not convinced that you build up an image of someone as an authentic leader in a moment. I think it's a series of moments. It's unlike some other models of leadership like charismatic leadership, where you can listen to somebody and after two minutes you are struck by a person's presence, and can build an impression of them as a certain kind of leader. I think authentic leadership takes a little longer to build up. So perhaps what I need to emphasise is that yes, I am absolutely a follower of hers, but I haven't worked with her. My impression of Thuli Madonsela has been built through the media, and being fortunate enough to listen to and observe her in person. I'd done some research around her. I had looked at what she had said in the press and what had struck me were a couple of things. The first thing is her courage and ability to focus despite a number of distractions and the pressures that she's faced. Her sense of purpose is for her office. It struck me enormously that she actually used the term – about making a difference to 'Gogo Dlamini's'[1] – underscoring the notion of who are you here to serve, and what you are trying to do. We have so many examples of people, particularly in political office, jostling for favour and not seeking particularly to serve the greater good, but to serve their own self-interests. The thing that struck me about her leadership style was this sense of purpose and the bravery that she has, to continue to serve that sense of purpose.

I think the second thing is her lack of sense of self-importance. Her emphasis on the importance of her office, and how work would continue even if she weren't there. Now that is self-deprecating and I think she's being generous. She has had a profound impact. This notion that it's not all about that person, is something that resonates deeply with me. A good leader, an authentic leader knows when their time is up in a particular role, and I have absolutely no doubt that she will go on to serve in whatever she does really well.

The other thing that struck me the first time I heard her speak was her own demeanour. She's softly spoken, people lean in to hear what she has to say. What I find so notable is the way she influences people because nobody says 'speak up', everybody just leans in and listens harder. Now you have to have a remarkable presence for that, and that very soft, quite deliberate style is absolutely all her own. It differentiates her; it distinguishes her. She showed a level of comfort in that interview when she acknowledged that when she had a problem with a legal case recently,

---

1   Gogo Dlamini is a South African metaphor for a typical grandmother, or a single person who believes that he or she has been wronged by the state, but does not have the means to face the state head on.

that she wasn't the expert. Although she had some knowledge of it, she deferred it to somebody else in her office. This is a demonstration of authenticity; there are situations where we don't have the answers. That level of comfort that says despite the pressure of the office to have the answers and to provide these even when the whole nation is waiting for them, it is in order to consult and defer, I think builds a sense of confidence and trust. She knows a lot, but when you compound that with the impact of knowing that you are not the font of all knowledge is very powerful, so her quiet energy, and her silence gives her power. Ultimately, it is the human trait that says no human being knows it all. There is a lovely quote by Neil Postman that says, "Everything we know has its origins in questions. Questions, we might say, are the principal intellectual instruments available to human beings"; being able to question is a very important skill. You cannot ask good questions if you are convinced you know the answer. She is able to ask very good questions.

This example indicates that positive psychological states (PPS) in authentic leaders inspire trust and confidence in followers. Examples such as moral courage and humility are demonstrated by Adv Thuli, realising that her office and position were more important than the person who filled these. Furthermore, strength-based vulnerability and relational transparency in Adv Thuli were noticed, as well as her sense of purpose, which was to serve the ordinary citizen who might not have the means to face the state head on when possibly being wronged, was evident.

The next questions in my interviews focused specifically on the effect of AL on trust. My doctoral research, combined with my AL practitioner experience, confirmed my belief that practising AL has a considerable impact on inter-relational trust between leaders and followers. AL and resultant trust has a further positive effect on individual and team leadership effectiveness, and furthermore on the results that need to be achieved through those leaders.

How authentic leadership can enhance inter-relational trust

One of my experiential learnings was that everything starts with self, including the development of trust. It is near impossible to trust unknown quantities, and as one of my coaching clients had once shared with me, "Often, the most unknown quantity, is the self." Therefore, before we can trust others, or be worthy of trust by others, we need to trust ourselves. I asked the leaders the following question about the effect of those authentic moments on enhancing trust in self.

Question 3: How did those moments affect your trust in yourself?

Neo: At some point, I did question myself when I saw what was happening, but I just told myself that "Neo, just be who you are, let them get to know you as a person, I came into this world naked, when the doctors smacked my bum they said it's a girl, not it's a VP. So let them know that girl." That was my approach, and the more I let them know me as a person, the more they seemed to like being in this space working here. The more I felt good about myself because I was being myself, the more all these colleagues, instead of judging me, actually liked me.

That confidence grew. I realised that I didn't have to pretend in front of others; I will be vulnerable, I have weaknesses, but they told me they liked it. They said to me "None of the executives have ever talked to us and come and give us a hug. So why are you different?" And I said to them, "I'm being me and I love being me and I love the fact that you guys accept me for who I am."

Misha: What authenticity gives you is freedom. You feel light-hearted or unburdened, because you can say what you want to say, but the important thing with this is never to be arrogant but rather be humble about what you have to say. For me feeling unburdened, is being free to say what I want to say, with humbleness, with respect to others and to myself as well. When you are unburdened, it allows your creative juices to flow, and people listen to you more clearly.

The other thing about being an authentic leader is that you don't have to be right. The most important thing I have learnt, I can be open with people, and have people say, "Let's not do it this way, let's do it that way", and then it is not about it being my idea, or someone else's idea; it's everyone's idea, and everyone is prepared to get going. It is not about being right, it is about working with people to get to a right solution. So sometimes you can say something and leave the discussion wide open so that the people who want to add, can add their thoughts as well. It is so liberating! Previously, I always took more responsibility, and sometimes I took the whole group's responsibility. Now when I don't do that and give everyone a chance, I actually realise there is a multitude of ideas and willingness to do work well, more than I knew others were capable of. The responsibility is cut in half even though the accountability for me as the team leader is still there, as I ensure that I guide everything, and bring everything together.

Noma: So it affected my trust in myself in two ways. The first way is that previously, I had never been someone who had confidence to voice what I thought, or things that should be done a different way. The fact that I was able to do this in that situation, already felt like trust in myself that I was on the right path and doing the right thing. Now I believe that if I do the right thing, even if I don't get the right results, I don't have a problem going back and apologising and suggesting that we do things differently. To have the confidence to go with what I believe is the right thing to do, is something that is new for me. I've already felt a lot of trust in myself just by making that step regardless of the practical results.

A couple of things allowed me to know that it was the right thing to do – the first thing was as we were having the discussion in the meeting, and my manager was talking about not consulting anyone, going down this path alone, immediately something within me just didn't feel right. But the other thing that I've also learnt how to do is to consider my leadership purpose and identity, and if I feel I'm not living up to my purpose and identity, then I know I'm not doing the right thing. I've realised that not every leadership style is the same. I'm confident to the point where I feel that if my leadership style was not going to work for him or was not going to work in the role, then I didn't have a problem not being in that role. I can look for other opportunities where my leadership style can add value, whereas previously I was always trying to change my style to suit the role and I thought that was the way to be successful. I've learnt for the first time that you can be authentic, and you can still contribute value and deliver results.

An antecedent to being able to trust oneself and one's thoughts and feelings is the presence of self-awareness and self-knowledge of one's internal AL Compass, which requires continuous introspection and reflection. Once this self-knowledge has begun to percolate, it then allows the regulation and alignment of our thoughts, feelings, and behaviours in order to remain authentic and congruent. These examples indicate that once a process of continual circumspection is in place, its combination with strength-based vulnerability and relational transparency allows us to reveal who we really are. Typically, we then discover that others actually value our ability to understand ourselves. This can then lead to further positive psychological states, such as a sense of freedom, of being unburdened, liberated, and relieved that it is actually okay to be authentic, especially when leaders are mindful of what is right for the greater good of all. Combining this with AL elements, such as our internal leadership identity and purpose, gives us the confidence and trust in self to be comfortable with our own AL style.

This leads to the question of how inter-relational trust is developed between an authentic leader and followers. Trust can be defined as "the mutual understanding between two persons that vulnerabilities will not be exploited and that the relationship is safe and respectful"[51]. This means we can take action, even where we risk putting ourselves into the hands of the other party. I have learnt that at times trust needs to start as conditional trust, as this provides fertile ground for developing unconditional trust. In time, through consistent behaviour that reflects congruence between espoused and enacted values, integrity is inferred, allowing trusting, authentic leader-follower relationships to be strengthened. The following question addressed the effect of authentic moments and increased trust in self, on enhancing inter-relational trust between authentic leaders and others.

Question 4: How did those moments affect the trust between yourself and others?

> *Neo: In the first couple of months, my Exco peers didn't know how to interact with me. I wasn't the norm that they were used to. I decided I needed to be myself with my colleagues. These mining guys are supposed to be tough; they've been in mining for 35 years. Even so, being myself affected how we worked, because we had this human-to-human type of relationships. They felt comfortable talking to me about things that they wouldn't want to talk about in Exco meetings. So we would be sitting in a meeting, and when asked whether they had any issues people-wise, they'd say "No". Afterwards there would be a queue outside my office, with a "please help me with this, I didn't want to say it in there, but I've got this and this and this...". I'd sort it out, and they would come back and say "thank you". It was weird because I did what I was supposed to do, and they said, "no, you didn't have to, previously we didn't get that", so it just made our working relationships so much easier.*
> *Misha: Previously, if someone new had to start here, my judgment would be that that person is not capable, and then what I would do first, was to over-explain and over-manage. They would feel frustrated, which would frustrate me even further, creating a vicious cycle. Now I give them a chance, and guide them. I have a positive regard for others first, give them a chance to ask, "how would you go with that?", and then guide them and coach them towards getting what we want.*

Managing your time is an important element; not everyone will get it first time; Now, I give people the first bite of the cake, and I guide them. Guiding them when you know how to do it properly, also grounds and unburdens you, because the skill of guiding and coaching in terms of how to achieve work, gives you freedom and less responsibility.

I trust people more now where previously I was more cynical. My default is to trust and then take it from there. From that sense, they trust me because I trust them. When they know that I ask them to do something, it comes from a good and authentic place. This is a good thing because people then tend to work and get their work done on time. It has become a mutual trust.

Noma: *My boss has very different personality traits to me. He is very bullish and confident, and when I joined the role, he actually said to me that he was looking for someone who could be very tough. He believed that to be successful you have to be someone who is aggressive, you take what you want, and that is how one can deliver results. When I joined, I had so much doubt whether this relationship was going to work out, whether he would see me as someone who could add value. I went to his office and I explained to him the reason why I felt that this wasn't the right thing to do and the reason why I was confident that my approach should be the right approach to work. I was amazed by his response as he actually said, "you know we're very complimentary. I can be the person who is aggressive and hard, but you are the person who is more focused on EQ and developing relationships, and so you are helping us to deliver our goals". So he's actually acknowledged from that experience and over time that he appreciated the contribution I brought to the team. He recognises that my leadership style is different from his style, but he can see that it gives results, so it's really been phenomenal for me.*

These examples showed the importance of human-to-human interactions with others, and even more so, of showing a positive regard for others, and being willing to invest the time to assist and empower them. Investing in others is an antecedent to being able to trust them, and such trust is often reciprocated with trust in the leader who makes that investment. Furthermore, having the courage to do the right thing for the greater good leads to respect from others, and has the potential to bring the results that are required from the leader and the team. Such leaders lead by presence, so much so that their seniors may well be prepared to be led by them. From a follower perspective, I asked Prof Nicola, in her opinion, how those authentic moments from Adv Thuli had affected her trust in Adv Thuli as a leader.

Prof Nicola: *I think we must distinguish between trust developed as a result of consistency, and trust as an expectation that somebody will do something positive. I think the one aspect that drives trust in her in terms of reliability is that she is entirely consistent. I've never heard her deviate from script and I think it's her own authentic script. She doesn't manifest one day as something and the next day as something else. She doesn't appear to be swayed by pressure, and in many cases she has spoken about some of her dark days. Of course, it's in those dark days that our leadership mettle is honed. She's been entirely consistent in the way she's projected, in the comments that she's made; she's deliberate, she's thoughtful, she doesn't fly off the handle. I think trust in her reliability and consistency is evidenced by that.*

> *There is another dimension of trust, where I trust the individual to carry the interests that they are meant to carry. What builds that trust is the courage to be the person who goes against the popular vote. There is no doubt that she has come out with verdicts that would not make her popular in current circles of political power in SA. Therefore, that courage builds a different kind of trust. It is not a trust in reliability, but a trust in doing what is right. It is a trust in her ethics.*

This response once again accentuates the importance of positive psychological states such as consistency, thoughtfulness, and the moral courage to stay true to one's leadership purpose, especially during challenging times. What these interview extracts have highlighted is that inter-relational trust between a leader and follower is developed when a leader is willing to be vulnerable. This means that the leader is sufficiently comfortable to reveal personal information if it may be helpful to others. Leaders who usually reflect relational transparency and balanced processing develop relationships of trust and mutual respect with their followers. Followers are then prepared to display vulnerability to that leader, knowing that the leader leads with integrity. Relational transparency can then to lead to organisational transparency. Characteristics that usually allow for trust-building include predictability, dependability, reliability, caring for others, and integrity, and these are qualities that are usually present in AL.

It could therefore be said that leadership authenticity is both a requirement and a consequence of trust building, and often I am reminded of the saying that we join an organisation, but it is the quality of a leader that will determine whether we wish to stay at an organisation, or not. Trust in leaders is a critical component that precedes organisational success. In organisations, this trust needs to extend to interpersonal trust between leaders and followers, where followers are not necessarily only subordinates, but any important stakeholders, such as peers, seniors, and even those outside the organisation that depend on good relationships with such leaders. Interpersonal trust is usually based on beliefs that others have about certain characteristics of a specific individual, and when such trust is broken, it could have serious adverse effects on a team or group's performance.

How authentic leadership can enhance individual leadership effectiveness

While authenticity has been posited as the root construct of positive leadership, it has been also equated to the highest leadership development levels (LDL), and it therefore aligns with the most effective forms of leadership. Following was the question I asked regarding the effect of authentic moments, resulting in an increase in trust in self and with others, on individual leadership effectiveness.

Question 5: How did those moments affect your individual leadership effectiveness?

Neo: It allowed people to be themselves around me; it allowed people to know that I would not judge them. I want to accept them the way they are because they brought different dynamics. People felt comfortable around me, and when people feel comfortable, seeing me drop my guard, and be myself, it allowed them to do the same as well, which had a huge impact on how we interacted, and how we delivered. People have fun at work and that is what is important. You want to wake up and go to a place where it's fun. Sometimes I would ask the team to do things that I knew were impositions, and they would say, "for you we will do this". You don't expect to hear this from your team.

Misha: Before I developed leadership authenticity, in terms of my work-life balance and responsibilities, I was heading towards burnout. Now I take on less responsibility because it has become shared responsibility. I have become more effective because I have become more people-orientated; people then tend to do their work better and quicker, and there is less work for me. This allows me time to think more, and come up with better ideas and to guide people more. Previously, I was in a leadership position but still working at an operational level. Whereas now in leadership I am more visionary, bringing ideas to the table, working with the team, and guiding my team through their and my ideas. I am a creative person, and I feel that if you are too operationally involved, you stymie your creativity, because you are inundated with detail. A creative mind needs time and space, so the pleasure of knowing that the operational stuff is being done, gives me more time to think.

That is why I have come up with dynamic ideas. Instead of working below my level of leadership by becoming too operational, increasing leadership authenticity allows me to trust others. I am now working not only at my level, but also at levels above that. I am not afraid of failure because I am happy to work on something that might not work out. I am also now more prepared to work in areas that are not my areas of expertise, in areas above my level.

Noma: I think that this authentic moment has given me confidence that I can replicate that same approach. Whenever I am faced with a difficult decision I ask myself, what would 'Confident, Inspirational Noma' do. I'm confident that I can apply that test, and the outcome would be positive. The other thing that moment has taught me about authentic leadership is the importance of applying that same principle across multiple areas. This is an example where I was doing it while leading upwards, working with my manager, but I've now also started to do the same thing in the way that I manage my team. Again, I ask whether I am being confident, am I being inspirational, am I inspiring them to do the right thing. It's so interesting because the buying role that I'm currently in, is a role where you have to enforce policy. You have to ensure that a fair and transparent buying process takes place, and that we're not awarding contracts to the wrong people. I've seen that I can apply all of those same principles across multiple areas of leadership, whether I'm leading my boss, my team, the organisation, or even myself whenever I'm trying to evaluate whether I'm making the right decision for myself.

The responses from the leaders indicate that authentic leaders lead by example, and when an example is a positive example, others wish to follow; even more so, as in the case of Neo, wish to go the extra mile for the leader. Balanced processing in authentic leaders also allows them to empower and thereafter trust others to take accountability for their areas of responsibility, which frees a leader to work at their own level, or even levels above. In the case of Misha, this allowed her to move beyond the operational level and to become more visionary, whilst having the confidence that operational issues would be dealt with. Her increased confidence also allowed her to venture into areas that were new to her. In the case of Noma, being guided by her internal AL anchor resulted in an increased trust in self, allowing her to try out her AL approach across multiple contexts, only to find that she was able to lead not only herself, but also her manager, her team, and her organisation. From a follower perspective, I asked Prof Nicola how, in her opinion, those moments affected Adv Thuli's individual leadership effectiveness.

> **Prof Nicola:** *There are multiple models of strong leadership. I do believe that we need different kinds of leadership under different circumstances. It is not for me to validate whether how she articulates her leadership style, is in fact what is practised in that office. But I would imagine that if you provide an environment where ultimately you are all aligned to serve a greater purpose, that is far more inspirational an environment than when one is purely serving self-interest or having to bend to the whim of the leader who has their own agenda. I think ultimately, followers seek meaning, and a greater sense of being able to give followers a sense of purpose that is greater than purely the existence of the Office of the Public Protector in this case, speaks to the impact that it has, and creates an enormous sense of energy.*

This response illustrates that a leader, who stays on purpose and leads by example, has the potential to be inspirational to followers, as human beings mostly need meaning in life, and they need to know that their contribution makes a difference. Followers trust leaders who are true to themselves, and respond more favourably to interventions they identify with.

The fact that authentic leaders are confident, optimistic leaders of high moral character who are aware of who they are, what they value, and how they behave, and who are also attentive to these in others in the context in which they operate, allows them to command follower loyalty, trust, and respect. This further leads to these leaders being able to assert a powerful influence during challenging and extraordinary times, for instance in the organisational context, when there is uncertainty regarding the organisation's survival.

In business, leadership is often approached as a skill with which to increase the effectiveness of the organisation and increase the bottom line, as was illustrated in the examples of inauthentic leadership moments. Such an approach is inherently transactional because the primary motivation is known to be profit-based. Followers in extreme circumstances move beyond transactional concerns; coercive leaders are eventually ignored, and bonuses or promises, or other tangible rewards become less relevant when they have to place their future in the hands of the leader. Business leaders who find it difficult to make the transition from transactional to a more authentic and perhaps transformational leadership may gain both understanding and inspiration from authentic leader role models. Followers are certainly able to recognise the difference between genuine and false authenticity in any leader.

How authentic leadership can enhance team leadership effectiveness

Authenticity is a leadership multiplier, as follows. As an authentic leader's ethical behaviour is infused into the organisational norms and relationships, the inter-relational trust between the leader and followers increases. This has proven to be an important component in predicting various attitudinal, behavioural, and performance outcomes, such as job satisfaction, team commitment, and organisational involvement and commitment. The positive impact of leadership authenticity on the levels of trust, and overall quality of leader-follower relationships ultimately leads to a positive influence on the development of a culture of authenticity. As this is an iterative process, it in turn, serves as a verifying reinforcement through leader-follower feedback, as authenticity encourages further consistency and transparency in the leader's behaviour, allowing the behaviour to become increasingly authentic. Following was the question I asked on the effect of authentic moments, resulting in increased trust and individual leadership effectiveness, on team leadership effectiveness.

Question 6: How did those moments affect the effectiveness of your team?

> *Neo: I think they all wanted to be so proud of themselves, and they also wanted me to be proud of them. It had that spinoff where people just felt "I want her to be proud of me and I'll do whatever it takes in terms of delivery, in meeting customer requirements, to make sure that she's proud of me." I was open in terms of public recognition; if someone did the smallest things I would send an e-mail to the entire department to say what that person did. That's how I interacted with the team. People used to say to me, "ah, you are going to the mines, and people at the mines are hard", but they're still human beings; they might wear this tough exterior, but inside they're softies.*
>
> *Therefore, things started changing! I felt that the level of how they did the work and the quality changed. When I started, it was gloomy; there were days when I would wake up and ask myself, "why did I take this job?" However, people perform when they are treated with respect, when they are shown appreciation daily, even for the smallest things. For me that was just a biggie and besides, I want to be in a work environment where everybody is happy. This year when our organisation did a culture survey, my team was one of the most engaged teams in the group of companies; the group, not just mining; 8000 in mining, 28 000 people in the group.*
>
> *Misha: This is not so much about the team but more about an individual in the team. I have always had a challenge with him. He is extremely smart, but very much a procrastinator. If something is due tomorrow, and you don't remind him, he never gives it to you. I sat with him one day and said, "if you don't do this, this is the risk for our section." I did not write him off or cut him out, and say "leave him, he is deadwood". Because I was thinking that there is value in him, and if there is value in him, how do I bring that out in him? It goes to the human-to-human level where it works. Nowadays people are shocked that he actually talks in meetings, and he actually contributes. I will say "great idea", and give him the responsibility to do it by asking him "do you want to run with it?'" That has been an incredibly positive thing for me. Now he realises that he can up his game and add value. People get into a rut and forget themselves. Now he has re-awakened himself.*

Noma: How that initial authentic moment affected my leadership or my team in a practical way is, for instance, I'm not afraid to be completely open with them. I tell them what we have achieved. I also tell them what concerns me. Because of my leadership vision and purpose, I'm a leader who tells the truth, so I'm very upfront and open with my team. I see that they appreciate that. It makes them more committed because they can see we are walking the journey together. At a place like our organisation, where we have had so much uncertainty, many people in the organisation feel that the leaders are not genuine, they don't tell them the truth, they lie, and then there isn't any security. Whereas my team feels confident that I tell them the truth; if there's a problem, I'll tell them that there is a problem therefore they can trust what I'm saying. The other thing about being confident and inspirational; I try as much as possible to provide opportunities for my team to be inspired not only by myself, because I work hard and I show a good example, but also inspired by other things. I look for opportunities for them to feel inspired in their roles so they can inspire other people as well.

It's made them more effective because every single person who was brought into my team came from other different functions in the organisation. We get really good recognition at group conferences, in the board meetings because of the progress that we are making towards achieving our goals. The other thing is that in the work that we do, we show high levels of professionalism, of willingness, of engagement, and we're constantly getting recognition for that in the organisation. I've managed to take a team of people who, if you looked at them and myself in the beginning, you might not have thought that we could ever succeed. We've actually succeeded, and it's given the team confidence where they feel that they belong, they feel that they can contribute and that's something that's really been a great experience for me as well.

These responses indicate people are only human, and that when authentic leaders show respect, appreciation, and a positive regard for others, they inspire others around them, and then those others are likely to become more engaged, and take pride in the quality of work that they produce. When these leaders display relational transparency, truthfulness, they are trusted by others, and they create a feeling of belonging in others. From a follower perspective, I asked Prof Nicola how, in her opinion, those moments impacted on the effectiveness of Adv Thuli's team and office.

Prof Nicola: The example that we've already touched on is around working as a team that is trying to implement processes that are as effective as possible, despite severe funding constraints. This speaks to the fact that she is not just a leader with a visible face, but she is a leader who has spent time ensuring that the organisational processes, policies, and systems that are in place, receive due consideration. It would be most appropriate to hear from the people themselves, but certainly, there are signs that typically would say that her impact has not been only on the greater public and those Gogo Dlamini's that she has served, but also I would imagine on her own team. Thuli Madonsela has also never come across as somebody who needs to be liked, but her actions instil respect and admiration. Her sense of resolve might not always make her the easiest person to work for, but at the end of the day meaning doesn't come from someone who makes our lives easy. Meaning comes from someone who makes us advance towards our higher purpose.

It is clear from this response that, in spite of severe funding constraints, Adv Thuli ensured to the best of her ability that as many obstacles as possible are removed for her team to be optimally effective, by ensuring that the necessary organisational processes, policies, and systems are in place. Together with her own sense of resolve, it would be very likely to inspire her team to give their best, as well as to leave a legacy that would make the world they serve a better place.

Often when I ask my clients to describe their teams, they refer to the teams that report to them rather than the leadership team of which they form part, and this is often how *silo* effects are created. It is important to consider not only *vertical* team effectiveness, which refers mainly to the effectiveness of how a leader leads the reporting team below, but also *lateral* team effectiveness, which refers to the effectiveness of the team of which that leader is a member. Even if the leader's peers have their own teams to lead, it is important to establish the impact that an authentic leader can have on his or her peers as this enhances organisational effectiveness.

How lateral team leadership effectiveness can be improved: Katzenbach and Smith had the following to say about the notion of a team[52].

> The word team gets bandied about so loosely that many managers/leaders are oblivious to its real meaning – or true potential. With a run-of-the-mill working group, performance is a function of what the members do as individuals. A team's performance, by contrast, calls for both individual and mutual accountability. Though it may not seem like anything special, mutual accountability can lead to astonishing results. It enables a team to achieve performance levels that are far greater than the individuals' bests of the team members. To achieve these benefits, team members must do more than listen, respond constructively, and provide support to one another. In addition to sharing these team-building values, they must share an essential discipline.

Unlike work groups that might work together on a temporary basis, ideally real teams are deeply committed to their purpose, goals, and approach. High-performance team members are also committed to one another, with the understanding that the collective wisdom of teams comes with a focus on collective work outcomes, personal growth, and performance results. By focusing on performance in addition to becoming a team, most teams can deliver performance results that rely on effective team behaviour. Such results require that individual members identify with the team purpose and vision, and that they are willing to make individual sacrifices for the team.

In authentic team leadership, there is a shared leadership approach where all team members, including the leader, share responsibility, and there is a strong reliance on shared mental models, knowledge, and cognition within the team. Leadership roles and responsibilities are shared and distributed throughout the team, depending on contextual requirements at any time. This fosters faster agreements on problem definitions and strategic decisions, resulting in enhanced team effectiveness and efficiency. This becomes possible only once team members develop a collective belief structure and a value system that are shared and adhered to by all team members.

Leadership, both hierarchically (formal leader) and collectively, is central to team effectiveness, as team effectiveness depends not only on the technical skills that members contribute, but also on collective positive psychological states, such as inter-relational trust, which are required to work together as a team. Authentic team effectiveness becomes possible when authentic leaders provide support for the self-determination of each member in the team. In my experience, that almost becomes the main purpose of leaders – to empower every team member to be a leader within his or her own right. Rather than coerce members, these leaders use their values, beliefs, and behaviours to develop others through choices that benefit the greater good of the team and outcomes. By further promoting relational transparency and balanced processing of information amongst team members, a rapid and more accurate transfer of information occurs amongst team members, resulting in the development of trusting relationships, which then further impact positively on individual and team performance.

Therefore, leadership authenticity is an antecedent to team authenticity and team effectiveness. It is what is required to build a solid foundation of the trust required in any effective leadership team and organisation. A team is never created merely for the sake of being a team, and is usually required to reach certain goals. I am deeply influenced by Patrick Lencioni's thoughts on the five dysfunctions of any team[53]. He pointed out that the true measure of an effective team is whether it accomplishes the results that it sets out to achieve. He concluded that the foundation of any effective team is that each member is worthy of trust; not only lateral trust (trust between leadership team members), but also vertical trust (trust from levels above and below current leadership level). More specifically, based on Lencioni's observation regarding ineffective teams, insufficient attention to results is often due to:

- absence of trust within the team, which leads to
- fear of conflict, and therefore a
- lack of commitment, resulting in
- an avoidance of accountability.

It therefore follows that the pyramid of strength in an effective leadership team requires:

- a solid foundation of lateral trust at the bottom of the pyramid, which leads to
- freedom to have healthy disagreements, resulting in
- commitment to a course of action, and
- a willingness to be accountable, which leads to
- achieving (and often exceeding) expected results.

Often, team members fear the exposure of their own and others' vulnerabilities, leading to a lack of communication, which results in difficult issues not being resolved. This then leads to reduced commitment, avoidance of accountability, and, ultimately, a reduction in performance and effectiveness. Archer[54] performed an empirical study on the effect of more candid conversations in a company with severe financial difficulties. The senior management team at the time had a low level of trust, with many unresolved issues. Archer performed one- and two-day off-site teaming sessions with the team over a ten-month period, and then allowed the team to continue with further integration of what they had learnt. The findings of the study were that, although the team had gone through the study, the teaming was not successful, and that one of the key factors was authority issues around the leader of that team. It appeared that the leader was not prepared to be appropriately vulnerable; she was not comfortable enough to acknowledge her own shortcomings.

In my experience, it is not uncommon for an organisational leader to be uncomfortable with displaying balanced vulnerability. It is therefore important to establish before a team intervention of this nature whether the leader is fully prepared to commit to further growth. This might require strength-based vulnerability from all, and especially from the leader. It is at times like these that it is important for the leader to go first, and to be an example of what is expected of those who follow.

Authentic leadership team effectiveness needs to be in place before a leadership team can hope to lead their reporting teams effectively towards delivering the required results. The leadership team members therefore need to be the change they wish to see within the organisation. For the team to become authentic and effective, its leader has to become an authentically effective leader.

How vertical team leadership effectiveness can be improved: Authentic leaders tend to have a positive influence on group performance as they use their values, beliefs, and behaviours to become role models to others. In addition, promoting relational transparency and balanced processing of information allows for a more rapid and accurate transfer of information amongst the group members, allowing individual team members to attend to their tasks, which enhances individual and team effectiveness. There is therefore a strong link between leadership authenticity, individual and collective positive psychological capital, inter-relational trust, and individual and collective behaviour and performance. Individuals in groups that have more trusting relationships are willing to be more transparent and share helpful knowledge.

Leadership teams do not work in isolation, and any expected results are typically delivered through individuals outside of the immediate leadership team, usually by those who report to the team. The trust that needs to be in place needs to be both lateral and vertical, meaning that there needs to be peer-to-peer inter-relational trust within the leadership team, but also between each leader within the team and his or her followers within the organisation. Trust has a positive effect on interpersonal communication, follower attitudes and behaviours, individual and collective performance, and achievement of outcomes.

How authentic leadership can enhance organisational outcomes and results

AL and trust in leadership are therefore associated with numerous important organisational outcomes, which include a general belief in information offered, a commitment to the organisation, task engagement, and job satisfaction. I asked the following question on the effect of authentic moments on the effectiveness of followers, meaning those with whom the leader comes in contact.

Question 7: How did those moments affect the effectiveness of your followers (those that you are in contact with, including your peers and leaders)?

> *Neo: Our organisation's housing project is an example of that. These houses had been delayed for some time and it was small little things. Somebody needed to un-break the deadlock with the local authorities. I remembered that I knew Scarlet. Scarlet has connections with the authorities as the Vice-President of public affairs. Why nobody had spoken to her, I don't know. I met with her outside work, and put that on the table. She said, "that's so easy; tomorrow morning send me a text, but it's done. You guys can proceed with a project." It's small things like that, and people don't realise that human relationships are the key to everything.*
>
> *Misha: People now want to achieve. I want others to be authentic and inspirational, and so they become authentic to themselves. When you lead yourself, and you lead others authentically, people start wanting to become like you. If you think of the initiative of 67 minutes for Mandela, everyone want to become like him, not by trying to be him, but by being our best selves, and that is what an authentic leader tries to get out of people... to be their best selves. Mandela's no longer there, but his spirit is still here... So yes, it breaks down boundaries, and hierarchy lines become softer. Instead of sitting across the table, we are sitting around the table... working towards that thing there, but we all interacting around the table as human beings. The whole becomes more than the sum of the parts.*
>
> *Noma: If I start with my direct boss – when I joined the team, he was well known in the organisation for a distinctive management style. I see his leadership style towards me, and even towards the team, has changed. He is giving people more space to perform in their natural leadership style. In terms of my team; they are people who came from a bad place, and now they feel confident; they feel they're producing and they are learning new skills as they go. One of the central points of the culture of our team is that I always go back to the same thing. When the situation is tough or something has gone wrong, I ask them what the right thing is to do. I see those values also coming through because they're starting to practise the same things.*
>
> *In terms of the wider organisation, for a very long time we have been struggling with performance. What my department has managed to do is to create an example that you can actually achieve something. There is strong talent in the business, people who are engaged, who are willing, and I think it's set an inspirational example for the rest of the organisation. We recently had a group conference where the CEO called everyone in the organisation, and he was talking about the strategy. I was one of the people who had to present what we were doing, and he asked*

me questions afterwards. It was so amazing coming out of that session and having people who I didn't even know, coming up to me and saying "I'm so inspired for what you and your team have done". And it's not just about the organisation, because I had a lot of Black females coming to me and saying "you are a Black female in a position of leadership, and it looks like you're doing well and we now think that we can do it too".

These examples once again reflect that authentic leaders lead by a presence rather than position. They do so by remembering that they interact with human beings rather than human resources, and as they lead themselves first, they become inspirational not only to their teams, but also to their seniors, and as in the case of Noma, to others with whom they do not necessarily have a direct relationship. Interestingly, leadership such as theirs has the ability to soften hierarchical boundaries, as they inspire followers to engage and work together for the greater good. Misha reminds us of the legacy of another authentic leader, Nelson Mandela, who inspires us still today. However, she points out that rather than his legacy encouraging us to be a replica of Mandela, it encourages us to endeavour always to be the best we can be. I asked Prof Nicola how, in her opinion, Adv Thuli had affected follower effectiveness in general, and specifically, her own effectiveness as the Dean of GIBS, as follows.

Prof Nicola: for me there would be the two areas – the one is the courage to speak, and the other is the way in which she is inimitably herself and the power that that gives her. We're operating in an environment where there are enormous challenges on the system, whether that is the political system, or whether it's around the absolutely unacceptable levels of inequality, of corruption, of poverty that we face. It requires determined energy over the longer run, and so to me she demonstrates not only intelligence and courage and ethics, but actually role model persistence. The one other thing that struck me was her amazing energy. It would seem that she gets up at 3am in the morning. She has what she calls her TIPTAT list – "things I plan to achieve tomorrow". There is on the one hand this sense of purpose but alongside this is constant resolute translation into daily activity. It is all very well having wonderful, great aspirations, but unless you are actually working on those every day, that's not effective.

The paradox inherent in my admiration is that following the practices of other leaders destroys your own authenticity. One can look and one can admire, and what we have to look at is admiring the quality of that leader. I know I certainly couldn't get up at 3am, but what we can look at is the sense of resolve, her sense of focus, and that certainly we can translate into our own lives. The challenge is the moment we simply try to plug what a leader does into our own life, it's not going to work. It's about being our best authentic self but in the context of something purposeful.

Her sense of resolve, what she wants to achieve, her ethics, she is her own person; she owns her own energy. Her emphasis on listening, we haven't touched on that. She has commented on how her quietness enables her to listen. I think this notion of good leaders being able to listen, is critical. Her comment about "a person can never be more important than the office" is something that we all need to take very, very seriously. Her sense of humility; she made a quote in an interview, "like any other member of the team". She doesn't create power distance, but in her own way she takes power or she has power. My sense of her is she has deep self-awareness; she comes across as being somebody who understands, and who has managed to reconcile her sense of self, her strengths with what she's trying to achieve.

Prof Nicola refers to Adv Thuli's *role model persistence*, and indicates how experiencing moral courage, authentic power and enacted ethical considerations and behaviour in a leader, is inspirational to followers. Furthermore, she refers to the fact that this leader *walks her talk* by ensuring that her great aspirations are consistently translated into accompanying actions, whatever it takes. She is further inspired by the inimitable sense of authenticity in Adv Thuli, her awareness and understanding of self, and of what her leadership purpose requires of her. She refers to Adv Thuli's humility when stating that she simply fills her position, just like any other member of her team, rather than that she *is* her position. Adv Thuli is a leader by presence that transcends the power that her position gives her. Prof Nicola warns us, however, that the intent of feeling inspired by a leader such as Adv Thuli should not translate into trying to be like her, but rather to be the best self we can be, echoing the thoughts shared by Misha.

Finally, I asked leaders about the effect of authentic moments on the achievement of organisational outcomes, towards which, after all, organisations aim.

Question 8: How did those moments affect your organisational outcomes?

> *Neo: Whenever a new union enters in our organisation, there is normally negativity towards it. I used the same approach as to my team, to welcome a new union, ABC, into our mining organisation. When ABC started recruiting at the end of 2014, I would hear Exco members say, "We need to destroy them". I would respond, "Colleagues, our job is not to obliterate unions. Let employees make their decisions, and then we decide, once they've received the threshold percentage, how we will integrate them in with the rest of the other unions, and how we manage it. The closer we keep them, the better we manage the solution. If we push them away, we are going to have unrest, not only in our operations, but also in our local communities, making this a socio matter and no longer just a labour issue – look at the poverty in our local township. It won't take a lot to spark a huge protest. We need to show our employees that we care about them and that we are not vindictive".*
>
> *ABC got their percentage, but because we kept them close, we neutralised them. ABC wanted a strike in January 2015, it has never happened until today. I sat and had coffee with the ABC shop stewards. They were very perplexed, and said, "we're not used to management treating us like this?" They expected management to have this ambivalent relationship with them. I told them "guys at the end of the day, we get paid by the same company; at the end of the day we are still human beings." I kept saying to them, "guys, you are business leaders; you are not shop stewards. You have people that follow you, whatever you say they will do. They believe in you. Therefore, you have the responsibility of ensuring that those people that you lead have jobs. You can't destroy the goose that lays the egg for those poor people because then it is not that guy that loses a job; it's him, six children, grandparents – there's about 30 people behind that guy. Think of that!"*

That had an impact for the business – we expected a huge strike, but it never happened. I think it was just how we related to them. Unions usually thrive on adversarial relationships. Give them the opposite. Show them respect!

Misha: *We are one out of many departments in the organisation. What it means for our department, it brought more effectiveness and less wasting of time and energy. If one of the pilot projects mentioned proves itself, our organisation will potentially become much more impactful.*

Noma: *Our team has a target of considerable saving in this financial year. We are already tracking in this second quarter to over-achieve our annual target, and I believe we can get to double the target. This is made even more special by the fact that, where we came from, from different areas, no one had done buying before. These were disillusioned people; they had been through tough situations in the organisation. I can't even quantify the return on investment, it's been phenomenal.*

These responses indicate that authentic leaders do not only lead those who report to them, but also their colleagues, and in this case, even the union members, doing so with respect and care. In the case of Neo, this averted huge protests, potential strikes, and a loss of income both for the employees involved and for the organisation itself. Misha indicated that the pilot projects introduced by her could make her organisation, a strategic organisation in SA, much more impactful. Noma indicated that allowing her AL compass to guide her, allowed her to build from scratch an effective team who was not only meeting, but also exceeding their annual targets, which was very important for this organisation in a turnaround phase.

I asked Prof Nicola how, in her opinion, those moments affect the outcomes against Adv Thuli's mandate for the greater good of SA.

Prof Nicola: *I don't know enough about the constitutional mandate, but what we know is that this office has a very clear mandate. I have no knowledge of the backlog of cases, but certainly, what we do know is that she hasn't shied away from tackling with gusto, intelligence and ethics, very difficult questions to investigate. So, if one goes by public opinion, if one looks at the evidence of the cases that she has addressed, that would lead me to conclude that she's been effective in achieving her mandate, given the limited funds she has. What she has constantly alluded to without complaining, is the fact that the office cannot solve everything it needs to solve in terms of funds, and that's a reality of modern day life.*

These examples reflect that irrespective of the level or the context in which authentic leaders operate, allowing themselves to be guided by their internal AL Compasses allow them to create more authentic moments that positively affect not only their trust in themselves, but also inter-relational trust between them and others. This results in increased individual and team leadership effectiveness, and a better delivery against organisational outcomes. A more detailed case study on the powerful effect of ALE on business results can be found in case study 1 in Chapter 9.

CONCLUSION

This chapter focused on the considerable effects of inauthentic moments in prominent international leaders, on others' trust in them and on organisational outcomes. The key points highlighted in this chapter illustrate that AL allows for an expansion of the traditional concept of followers, since those more senior, whether in terms of organisational hierarchy, age, skills or social context, may decide to pattern themselves on these authentic leaders. "Good" leaders move beyond the achievement of results to creating environments that are characterised by what is in the best interests of everybody. Authentic leaders often lack self-importance and are able to influence others positively through their presence alone. This reflexively increases the authentic leader's own effectiveness, the effectiveness of followers and, ultimately, the effectiveness of the team. Ultimately, AL has a positive effect on the achievement of organisational results, as will be illustrated in a case study outlined later in the book.

GROUP DISCUSSION: WHAT IS THE EFFECT OF LEADERSHIP IN YOUR ORGANISATION?

Consider inauthentic leadership moments in your organisation. How have these affected:

1. Your inter-relational trust in your leadership?
2. Individual and team leadership effectiveness in your organisation?
3. Organisational outcomes and business results in your organisation?

Now consider AL moments in your organisation. How have these affected:

1. Your inter-relational trust in your leadership?
2. Individual and team leadership effectiveness in your organisation?
3. Organisational outcomes and business results in your organisation?

PART II:

DEVELOPMENT OF AUTHENTIC LEADERSHIP

Chapter 4

DEVELOPMENT OF AUTHENTIC LEADERSHIP

I am often asked whether leaders are born or whether leaders can be developed. The answer is a bit of both. We all have strengths in different areas, and for some more so in leadership than others. Depending on our willingness and ability to develop further, we can all increase our ability to lead, starting with leading self, followed by leading others and organisations. I also do believe that we can continue to develop as leaders for as long as we are able and willing to do so. I therefore never refer to one's best self and instead, refer to the next level of one's possible self.

In this chapter, I focus on the development of leadership authenticity. I introduce the concept of varying leadership effectiveness levels, and the link between these and leadership authenticity. I continue with a discussion on the development journey towards leadership authenticity as long as there is a sufficient level of leader developmental readiness and commitment. I also explore how leadership authenticity can be enhanced by the development of AL political acumen. I conclude this chapter with an overview of the various lenses through which we can measure AL development.

DEVELOPMENT LEVELS TOWARD LEADERSHIP AUTHENTICITY

AL is related to characteristics such as self-awareness, self-esteem, trustworthiness, integrity, respect for others, and high emotional intelligence, which are the characteristics that one expects to find at the highest level of leadership. However, one has to bear in mind that the level of authenticity within any leader varies along a continuum, from complete inauthenticity towards full authenticity. Eigel and Kuhnert[55], having done research on AL and leadership effectiveness levels, remind us that many distinctive features of authenticity, such as the afore-mentioned, and other noble characteristics, are the outcomes of a developmental journey, and it is at the highest leadership development level that leaders are most authentic in whom they are and what they have to offer.

It is therefore useful to understand the various leadership development levels[56] of maturity that shape the moral and cognitive capacities of any leader. The underlying rationale for the leadership development theory is that leaders grow through an increasingly better understanding of who they are and how others see them. Individuals develop over the course of their lives, through life events and, in the case of leaders, leadership episodes, and do so in predictable ways. It is for this reason that there are measurable differences between leaders, which account for the differences between less and more effective leadership.

Rather than having an objective experience of the *real* world, humans construct a subjective understanding of the world that shapes their experiences.

If we then extend this theory to include development, it assumes that the more life events that individuals experience, the more these allow them to progress from simple to more complex modes of understanding their reality. A leader's constructive development capacity runs along a development continuum known as *leadership development levels* (LDL), ranging from LDL2 to LDL5, with LDL1 being *pre-adult*. Following is a brief description of the defining characteristics at each of the leadership development levels, from LDL2 to LDL5, which are characterised by alternating periods of stability and growth, as illustrated in the following figure.

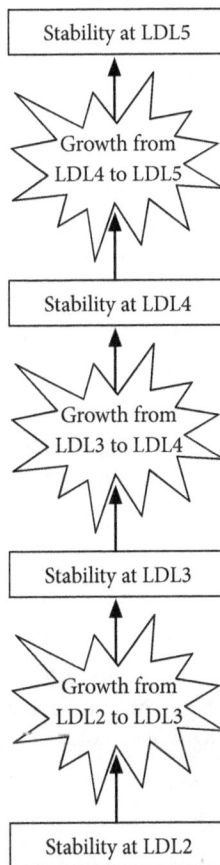

Figure 1: Leadership development progression[57]

A LDL represents a measurable capacity to understand others, our situations, and ourselves. Each LDL is the total of who we are, how we think about leading others, the way we see and solve problems, and what we know to be important and true. This capacity to understand is more than the sum of what we know; it is *how* we know what we know that defines our LDL.

What we know is what we learn from our experiences. *How* we know, or the frame for our understanding, is how we understand or make sense of our experiences. The way in which we differentiate levels of *how* we know determines our LDL. More specifically, when new experiences contradict our current way of thinking and understanding of ourselves, others, and our situation, those contradictory experiences potentially become the catalysts for further development, helping us to develop increasingly more effective ways of knowing, processing, deciding, and relating over the course of our lifetime. This developmental phenomenon explains why some leaders lead more effectively than others.

The differences between the lower and higher LDLs can be determined by grouping the characteristics of the development progression around three areas of experience – intrapersonal, interpersonal, and cognitive – referred to – as knowing ourselves, knowing others, and knowing our world respectively. The ways of knowing differ significantly for each LDL. As leaders move from lower to higher LDLs, there is a transition in the *knowing self* realm (intrapersonal), from an externally defined understanding of self to an internally defined understanding of self; in the *knowing others* realm (interpersonal), from self-focus to other-focus; and in the *knowing our world* realm (cognitive) from simplicity to complexity.

Thus, the lowest LDLs present in adulthood can be described as cognitively simple or concrete, interpersonally self-centred, and intrapersonally defined by the immediacy of the moment and the external factors that dominate at the time. Less than 10% of leaders operate at this level. In contrast, the highest LDLs represent an ability to determine what is important in a situation, and do so with an understanding that is complex, principled, inclusive, and stable. This is more authentic, as such leaders know better who they are and how to make a significant contribution. With all other things being equal (traits, knowledge, skills, and ability), individuals who know, process, decide, and relate at the highest LDLs, not only respond to life's dilemmas more effectively, but have an increased capacity to lead others well.

In order to produce sustainable and effective solutions in a complex environment, it is imperative that the leader knows self, others, and the environment at the highest LDL. Usually in the development from the lower to the higher LDLs, one can only grow and not regress, and levels cannot be skipped. What does vary from person to person is the rate of development; for instance, where each person stalls at any level and for how long. This might well depend on the challenges each person encounters, and how they choose to respond to these. It also depends on the level of leader development readiness, and the commitment of the leader to further growth. Only 5-8% of the adult population between 40 – 60 years operate at LDL5. Research has shown that characteristics required at this level are associated with leadership authenticity[58].

JOURNEY TOWARDS INCREASED LEADERSHIP AUTHENTICITY

The characteristics that need to be present at the various leadership levels beg the question of how one gets from one level to the next, especially if we are to assume that our rational intelligence (IQ) and personalities do not change much in adulthood. Usually, the catalyst for the further development is an event that threatens to challenge the leader's current worldview and destabilises the equilibrium at the leader's current level. The challenged leader will construct a new understanding, which will either limit or empower the leader. As leaders respond to these challenges, they can either resist or grow. Assuming that we are systems within our own right, systems thinking suggests that we are never static; we either grow or diminish. Rather than allowing entropy to set in, leaders should be continually encouraged to seek further growth.

In my experience, two major categories of triggers result in leaders approaching me for AL development. The first trigger is when something has occurred in their leadership context that threatens their continued leadership practice. The second category is when they are no longer fulfilled in their current leadership role, and something needs to change, but they are not sure what that is, or how they can change it. At times, it can simply be that they no longer experience meaningful success; they are no longer eager to jump out of bed in the morning to practise their role as a leader, and this has a potentially limiting impact on their leadership effectiveness. Often, my clients simply feel that their organisations have squeezed *the self out of the self*, leaving them to question, "Who have I become?" or "Who am I really?" Often a journey of AL development can address such an existential dilemma.

AL development and the emergence of AL behaviour needs to be divided into 1) the intrapersonal processes, followed by 2) the effect of that on self, others, and outcomes. This requires that the process model of the emergence of authentic behaviour needs to start with self. As every leader also forms part of a bigger system, they interact, influence, and receive feedback from other members in their system. An important consideration in the development of leadership authenticity is to bear in mind that the leader's worldview, or internal compass, can range from being relatively flexible to being very fixed and rigid, in which case the leader is not necessarily open to innovation or creativity. Dweck[59] refers to this as fixed and growth mindsets, and indicates that as part of one's worldview, one needs to believe that one can grow further as this allows one to step into a growth mindset. Mindsets are influenced by these worldviews; in turn, worldviews remain limited when mindsets are rigid as rigid mindsets can bring learning and growth to an end.

Our worldview forms part of our internal compass. So often, we are told to be more self-aware, but this begs the question of exactly what aspects of ourselves we need to become more aware. In the context of AL development, I introduce in Chapter 6 the various elements, such as our internal identity, our purpose, vision and legacy as leaders, our values and ethics, our beliefs, and our thoughts and feelings that comprise our internal AL Compass. All these elements inform our leadership behaviours.

This development often requires the leader to develops a muscle not often focused on, which is to grapple with the various aspects of their internal AL Compass, not only to increase self-awareness, but also to increase self-regulation in terms of the changes that might be required within that internal compass, which ultimately needs to reflect in the leader's behaviour.

LEADER DEVELOPMENTAL READINESS

As already discussed, whether further development happens in response to a catalyst, such as a life event that threatens to challenge the leader's current worldview, or in response to a leadership development intervention, it is important that the leader engage in balanced vulnerability that allows readiness to engage in such a development journey. This becomes especially challenging in the organisational context when a leader is instructed to engage in such development. A leader's developmental readiness is a function of two parameters, namely motivation and ability to develop. Motivation to develop is enhanced by interest and goals, learning goal orientation, and developmental efficacy, whilst ability to develop is promoted by the leaders' self-awareness, self-complexity, and meta-cognitive ability.

In my experience as an AL development facilitator, I have learnt that not every client leader embarking on the AL journey is at the same level. Nor do they have the equivalent skill to develop further, which was highlighted during my doctoral research study. This could be linked to leader developmental readiness, and as a result, commitment to further growth. The will and the skill to develop further, as indicated in the level of leader developmental readiness, requires intrinsic motivation to want to focus on achieving or aligning to interests and goals, underpinned by a belief or confidence that the leader can change and develop by engaging in new experiences (developmental efficacy). The ability to develop requires high levels of self-awareness, and cognitively complex leaders who can process developmental information more thoroughly, and who can derive meaning from developmental experiences. This is discussed in more detail in the following chapter.

DEVELOPING AUTHENTIC POLITICAL ACUMEN TO ENHANCE AUTHENTIC LEADERSHIP EFFECTIVENESS

Politics forms part of any organisation, and it is therefore necessary for any effective leader to take cognisance of this. The higher the organisational level of the leader, the more evident and complex are the political dynamics. My AL clients often share how they prefer not to engage in the political dynamics of an organisation, as they find it manipulative and self-serving. However, at best, a leader needs to understand how to navigate a political minefield in order to remain effective. I often refer my clients to the chapter called "Political Coaching" in one of my books for coaching leaders, which points out that leaders often deal with the following political situations[60]:

- Peers are envious of a leader's promotion and even hostile.
- The leader is influenced by his peers' turf-guarding behaviour.
- The leader's manager favours specific colleagues.
- The leader is required to get buy-in from other departments.

I have personally found other scenarios, as well, that lead to destructive politics. An example that comes to mind is when a leader feels very insecure, and is therefore inauthentic, and uses positional power to divide and rule. Often such behaviour can create a destructive political climate in the levels below that leader. In all these instances, it becomes important for those affected by such dynamics to develop sufficient social awareness to navigate the minefields that might have been created, so that they can remain effective. In particular, leaders need to develop insight into the power relationships in organisations, as it assists them in reading the environment in order to understand how things are done in the organisation. This includes the development of social awareness of the politically destructive and constructive forces at play. It is important for any leader to be mindful not to become so enmeshed in the political ploys that they and their teams become less effective. Scheepers[61] recommends three high-level themes that need to be considered in order for a leader to become politically more astute. These are to:

1. Consider in a credible way his/her position in the organisation, together with his/her connections and relationships across the organisation.
2. Set boundaries by deciding where to draw the line when engaging in political manoeuvring.
3. Network and build alliances to help proactively manage his/her career and position his/her team internally and externally to the organisation.

Just like the development of authentic leadership runs along a continuum, so does the development of political skills. Both leadership authenticity and leader political skills run along a continuum from low to high and, ideally, the combination of high leadership authenticity and high leader political skill produces positive and lasting perceptions of trust in leadership credibility and reputation. The political skill enables leaders to transition from "I" to "We", and authenticity allows leaders to enhance trust, credibility, and reputation through consistent behaviour.

The question that remains to be answered is how a leader can combine leadership authenticity with political skill so that the leader develops *authentic leadership political acumen*. It is important to remember that when using political skills, the authentic leaders continually self-regulate rather than self-monitor. This requires that they ensure that their chosen behaviour is appropriate for any particular situation, whilst continuing to align their behaviour with their working compass within the overarching internal AL Compass. This allows their behaviour to remain consistent and credible.

In Chapter 9, I share a case study of how an authentic leader with a low score on political acumen developed her political acumen in alignment with her internal AL Compass, and furthermore, how this affected her leadership effectiveness.

MEASURING THE DEVELOPMENT OF AUTHENTIC LEADERSHIP

How do we measure what impact ALD has had on the leader? Chan[62] offers four perspectives in terms of measuring AL development, as follows:

1. *Intrapersonal:* considers AL as a system of internal processes such as self-awareness, self-regulation, meta-cognition, and values.
2. *Interpersonal:* considers AL as a positive relational influence by means of relational transparency, behavioural consistency, and relational orientation.
3. *Developmental:* considers AL as a personal journey of growth by means of narratives, lifestories, insight, themes, and self-reflection.
4. *Pragmatic:* considers AL as a means of veritable outcomes by means of growing performance beyond the usual.

It is therefore important to understand what perspective we wish to consider when measuring the increase in authentic leadership. It is even more important to understand that when one is measuring the development of AL from a pragmatic perspective, due to the very individual nature of AL, instead of a *normative* measurement approach where change is measured against a set of established norms, a more suitable approach would be the suggested *ipsative* measurement approach. The ipsative measurement approach allows for the measurement of the self-development of AL as a personal journey of personal growth. It is more meaningful to compare within-person change using the person's unique set of measures as the yardstick, preferably with some input from his/her organisation. This will be discussed further in Chapters 6 and 7.

CONCLUSION

All leaders, no matter what their current leader development level is, can develop further as long as they have a sufficient level of leadership developmental readiness. It is however a journey that requires deep introspection and continual self-regulation against their AL internal compass. Combining AL with AL political acumen can increase AL effectiveness even further. It takes time to depend on life events or leadership episodes to provide opportunities for further growth; organisations need true leadership now. Appropriate leadership interventions can assist in the acceleration of development towards higher leadership development levels.

PERSONAL REFLECTIONS: YOUR DEVELOPMENT OF AUTHENTIC LEADERSHIP

Consider the following:

1. How well do you really know yourself, and what do you believe about your own leadership development level?
2. How well are you able to regulate your behaviour to reflect your values, purpose and vision?
3. How ready are you to embark on a journey towards increasing your ALE?

GROUP DISCUSSION: DEVELOPMENT OF AUTHENTIC LEADERSHIP IN YOUR ORGANISATION

Consider the following:

1. What do you believe about the leadership development level of your organisational leaders?
2. How well are your leaders' values, purpose and vision reflected in their behaviours?
3. How ready are the leaders in your organisation to embark on a journey towards increasing their individual and collective ALE?

Chapter 5

CRITERIA FOR LEADERSHIP
AUTHENTICITY PROGRAMMES

Being able to lead self and others with awareness and authenticity often requires a journey of transformation where we need to explore the internal identity that drives us, and where we need to integrate all of life's experiences into a meaningful context. The development of such awareness requires that we explore what is happening below the emotional soil-line, and it is often a very challenging journey, near impossible to undertake on our own. It requires the skills of someone who will listen in a way that we feel heard, and ask those questions that ignite our minds in order to uncover important aspects of ourselves that we have overlooked; someone who will challenge us to move outside our comfort zone whilst supporting us when we do so.

New self-awareness does not automatically lead to change. It needs to be supported by self-regulation by means of aligning to an internal compass that enables us to remain "*True North*", as Bill George describes it. Our existing ways are often habitual, requiring a partnership with an external experienced person to facilitate the journey towards change from limiting to empowering habits. A leadership coach, for instance, could play this role, as discussions with such a coach can help leaders to increase their self-awareness about what is important, and identify the gaps they need to attend to, in order to achieve their desired outcomes.

The metric of time for the development of AL is typically very long, and it usually takes time for the characteristics of AL to emerge. Therefore, whilst perceptions of authenticity that occur may be instantaneous (self-awareness), the development and execution of actual AL behaviours may take longer (self-regulation). This therefore means that, as conventional leadership interventions might often be short and training-based, they would be insufficient for the transformative nature of developing AL.

I have often found that organisations hope for silver-bullet programmes when considering the development of effective leadership. However, for the afore-mentioned reasons this becomes an unrealistic expectation, and those who truly wish to invest in the development of more effective and sustainable positive leadership need to consider the appropriate investment required for such leadership development. Authentic leadership development involves complex processes that cannot be achieved through normal training programmes. Until recently, the opinion was that AL development, compared to the development of other transformational leadership forms, could not be achieved in a programme format unless that programme could broadly be labelled as *life's programme*. At best, the programme that life offered us, consisting of learning through leadership episodes and life events, could be supplemented with some training. However, there has been a proliferation of new leadership development methods and since then a growing recognition of the importance of leaders' emotional resonance with others, moving the focus of leadership development towards coaching and mentoring whilst focusing on both individuals and teams.

Whilst developing this ALE programme over a number of years, the AL guidelines offered by Cooper et al.[63] and Chan[64] resonated with me, and I ensured that my ALE programme adhered to those guidelines, which has proven to be very effective. I outline these, enriched with my own thoughts, and elaborate further in Chapters 6 and 7 on how this ALE programme aligns to these.

IMPORTANT PROGRAMME CONSIDERATIONS

To date, the guidelines offered by both Cooper et al. and Chan on the requirements for leadership authenticity interventions are still very relevant. Cooper et al. suggested four major issues that need to be addressed by any AL development intervention.

1. *Ensuring the programme itself is authentic:*
    a. Authentic leadership development needs to be underpinned by a valid theoretical and conceptual model, and the key processes need to align adequately and truthfully with the underlying theoretical and conceptual model.
    b. For the programme itself to be authentic, it needs to be mindful of systemic and contextual concerns and specifics that affect individuals. There is no one fit for all in ALD, and for that reason, conventional training programmes are unsuitable. In my experience, whilst authentic leaders might have aspects in common, these programmes also need to recognise the uniqueness of individual and team authentic leadership and their interactions and responses to their environmental and systemic contexts. Not only do their environments and the elements therein affect them, they also influence their environments. A suitable programme needs to be cognisant of such dynamics. Furthermore, the uniqueness of human beings is that they usually form part of more than one system. For example, not only are they are part of their system at work, they also form part of family and social systems outside work, and what happens in one system can cross-influence their responses to others. Finally, their physical bodies are systems within their own rights and are therefore affected too. A programme needs to consider systemic feedback from all of these.
    c. Such programmes cannot be one-time training events. Unique designs might be required to evoke responses required to develop authentic leaders. Such interventions might involve training, one-on-one coaching, and the need to be mindful of trigger events, such as leadership episodes and life events that can test and further develop AL.
2. *Determining how trigger events can be replicated during training:*
    a. Often certain work episodes or life events have an impact on the worldview or leadership style of any leader. These might be smaller events, which accumulate until they trigger a response from leaders who allow these to test or further develop AL in their behaviour.

a. Highlighting and using those events and their responses allow leaders to reinforce new behaviours, either through 'chaining' (reinforcing the simpler behavioural processes that collectively comprise a more complex pattern) or 'shaping' (rewarding successively closer approximations of desired behaviours).

3. *Deciding whether ethics-based decision-making can be taught:*
    a. In the wake of the ethical organisational challenges highlighted in the media, the ethical and moral component has become a central component of leadership authenticity. Can ethics-based decision-making be taught? In my own experience, my leader clients are continuously faced with ethical dilemmas, and it is by assisting them in finding their *True North* internal AL Compass that they learn how this can guide them in making ethically-based decisions. Usually, when individuals aspire to be positive leaders, it goes hand-in-hand with desiring a well-developed moral compass.

4. *Determining who should participate in AL training:*
    a. The question asked is whether all have the innate ability to become authentic leaders. Although I believe that most people have the innate ability to become moral, authentic leaders, it is important that there be a certain level of leader developmental readiness, and this can be tested upfront. In my own practice, I test for leader development readiness and the willingness to be appropriately vulnerable that allows for relational transparency. This needs to be accompanied by a commitment to take ownership of the ALD journey.

Chan offered four working assumptions regarding the requirements of effective AL programmes, which corroborates and builds further on Cooper et al.'s guidelines for AL interventions, and being mindful of my own experience as AL practitioner, I discuss these further as follows.

1. *Targeted and customised.* There can be no default, one-size-fits-all AL training system. Individually considered approaches that are targeted to the specific needs of individuals and requirements of the organisational contexts or cultures in which those individuals are situated, need to be considered. These types of interventions should result in the greatest buy-in, learning, and transfer, and generate the greatest improvement in results. This also accommodates the notion that a programme should be able to be refined along the way to accommodate the emerging needs of any specific leadership situation. I have recently worked with a team to develop team authentic leadership effectiveness, and for the first time, due to budgetary constraints, I did not precede the team development with individual development. During the team intervention, we realised that some individual development was required, and the team development was put on hold in order to allow individual work to be completed. The ability to bring such flexibility into the journey will ultimately yield the most effective results.

2. *High-frequency micro-interventions.* One way to model what authentic leaders go through in real life is to simulate these learning episodes in high-frequency micro-interventions, which would shorten the time required to develop leadership authenticity. In my own work that is always underpinned by a coaching and reflective approach; we do not necessarily always simulate learning episodes. However, as part of the overall journey, we do consider the events that happen in between our sessions, and we do reflect on whether the leader's responses to leadership episodes and life events limited or empowered their ALE. We then consider how this further informs their response to a similar event in future. The coaching approach allows the ball to remain in the leader's court, where the leader reflects on the effectiveness of earlier responses and the way forward regarding future responses.

3. *Self-reinforcing interventions (over time).* AL interventions need to be self-reinforcing, in order to sustain development over time. Three pathways were suggested:

    a. *Development of self-mastery*, which leads to more engagement in the particular leadership development activity, thereby creating a continuing cycle of self-development. I believe that this starts with the enhancement of self-awareness.

    b. *Self-reflection* regarding past leadership episodes, thereby raising further self-awareness and reinforcing the leader's implicit leadership theory held in long-term memory.

    c. *Self-verification,* by means of receiving positive feedback from followers regarding one's AL, thereby bolstering one's sense of self as an authentic leader. It is important to bear in mind though that not all feedback will necessarily always be positive, and it therefore becomes important to consider how we view the feedback we receive. I always tell my clients that feedback can be considered like a tray or coffee/tea, with milk and sugar, and some cookies to round it off. When it is offered to us, we do not drink all the coffee and tea, have all the sugar and milk, and round it off by munching all the biscuits. That could well lead to stomach ache. The same could be said of feedback. It is useful to remember that all feedback is worthwhile considering before taking out of it that which will contribute to further self-development. Finally, no feedback can also be feedback, in that followers might not be comfortable to give the leader feedback. The question then would be "What is it that they are not telling me?"

4. *Multilevel, nested interventions.* Leaders never operate in isolation, and whilst the contexts in which leaders operate impact on the leaders, they also need to acknowledge that they are able to be agents of change. AL development interventions therefore need to incorporate the context, and take levels of complexity into account. This could be accommodated by a nested mix of individual and team interventions.

RATIONALE FOR A COACHING FACILITATION STYLE IN AL PROGRAMMES

Whilst coaching is a conversation, it is not simply a chat, nor is it teaching, training, telling, counselling, or mentoring. Coaching is about facilitating change through listening, challenging, supporting, questioning, testing, and giving feedback. It is about understanding how we manage our brain for more effective performance in life and work. It is about facilitating new awareness, new solutions and outcomes, through dialogue.

Coaching needs to support individuals' growth by helping them to understand themselves better, to reflect on their work, to challenge their assumptions, and to experiment with new behaviours and attitudes. Not only does this allow *individuals* to build more power within, to have a better understanding of self and others, and build up a self-coaching and -development toolkit, it also gives *teams* and *organisations* the advantage of having compelling role models, ideally resulting in a positive impact on their organisational outcomes.

According to Sieler[65], who focuses on ontological coaching, there has been a gradual realisation of the importance of attending to communication and behaviour in organisational learning as it is people who implement systems, structures and practices. Efficient organisational practices depend on human behaviour and communication. The quality of conversations in the workplace affects the quality of relationships, and workplace relationships have a major impact on performance, creativity, and productivity. Conversations and relationships are the lifeblood of organisations. Organisations can be thought of as networks of conversations and relationships. Organisational health is directly tied to conversations and relationships, for they affect key issues of trust, morale, and performance.

Therefore, conversations and relationships are key variables in organisational performance, and building a coaching underpinning into these can increase their effectiveness. However, there are different types of coaching, and it is important to understand what these are and where these fit. In the context of ALE development, the three types of coaching categories of relevance are individual leadership coaching, team leadership coaching, and leader as coach.

The first type of coaching, *individual leadership coaching*, between an external coach and a leader within an organisation, is usually anchored in a one-on-one relationship of trust aimed at fostering learning and professional growth. This relationship often provides an impetus for professional breakthroughs. This type of coaching is often *transformational* or *developmental* in nature.

The second type of coaching important in ALE development is *team coaching*, often confused with similar interventions such as group coaching, team development, team building, and team facilitation. Although there might be overlaps, team coaching is a very distinct coaching development intervention with natural teams. Hawkins, a respected researcher-practitioner in the area of team coaching, points out that team coaching can also be narrowed down further into leadership team coaching, transformational leadership team coaching, and systemic team coaching. He places these along a continuum, and defines team coaching as[66]:

enabling a team to function as more than the sum of the parts, by clarifying its mission and improving its external and internal relationships. It is therefore different from coaching team leaders on how to lead their teams, or coaching individuals in a group setting.

He further suggests a continuum in team coaching, starting with team performance coaching, where the coach focuses on team processes and performance, leadership team coaching, allowing the team to develop collective leadership, and transformational leadership team coaching. He follows on by mentioning systemic team coaching, and refers to it as a newer approach that needs to replace the more traditional team coaching approaches that do not go far enough in their considerations in transforming leadership teams. Aspects of the latter two approaches are appropriate for the collective development of ALE.

The third type of coaching that is important in the development of ALE is that of a *leader as coach.* Using a coaching style of leading, this often enhances leadership effectiveness. A successful leader usually plays two roles, *that of boss, and that of coach.* In the role of the boss, a leader needs to ensure that departmental and organisational goals are met and tasks towards those goals are completed. In this role, the leader attends to outcomes, and the requirements towards achieving those outcomes. This role is therefore *task-focused.* In the role of coach, a successful leader attends to the *how* part of getting things done. In this role, a leader needs to be *people-focused* and believe that those who report to him or her are talented and competent with multiple strengths, and help them through coaching to unlock that potential to maximise their performance.

The leader therefore needs to help them to *learn* rather than *teach* them. Here the leader needs to draw more on non-directive skills, which help individuals to solve their own problems, empowering them to take responsibility for their own performance and development. The leader needs to support these individuals by helping them to understand themselves better and to reflect on their work, by challenging their assumptions and supporting them to experiment with new behaviours and attitudes. Leaders often coach towards improvement of *performance.* Not only does this allow those they coach to build more power-within, to have a better understanding of selves and others, it also helps others to develop self-coaching toolkits. It allows organisations to have compelling role models ideally resulting in a positive impact on bottom lines. Whilst I will discuss the leader as coach in detail as part of the ALE programme in Chapter 7, the following elaborates on the first two categories, namely individual leadership coaching and team coaching.

Individual leadership coaching

In her book, *Business Coaching: Wisdom and Practice,* Stout Rostron[67] outlines the history of coaching, and the coaching process. She highlights the different schools and models of coaching, that one can find single-school coaches, but also eclectic coaches who can blend and use models as they see fit for the coaching conversation required at any one time. I fall into the latter category and always explain to my clients that whilst I might wish to dance the Tango with my client, what the client might require is a blended waltz/foxtrot. During my academic Masters journey, one of my professors explained it in a simpler way; he suggested that if all one had in the toolbox was a hammer, then all else one would need would be nails! Sometimes we might need a screwdriver or a saw – it all depends on the outcome that one wishes to achieve.

Although she refers to it as business coaching, much of what Stout Rostron outlines, applies to executive or leadership coaching as well, as these simply refer to coaching in a more complex environment occupied by executives and leadership in general. Usually an executive or leadership coach would be a more senior or experienced coach, who requires some gravitas in his or her coaching presence, as this allows a senior client to feel safe with such a coach. Coaching originates from the Socratic Method, which is characterised by questioning and self-analysis. It is the role of the coach to facilitate such a process. This requires time and space to think for ourselves, a much-needed luxury, for which leaders seldom make time. Kline[68] refers to this as creating a *thinking environment*, and in the coaching context, the coach creates the safe space for the leader for a thinking environment in which the coach becomes the thinking partner. This requires that the coach understands both the leader's context and the coaching process, which commences with contracting the leader's desired coaching outcomes, and how the achievement will be measured by the leader. The coach and coachee agree on the nature of their coaching partnership and what it is that each one will contribute to the partnership.

There are a number of coaching frameworks in which coaches can be trained. For instance, some coaches are trained in Neuro-semantic meta-coaching[69], which believes that thinking and feeling in human beings occur both at primary- and meta-levels, and which builds on the foundation of Neuro-linguistic Programming (NLP). NLP, in turn, is based on one of the newer schools of psychology, cognitive behavioural psychology, which examines the cognitive processes that precede and inform behaviour, and whether those are empowering or limiting behaviour. This allows the client to notice and change thought processes, which can then further benefit their emotional states and behaviour. There are also coaches who are trained in Ken Wilber's four quadrant Integral Coaching techniques[70]. Results Coaching, on the other hand, bases its techniques on John Whitmore's GROW (grow, reality, options, way-forward) model[71]. Some coaches follow Peter Hawkins' CLEAR (contracting, listening, exploring, action, review) model[72].

The most recent sought-after coaching training is based on Neuro-leadership brain-based coaching, with David Rock, who more recently developed the SCARF (status, certainty autonomy, relatedness, fairness) model[73], which refers to how each of these domains impact on the threat/reward elements that affect the Neuro pathways of our mind. The knowledge of Neuroscience and Neuro-leadership is currently sought after by leadership coaches, as research has shown that if any of the five domains in the SCARF model is perceived to be threatened, it can send us into fight or flight mode, which can diminish leadership effectiveness. More recently, Rock and Cox[74] published some further research on how the knowledge of social neuroscience can help individuals and teams to detect threats in the five SCARF domains, and regulate and adapt, if necessary, their individual or collective emotions and behaviours, to ensure that they remain healthy and effective.

Initially when I was trained as a coach, I thought it important to define myself in terms of the coaching school of training I had received, which is what coaches tend to do. For instance, am I a Neuro-semantic coach, a results coach, an integral coach, or a Neuro-leadership coach? Whilst that creates good (or not) advertising for the various coaching schools, I did not find it very helpful when introducing myself to any new client, especially when every coach they meet feels that he or she had undergone the most definitive coach training available in the market place. During my post-graduate practitioner-based Masters research, we were encouraged to define ourselves in terms of what we can offer to the client in helping them to improve their lives and to become more effective. As part of this journey, I could start considering what coaching tools, techniques and processes I required in my toolbox as a transformational ALE coach. This process helped me to understand the unique purpose and value-add that my coaching could offer to any client.

It is just as important for clients to understand what value they wish to derive from a coaching relationship. When meeting with coaches in introductory sessions, clients need to ask themselves whether they would feel comfortable to work with a particular coach, both in terms of the chemistry they experience in the initial coaching session, and their sense of the fit between the coach's coaching purpose and focus, and their coaching needs. Over and above that, the core coaching skills are common across the various coaching schools, both in individual and team coaching.

Team leadership coaching

As in individual coaching, there are also numerous models in team coaching, and many of the underpinnings in individual coaching can be transferred to team coaching as well. This is well illustrated in Dolny's[75] book *Team coaching: Artists at work*, where seven coaches discuss their coaching models, such as Meta-Coaching, Nancy Kline's Thinking Environment work, Integral-Experiential Coaching, and other models. As in individual coaching, there are numerous team-coaching models, but ultimately one has to ask what the purpose is of the team coaching intervention, and find the best employment of various coaching tools and processes in order to achieve the desired team outcomes.

Systemic transformational leadership team coaching, as described by Hawkins, is appropriate for the collective development of ALE. Hawkins explains that transformational leadership coaching focuses not only "on how they want to run their business, but also how they want to transform their business"[76]. It is only once he refers to the systemic aspect of transformational leadership team coaching that he considers the purpose, performance and processes of the team, with the focus primarily as a collective, and thereafter the personal and interpersonal development within the team. He defines systemic team coaching as follows[77]:

> *Systemic team coaching is a process by which a team coach works with a whole team, both when they are together and when they are apart, in order to help them improve both their collective performance and how they work together, and also how they develop their*

collective leadership to more effectively engage with all their key stakeholder groups to jointly transform the wider business.

In ALD, the thought is that it is not easy to lead others until we can lead ourselves, and that is why it is advisable, at least for the leader of the team, to develop personal and interpersonal leadership on an individual coaching level, before continuing with the collective team ALE development. This can be done either by means of one-on-one coaching sessions, or by commencing with individual development work within the team context.

Skills required across the board in individual and team coaching

As the afore-mentioned sections have highlighted, there are different types of coaching, underpinned by different schools of coaching. Even so, across the board there are certain coaching skills that are required by all coaches. These include skills such as the ability to create rapport with our clients, to listen well to what our clients are saying (or not saying), to question in a way that ignites the mind of the client, to clarify our understanding of what we are hearing, and to support our clients. Finally, a less mentioned skill is called bracketing, where we bracket our own worldviews and assumptions, and focus on those of the client. Other than the skill of bracketing, if one were to compare the competency frameworks of the better-known coaching federations, such as the International Coaching Federation (ICF), the European Mentoring and Coaching Council (EMCC), and the Worldwide Association of Business Coaches (WABC), one would find in each the core coaching skills of creating rapport, listening, and questioning. One could even create benchmarking scales for each of these to help coaches to enhance these skills and measure these during their continual professional development (CPD) sessions.

Creating rapport with the client: Based on Carl Rogers' person-centred approach, it is extremely important in coaching to create rapport with the client as part of building a trusting coaching relationship, because after all, that is the foundation upon which the coach and client will achieve the coaching outcomes. Building rapport by having a person-centred approach allows trust to develop between the coach and client. Rogers maintained that three elements in a coach allow for the creation of rapport with the client, those being[78]:

1. *Congruence:* This is especially important in ALE coaching, and it means that the thoughts, feelings and behaviours in a coach are aligned.
2. *Unconditional positive regard and acceptance:* It is about setting aside one's own assumptions and preferences, and accepting the client as they are. The coaching skill of *bracketing* is very helpful in achieving this.
3. *Accurate empathetic understanding:* This can be done by clarifying one's understanding and playing this back to the client so that the client can firstly check that what the coach is understanding is what they had intended to communicate. A further advantage is that

the client can hear a playback of what they themselves might be expressing for the first time, helping them to create more self-awareness.

All the following qualities are required for building and maintaining rapport in a coaching relationship. These assist towards creating a safe space for the client and a trusting relationship with the coach, allowing the coaching process to work faster and more effectively.

Listening to the client: Deep and active listening allows the coach to listen to what the client is saying, but also to what they might not be saying. It means that the coach allows the client, or coachee, to do most of the talking.

Questioning to ignite the mind of the client: This refers to powerful questions that will highlight information required for the client to increase self-awareness and find solutions he/she might never otherwise have considered.

Bracketing the coach's worldview: Bracketing in coaching, although not often mentioned as a coaching skill, can be described as the skills of exploring the reality of others without the interference of one's own worldview. This can be done by stepping into a mind state of 'know nothing' (meaning the suspension of one's own assumptions), combined with a deep sense of curiosity about the reality of another. This often allows others to feel comfortable in sharing their views with the coach, as they do not feel judged. As coaching is underpinned by various schools of psychology, this aligns with the Rogerian view of holding a positive regard for the client, allowing for a relationship of trust and rapport to develop, wherein the client can safely explore their own limiting and empowering thoughts and feelings, and how to transform those towards achieving their outcomes. This method of bracketing can be applied in both individual and team coaching.

Finally, coaching, and especially ALE coaching, requires considerable commitment of resources in terms of time and finances. Where coaching mainly differs from alternative modalities such as mentoring or training is that whilst the coach plays a facilitative role in the development of leader coachees, it is the leader coachees who need to take ownership of their development journey towards leadership authenticity. Often this requires considerable time, and at times even very challenging work. Therefore, for coaching to be effective, the coaching client needs to be ready for the journey. In response to the question of whether leaders are born versus developed, my response is that leaders can be developed, on condition that they are ready to commit to their development journey. This will be discussed in more detail further on in this chapter.

The role and presence of the coach

The role of an individual or team leadership coach is multi-fold. Firstly, the coach needs to ensure that he or she creates a safe space in which individuals or teams can do whatever work they need to do in order to achieve their outcomes. The coach does this by contracting with the individual or collective leadership client. This means that the coach engages in an initial discussion with the client on what the journey entails, what will be expected from the client, and what can be expected from the coach. I usually explain to my clients that I will do my best to facilitate the journey in the most empowering way to my clients, but that I cannot do the clients' work for them. They need to bring their part of the journey towards achieving their outcomes. We usually then sign a coaching commitment document wherein both parties commit to what they will bring to the journey towards achieving their outcomes. I usually then do an initial and midway review with the client and if appropriate, with the line manager in order to establish what needs to and has been achieved, and what outcomes require further work.

A coach also requires a signature presence, a phrase initially coined in the coaching context by O'Neill[79]. She refers to coaching with backbone and heart, and explains that bringing ideas and challenging suggestions to your clients, whilst maintaining strong relationships and connections with them, is what creates a signature presence as a coach. Van Coller-Peter[80] explains it very succinctly when she states that a coach's signature presence has to do with the use of their voice, presence, and influence, and doing so within moral and ethical boundaries. Not unlike AL, this requires that coaches reflect on whom they are, the roles they wish to play, and an understanding of how to lead themselves.

Both O'Neill and Van Coller-Peter's sentiments resonate with me. As coaches, we sometimes do have to coach with backbone, as dynamics with individual and team clients are not always plain sailing. Both in the individual and team context, our clients might play out limiting or challenging behaviours in the coaching context that play out elsewhere as well. In such instances, a coach needs to challenge the client about that behaviour in such a way that the client is compelled to reflect on what beliefs, thoughts and feelings might be informing such behaviour. A coach needs to suspend assumptions, and always remain authentically curious, for the benefit of the client and the coaching relationship that is intended to achieve agreed outcomes. Simultaneously, the coach always needs to balance backbone with heart, which can be a delicate balancing act. Ultimately, as coaches we also do need to model the behaviour we expect from our clients.

I personally have always felt very blessed to work with my clients, and I see our relationship as a sacred partnership, in which we work side-by-side to achieve the client's outcomes. I also believe that when I start working with my clients, I often can already see the immense potential in them that even they themselves cannot and do not yet see. As long as they are prepared to work hard towards achieving their outcomes, I am 100% comfortable that they will move a long way towards achieving those during our journey. I also continually transfer self-coaching tools, so once our journey has concluded, my clients have developed the ability to self-coach that will allow them to continue further growth on their own. I therefore see my purpose as a coach as becoming redundant to my clients in the most empowering way.

In my coaching commitment document, I also ask my clients to commit to paying forward; meaning that whatever benefits they have gained during our coaching relationship, they will pay forward to others with whom they interact, as not everyone is equally fortunate to experience individual and team leadership coaching.

THE ROLE AND REQUIREMENTS OF AN ALD FACILITATOR

In terms of the role and requirements of an ALD facilitator, I believe that the presence of the facilitator is even more important than usual. Although I was always aware that an ALD facilitator needed to experience a strong intrapersonal sense of authenticity, I never realised how important it was for ALE clients. During my doctoral study on evaluating my AL programme[81], I expected the research participants to limit their feedback to the programme itself, but they frequently referred to the impact and presence of the facilitator. For instance, they referred to the importance of the rapport that developed between the facilitator and each individual participant, and the level of trust and comfort between the facilitator and participants in both the individual and the team sessions.

One of the challenges I had experienced during one of my individual and team ALE programmes was with one of the participants whom I experienced as passive resistant throughout the individual sessions. My experience of this participant was similar to that which his own leader experienced of him – a phenomenon that is looked out for in coaching. This participant indicated his distrust in me, and I realised that I could take responsibility only for my own actions and not for the way in which these were perceived by this participant. As an ALD facilitator, I needed to remain true to myself. I realised that not all participants were equally ready for such journeys. Yet, the results showed that, despite his resistance, the journey did have some positive impact on this participant. Once the majority of the team members had increased their leadership authenticity, the critical mass effect resulted in a more authentic culture in which he needed to operate.

ADDITIONAL PROGRAMME CONSIDERATIONS TOWARDS SUCCESSFUL AL DEVELOPMENT

Two further factors are important when embarking on an ALE programme to ensure a successful outcome of ALD. Those are: 1) the importance of leader developmental readiness and commitment in a participant, and 2) sustainability of individual and team authentic leadership effectiveness in organisations where the only certainty usually is change.

Leader developmental readiness and commitment

Leader developmental readiness and commitment is crucial to successful ALD. Whereas in an individual leadership authenticity coaching programme the individual often identifies a need for further development, in team initiatives the need for team leadership development is more often identified by the leader or the human resource business partner, whether all team members are in agreement or not. At the outset of one of my ALE programmes with an executive leadership team, the General Manager had communicated the following to me in writing:

Years ago, I was asked to take over the management of the brewery due to a period of sub-standard performance. Due to the new members in the team, the team dynamics changed with a significant amount of distrust amongst members and a resulting negative impact on overall performance. Although as individuals, most members are recognised as high potential employees, but as a team the leadership and the direction and subsequent performance is lacking. It is clear that an intervention is needed to extract the potential from this team and get them to lead the brewery to the performance that is required.

It was agreed that they would participate individually and collectively in the ALE programme, and one of the team members felt aggrieved that he was invited to engage in this programme without the option to refuse. He admitted afterwards that he had not been prepared to engage, which stance persisted throughout the programme. The nature of a programme such as this one requires full commitment and participation, and in this case, the programme was introduced and launched quite suddenly, and team members were not given a choice of whether or not to participate.

Although the majority of participants indicated that the programme had had a considerable effect on the development of their leadership authenticity, not all participants were ready at the outset, or equally committed throughout, to derive the most benefit from the programme. Those who indicated readiness stated that it was due to the situations in which they found themselves, either individually or as a team. They had identified a need for further growth, and they were willing to engage in this programme.

At the outset of the programme, almost all participants indicated a lack of respect for their team members' abilities as there was little self-awareness of how the respective participants were contributing to the dysfunctional dynamics within the team. Bearing in mind that the programme was underpinned by a coaching modality, most, but not all participants engaged in continuous introspection, allowing for increased self-awareness and understanding of their respective contributions to the toxic team dynamics. What was true, however, was that some of the participants indeed had a higher cognitive ability to process complex developmental information, and with the introduction of the adult experiential learning process, could increase their reflexive meta-cognitive ability, meaning to 'think about how they think'.

Leader developmental readiness is not unlike coaching readiness. Kretzschmar[82] identified six main themes that could impact on coaching readiness. These range from the more situational and institutional variables, such as culture and class, knowledge about coaching, and access to coaching, to individual variables specific to the clients, such as psychological interpretations of whether they require coaching, whether they feel safe enough to open up in coaching and finally, how committed they are to take responsibility towards change. One of my programme participants, for instance, felt quite strongly that the programme was about 'fixing', and that he did not need to be fixed. Another participant initially felt very distrustful, and, despite assurances that all one-on-one conversations were completely confidential, she was initially hesitant to share information with me. However, this soon changed as trust was established between this client and me, and as the client realised that she personally stood to gain considerably from this ALE journey.

It is for this reason that leadership coaches usually offer an initial introductory (also called a chemistry) coaching session with new clients. The purpose of such a session is to address the afore-mentioned factors, and to establish not only whether the client is ready for coaching and leader development, but also whether there is a sufficient coaching fit between the coach and client to allow the client to feel safe towards opening up and being vulnerable with the coach.

However, leaders' initial levels of readiness are not necessarily an indicator of their commitment throughout the programme. Usually, once they have an experiential understanding of what the programme entails and how they can benefit, they will increase their commitment and engagement in the programme. Even so, it is important to be mindful of the fact that for most participants, levels of commitment can vary throughout the programme. In some cases, this might be due to circumstances, while in other cases it can be due to an intrinsic lack of commitment. There can be numerous underlying causes for wavering commitment. At times, it might be simply circumstantial, meaning that work and life gets in the way of allocating the attention that the self-work required, and this needs to be factored into a programme such as this one. For some leaders, it might be because they do not necessarily understand the importance of taking full ownership of the journey, or have a lack of leadership developmental or coaching readiness.

I now realise the importance of testing readiness and appropriate pre-framing at the outset of the journey, and even so, there will always be varying commitment between different leaders and at different times. It is important to note that there is usually a direct relationship between effort and time invested, and the immense benefits to be derived from such a journey.

Sustainability when the only thing that is constant, is change

The only thing that is constant is change! This needs to be factored into the equation; otherwise, all the good work done might yield temporary benefits at best. I started as an ALD facilitator by working with leaders on an individual basis. I realised that it was not enough to do only individual work, and then started to combine individual work with team ALE work. Only to find that as soon as the leadership team works effectively as a coherent team that the team members might change again. Leaders might be further promoted, find more senior positions elsewhere, companies merge, and restructuring could take place.

What I have found is that individual leaders do tend to sustain the authentic leadership effectiveness gained during their ALD journeys, but further measurements need to be in place for the same to apply to teams. It is therefore important to consider to what extent and at what levels an organisation wishes to introduce an AL culture, and thereafter, how ALE can be rolled out and sustained. This needs to be contracted at the outset of any ALD journey. An interview in Chapter 9 with a leader who participated with his team in an individual and team

ALE programme sheds some more light on how sustainability can be achieved when the only thing that is constant is change.

CONCLUSION

It is important to consider the criteria that need to be in place when considering an initiative such as an ALE programme that will allow for sustainable transformation in leaders. There are no silver bullets and organisations need to consider the investments that they are willing to make towards transforming their individual and team leadership to the highest level of leadership effectiveness.

Although it was previously believed that AL cannot be developed by means of a programme unless it is 'life's programme', this is not true, and I have proven this. However, such a programme cannot simply be a training programme. I have discussed the rationale for a coaching approach when facilitating such a programme, and I have outlined various individual and team coaching approaches. The role and presence of the coach is important, especially in AL programmes. Just as important is the degree of leader developmental and coaching readiness in the programme participants, as ultimately, it is their journey and they need to take ownership and make the time for the transformational work that they need to do.

I concluded this chapter by sharing some further thoughts on the sustainability of individual and team authentic leadership effectiveness in a world that is constantly changing.

Chapter 6

THE AUTHENTIC LEADERSHIP PROGRAMME – HIGH-LEVEL UNDERPINNINGS

Whereas the previous chapters focused on defining authentic leadership, the impact of authentic leadership, and considerations when developing authentic leadership and AL programmes, the next two chapters focus on what might be the first ALE programme that has been scientifically evaluated in a doctoral research study[83], and found to be effective and fit for purpose.

This chapter offers a high-level overview of the programme theory and conceptual framework of the ALE programme, with a specific focus on the systemic coaching facilitation style used throughout. I have already discussed the importance of the presence of AL facilitators, and I will therefore start by sharing a profile of myself as the developer and facilitator of this programme by using a narrative approach, very common in the development of leadership authenticity. I share the journey of how my underpinnings gradually developed over the years, bearing in mind that it is very difficult to facilitate a journey of leadership authenticity for others if it has not been one's own journey as well. Furthermore, I share how this programme aligns to the proposed guidelines for programmes such as these.

MY PROFILE AND UNDERPINNINGS AS AN ALD FACILITATOR

I was not always active in the field of leadership development. Initially I set out in the information technology field after founding my own consultancy where I served organisational clients in developing financial modelling solutions, and later on, business-intelligence software solutions of up to six to seven dimensions. I found this work all-consuming and mentally very stimulating, and it felt to me as if I disappeared into my computer for months at a time, peeping out occasionally to find new buildings had been built, people had gotten married, and babies had made their way into the world. One could have described me as a computer nerd! This worked fine until I became a parent, and some time later a single parent. I realised that I could not continue with work of this nature and be a good mother at the same time.

I was at a crossroad where I knew I had to change my career direction, but I did not know what that career could and would look like. In 2004, I received a giant wake-up call! I knew that if I did not take heed of this warning, I would receive a bigger smack. I found the moral courage to do the right thing, and that year I obtained an experiential understanding of taking a leap of faith. This was when I jumped ship, with no idea of where I would land. I left my career at that time without any idea of what new career to move into, and I was financially unprepared for this move. The road forward from there on was a very bumpy road of discovery, yet looking back now I understand that I was exactly where I was meant to be. I learnt to trust the fact that I was always supported by the universe and all that it contains. As being a good mother was one of my top values, this giant leap of faith allowed my espoused value to become my enacted value. I could not have done this had I not had the courage to take a leap of faith.

Another top value that evolved from this was to see a better quality of leadership in our world in all spheres of life. This led to an interest in exploring coaching, and in 2005, I was introduced to coaching training with the International Society of Neuro-Semantics. After some rigorous training, I developed the skills of good listening, supporting, and questioning, all required in facilitating empowering crucial conversations of discovery with my leader clients.

Unaware at that time of the literature on AL, I started to develop my own thoughts and practices regarding the development of leadership authenticity. It was only once I stepped back into the academic world in 2007, and embarked on a post-graduate Master's degree in Professional Coaching with the University of Middlesex, that I started exploring research in the area of AL. Also referred to by me as a *pracademic* journey, this process usually involved researching academic perspectives on the various topics that were introduced, and thereafter, we as students were encouraged to consider how these 1) *could* be integrated in a coaching process, 2) how they *had been* integrated in our own coaching processes, and 3) what we learnt from that. Furthermore, Kolb's[84] model of adult experiential learning was introduced into this academic programme, which was a learning style that suited me very well. During this process, I discovered the synergy between my own experiential learnings on AL and the thoughts shared by thought leaders on this topic. This, in turn, led to the gradual development of an individual and team ALE programme, which I facilitate successfully with my senior and executive leader clients. I evaluated this programme in an empirical study that formed part of my doctoral research, which I completed in 2014 with the department of Personal and Professional Leadership in the Faculty of Management at the University of Johannesburg, SA.

ALIGNMENT OF UNDERLYING PROGRAMME THEORY TO PROPOSED GUIDELINES

In my experience, the ALE individual and team coaching programme that I am about to outline aligns with the guidelines outlined in the previous chapter, as suggested by Cooper et al. and Chan in 2005, despite the fact that they did not ever refer specifically to coaching. As Chan recently admitted to me, this was because coaching was still a relatively new profession in 2005.

The standard format of this individual and team ALE programme comprises six individual sessions, followed by three team sessions. The programme itself is authentic, in that it is underpinned by a conceptual model that aligns with Chan et al.'s[85] model of leadership authenticity functioning and development, Cooper et al.'s proposed guidelines, and Chan's four working assumptions for AL interventions. For instance, the programme is targeted and customised in that participating leaders decide which outcomes they wish to achieve in this programme.

The programme consists of multiple sessions over time, allowing the leader to reinforce and grow from life events and leadership episodes, also called *trigger events*, between those sessions. Each session solidifies and builds on the self-development resulting from previous sessions, where self-awareness, self-mastery, and self-regulation are developed, with feedback from self and others as reinforcement of progress achieved. The programme has a strong ethical underpinning, where, for instance, congruence between espoused and enacted values is explored, and where the leader is encouraged to close the gap. These ALD coaching sessions, consisting of both individual and team sessions, may at times also include aspects of training. An AL programme such as this does not have to work in isolation; additional interventions might also be identified as helpful resources in attaining the leaders' chosen outcomes.

Whilst we need to bear in mind that each leader is completely unique, most have the capacity to move from their current LDL to a higher LDL in the development of increased leadership authenticity, with the proviso that they are ready for such a journey. I therefore usually test leadership developmental readiness, in this instance also called *coaching readiness*, by means of an initial introductory AL coaching session with each individual leader.

Furthermore, when clarifying the role that leadership events play, we need to be mindful that leadership episodes are both the outcome of ALD as well as the *raw material* for further ALD. Whilst the episodes themselves are non-indicative of development, it is the responses to, and the meaning attributed to these episodes by those involved in the ALD process, that make these episodes matter. This is an important consideration to bear in mind in a programme journey such as this one. The development of AL does not happen only within the individual and team AL sessions, it happens throughout the AL journey, and the intent is for it to become a life-long development journey, with the use of the tools that have been transferred throughout the duration of the programme. I always tell my leader clients that it is my outcome as facilitator to become redundant to them in the most empowering way.

We also need to be mindful of the fact that there is a difference between leader development and leadership development. Leader development is about the development of the individual leader by expanding his/her capacity to be effective in leadership roles and processes. Leader development then becomes one aspect of the broader concept of leadership development, which is the expansion of the organisation's collective leadership capacity to enact leadership tasks needed for collective work towards achieving collective outcomes. Whilst I sometimes notice debates about individual or collective leadership development, and which of these is more important, I do believe that both need to be available, depending on requirements within any particular organisation. In the ALE programme under discussion both aspects are incorporated, commencing with individual leader development, followed by team leadership development with the whole leadership team.

AL can be described as a leadership that comes from within; this implies that, instead of a normative measurement approach where one normally measures change against a set of established norms, the ipsative measurement approach is highly recommended to measure the self-development of AL as a personal journey of growth. Ipsative measures are useful for providing respondents with a frame of reference that is uniquely their own, thereby making development measurement extremely personalised.

CONCEPTUAL FRAMEWORK UNDERPINNING THE LEADERSHIP AUTHENTICITY PROGRAMME

In order to create some context, I outline my conceptual framework of AL, which underpins the AL programme. As shown in the following figure, the actualisation of ALE in organisations requires the underpinnings of interpersonal and, more importantly, personal leadership. Although individuals are usually promoted into professional leadership positions due to their requisite acumen, once in a leadership position, they need to deliver through others, which is not always so easy. It is important to note that the mastering of effective leadership needs to start with mastering self-leadership, before being able to lead others and, ultimately, an organisation or society, as the complexity in leading each level increases. It is not possible to successfully lead others if self- or personal leadership has not yet been mastered.

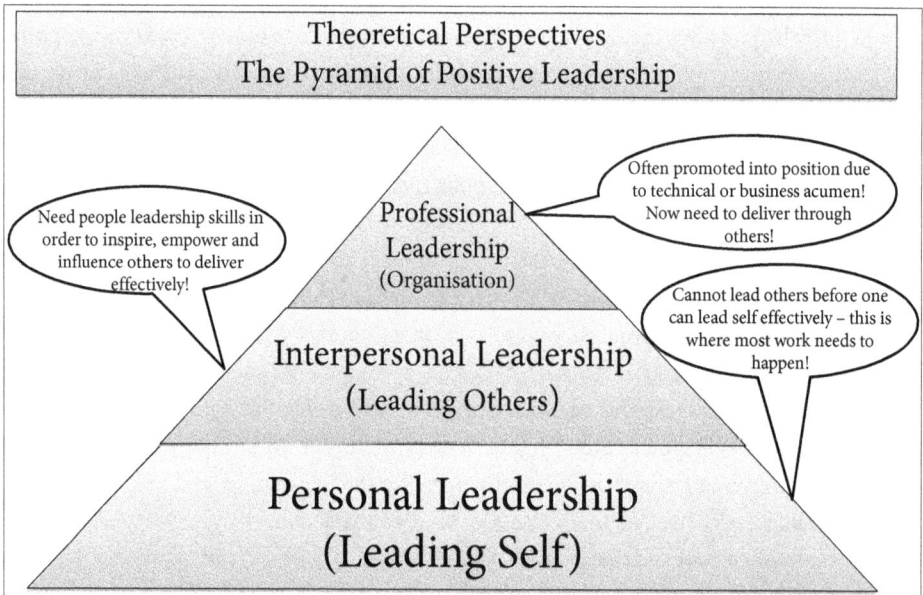

Figure 2: The pyramid of positive leadership

My research has shown that the majority of work required, not surprisingly, was in the enhancement of personal leadership. Personal leadership includes the processes of 1) being aware of one's internal compass for the *current self*, and 2) being committed to self-regulating so that one's internal compass becomes an internal AL Compass allowing further development towards more empowered possible self, which then 3) reflects in the behaviour of the leader.

As reflected in the following figure, the internal AL Compass referred to comprises our internal identity, purpose and vision, and our values. It also comprises our beliefs about self, others and our environment, and our psychological states, which are impacted by our thoughts and feelings. These aspects of our internal AL Compass are invisible to self and others as they fall below the soil-line. Even so, all of these affect and reflect in our behaviour and performance, which is the only aspect of our internal AL Compass that is above the soil-line and therefore noticeable to others.

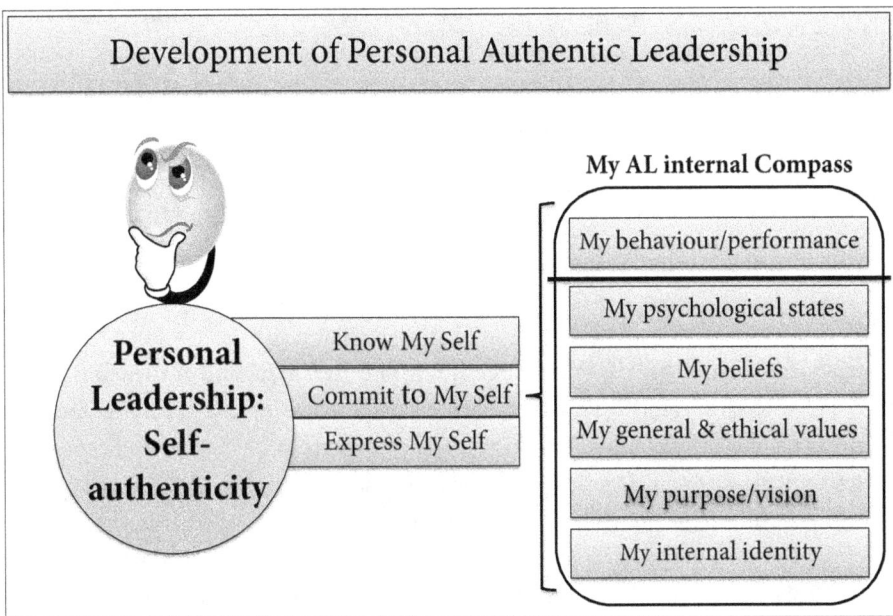

Figure 3: Personal leadership authenticity

It is important to note that we need to regulate what is below the soil-line before we can reflect such regulation in our behaviour. Although it might seem implicit and therefore of limited practical value to create this additional step, I have found this useful, as it has helped my clients to be mindful of ensuring their behaviour above the soil-line reflects their internal AL Compass below the soil-line. As others observe this expression of self, they make sense of the level of authenticity that underpins this behaviour (perceived authenticity, see following figure) as they ask themselves questions such as whether the leader's espoused values are reflected in his/her behaviour, or else whether they experience integrity, transparency, predictability from this leader, and finally, whether they can trust this leader.

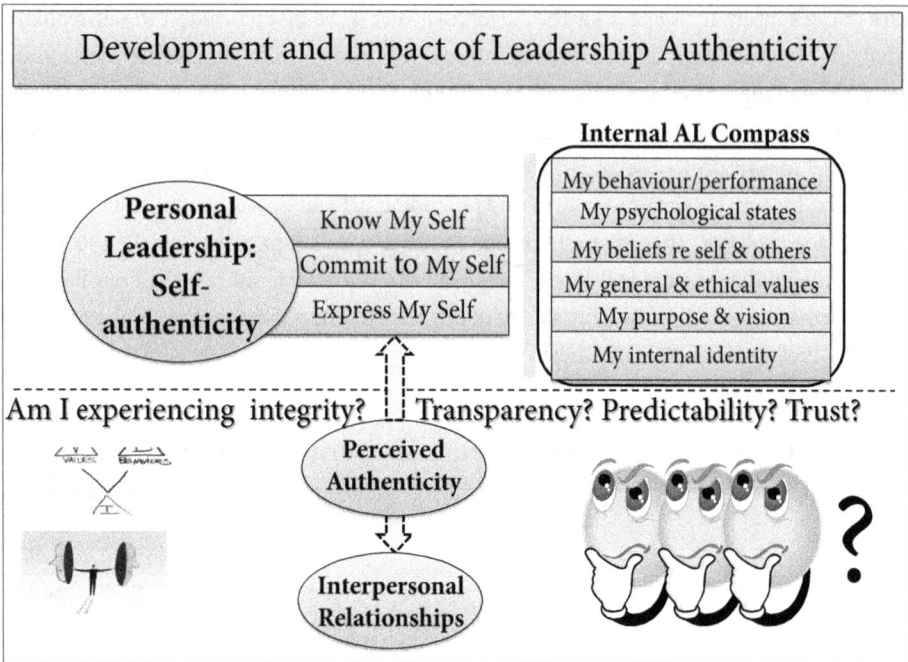

Figure 4: Perceived authenticity

Inter-relational trust forms the foundation of any effective team, and is therefore required to turn an ineffective team with inattention to results into an effective team that focuses on collective outcomes. I have often noticed an absence of trust in ineffective leadership teams, and concur with Lencioni (see following figure) that even though an artificial harmony might exist within the team, when it is needed most, an absence of trust leads to a fear of conflict where matters of importance are not sufficiently challenged, even at the level of board meetings. This can lead to a silent disagreement about the way forward, resulting in a lack of commitment, which creates ambiguity. Ambiguity, in turn, results in an avoidance of self- and peer-to-peer accountability, and often it is when this happens that the leader tears out his/her hair in frustration. Ultimately, it leads to an inattention to results and blaming others and external circumstances for the under-achievement of results.

Team Ineffectiveness

Leads to	Inattention to Business Results	Status and Ego
Leads to	Avoidance of Accountability	Low Standards
Leads to	Lack of Commitment	Ambiguity
Leads to	Fear of Conflict	Artificial Harmony
	Absence of Trust	Invulnerability

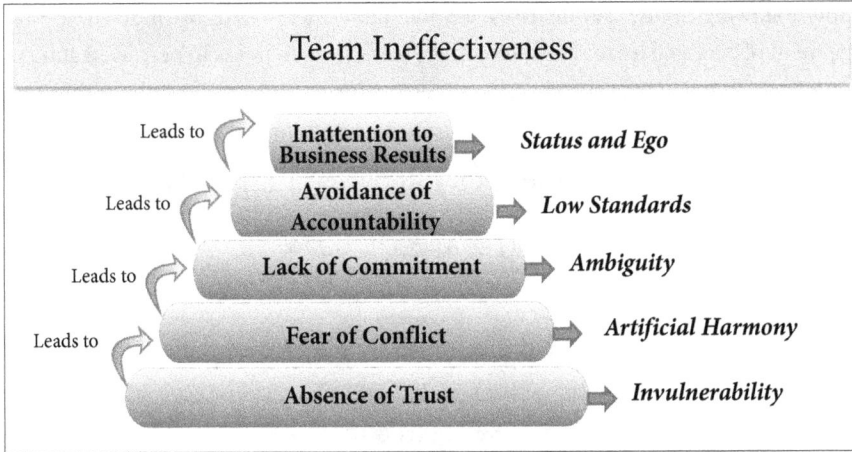

Figure 5: Team ineffectiveness[86]

So how can an authentic leader turn this around? As reflected in the following figure, an authentic leader, through being trustworthy, and with a focus on the greater good for all and the organisation, needs to focus the team on collective outcomes rather than just their own outcomes. This means that the leader needs to encourage team members to confront difficult issues so that self- and peer-to-peer accountability can take place. This can happen by forcing clarity and closure on issues so that team members can commit to the way forward. However, this is not possible until all team members feel that they have been heard and their standpoints and ideas considered. Therefore, the leader needs to mine for healthy conflict. Most importantly, the leader needs to *go first*, that is, be the example that the team wishes to follow. This includes the psychological state of balanced vulnerability that allows the leader to admit that he/she does not always know it all.

Leadership Authenticity and Team Effectiveness

The Role of a Leader

Leads to	Inattention to Business Results	Focus on Collective Outcomes
Leads to	Avoidance of Accountability	Confront Difficult Issues
Leads to	Lack of Commitment	Force Clarity & Closure
Leads to	Fear of Conflict	Mine for Conflict
	Absence of Trust	Go First

Figure 6: Team effectiveness (based on Lencioni's model)[87]

The following figure summarises all the afore-mentioned by indicating that the development of personal leadership authenticity leads to an increase in perceived authenticity in a leader, which impacts positively on interpersonal trust and relationships within teams.

Figure 7: Link between AL and team effectiveness

Once that trust has been built, it allows for robust and healthy disagreements, which form part of the process that leads to collaborative agreements. This, in turn, creates clarity and closure on the way forward as a team. It also allows for horizontal leadership development within a team where every member in the team can hold self and others accountable for their individual and collective behaviours and performance, towards achieving collective outcomes.

Once we understand more meaningfully what drives us in terms of our internal identity, our purpose and vision, our values and beliefs and our psychological states, we can then consciously decide how to use those as internal resources, resulting in more empowering leadership of self (personal leadership), of others (interpersonal leadership), and of the organisation and society we serve (organisational leadership). A journey such as this one is required to move to the next leadership development level or LDL.

SYSTEMIC COACHING FACILITATION STYLE USED IN THIS PROGRAMME

The following outlines the rationale for using a coaching style that also considers systemic thinking. For me, coaching holds the philosophy that individuals are talented, competent and with many strengths, which aligns with the positive psychology and strengths approach to developing leadership authenticity. Through one-on-one and team coaching, leaders are assisted in unlocking their potential in order to maximise their performance. Coaches help leaders to learn, rather than teaching. Coaching in its purest form therefore draws more on non-directive skills that help individuals and teams to solve their own problems, empowering them to take responsibility for their own performance and development.

All leaders work within a systemic context, and the success of any organisation is dependent on the communication and behaviour of its people. There has been a gradual realisation of the importance of attending to communication and behaviour in organisational learning as it is people who implement systems, structures, and practices. From this, we can deduce that the quality of conversations in the workplace affects the quality of relationships, and workplace relationships have a major impact on performance, creativity, and productivity. It is for this reason that leaders themselves often require training nowadays to use a coaching style of communication.

OVERVIEW OF THE USUAL STRUCTURE OF THE LEADERSHIP AUTHENTICITY PROGRAMME

The main systems thinking elements that underpin this programme begin with the future environment and the end in mind. From there the process then works backwards to trace who we are, and to explore possible paths to new behaviours and outcomes. This can be facilitated by engaging in the three ALD processes, those being: 1) becoming aware of one's internal compass (of the current self), 2) to self-regulate that internal compass towards an internal AL Compass (towards the possible self), and 3) to reflect that internal AL Compass in one's behaviour.

Unpacked in more details (see figure 8), this means that we start with our future environment, as follows.

1. **Output and evidence of success:** *Where do we want to be? How will we know when we get there?* What are the desired behavioural outcomes within the various contexts, environments and other systemic levels that surround us? What evidence in the feedback loop indicates that the desired behavioural outcomes have been achieved? This aligns with ALD process 3, as outcomes are reflected in, or are a result of, changed behaviour.

2. **Input:** *Where are we now, and from where have we come?* This question defines the gap between from where we have come (past self), where we are now (current self), and the desired future (next level of possible self). This aligns with ALD process 1, which is to become more aware of what is informing us below the soil-line.

3. **Thru'put:** *How will we achieve our outcomes?* This phase uses systems thinking to define and implement strategies and tactics that will integrate the processes, activities, relationships, and changes needed in our toolbox to close the gap and create desired outcomes. This aligns to ALD process 2, which refers to self-regulation to align all aspects below the soil-line towards being the leaders we need to be.

4. **Context:** *What other important factors could change in the future environment, which we need to consider?* This means that feedback continually needs to be sought from the environment in order to influence outcomes, as leaders influence their environments and environments affect leaders.

This concludes the high-level overview of the systemic structure of the leadership authenticity programme. In my experience, positive outcomes of development of ALE in a programme such as this one include the following:

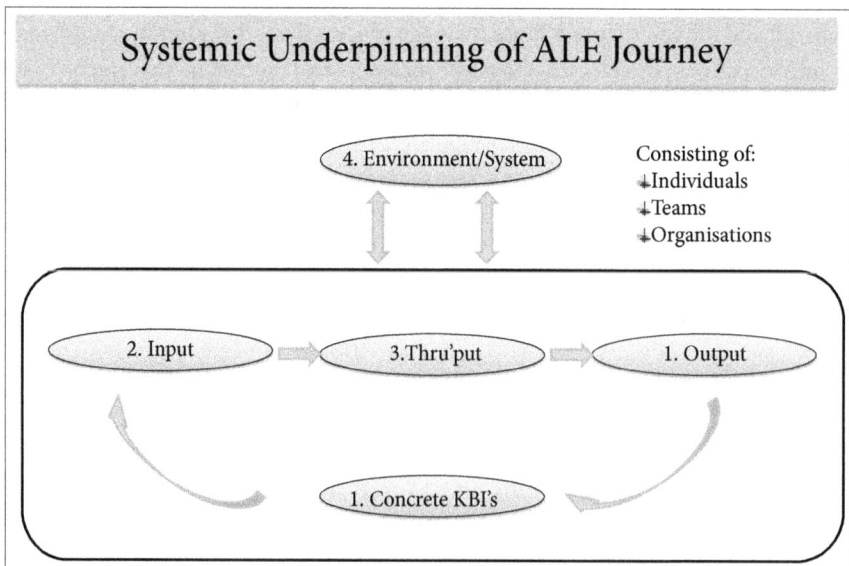

Figure 8: Systems Thinking underpinning AL programme

1. In order to develop individual and collective ALE, leaders learn in depth about who they currently are and who they need to become, and engage in the work required to achieve this.
2. As a result, leaders develop intrapersonal trust in self, and interpersonal trust relationships with others.
3. In order to achieve business results, leaders learn to engage in healthy conflicts towards agreeing on the way forward to which they can commit.
4. By means of courageous conversations, leaders are empowered to hold themselves, their peers and direct reports accountable towards achieving outcomes.
5. Leaders build integrity, transparency, moral courage, and resilience that they can sustain whilst leading change towards a high performance culture.
6. Leaders understand how to listen, and question in a way that is empowering to those with whom they interact.
7. Leaders develop three-sixty leadership, which is linked to the gravitas in their presence rather than only to position.
8. Leaders learn to deliver through others by developing balanced leadership.

It is therefore worthwhile to understand in more detail how a programme such as this one can achieve sustainable transformation to a higher LDL by means of developing increased individual and team ALE.

CONCLUSION

It is important that programmes of this nature are mindful of the programme requirements that need to be aligned to for developing the sustainable ALE, and that these are underpinned by a credible conceptual framework.

Whoever facilitates such a programme needs to some extent to embody the presence of leadership authenticity, and have the ability to use a coaching style of facilitation, as there is no one size for all in the development of ALE. Each participating leader needs to do considerable introspection to allow for increased self-awareness in order to develop their internal AL Compass against which to self-regulate their thoughts and feelings, speech and behaviour. A coaching style of facilitation supports leaders to do so, and in doing so, allows them to develop towards their next level of the possible AL self. With this global understanding now in place, the following chapter continues with a more detailed overview of the programme itself.

Chapter 7

THE AUTHENTIC LEADERSHIP PROGRAMME –
DETAILED OVERVIEW

Whereas the previous chapter focused on a high-level overview of this individual and team authentic leadership effectiveness programme, this chapter is devoted to a detailed systemic overview of the usual structure of this programme. The programme, designed, continually refined, and facilitated since 2007, comprises individual and team ALE development components.

I commence with a discussion on the overall programme in terms of its flow and purpose, followed by a detailed discussion on the individual ALE programme, concluded by a discussion on the team ALE programme. I discuss both the individual and team ALE programme, step-by-step. Within each step, I discuss both the theory behind the programme and process components employed, followed by actual experience, and feedback from the field. Feedback is provided from an international brewery leadership team who participated in my doctoral study in 2011 and 2012. The team comprised the General Manager, HR business partner, financial manager, operations manager, engineering manager, brewing manager, packaging manager, quality assurance manager, systems manager, and the brewmaster (see more on participant details in Appendix 1, with names changed to protect their identities).

OVERALL ALE PROGRAMME

The usual ALE programme commences with a number of individual coaching sessions to develop individual ALE, followed by a number of team sessions in which team ALE is developed. Although it can be tailored to the organisational needs, the programme usually assumes the format of six structured individual face-to-face coaching sessions per leader, approximately two weeks apart. These are followed by three team-coaching sessions, approximately one month apart, during which interpersonal and organisational leadership within the team is enhanced through collective training, coaching, and experiential learning. The content can be somewhat tailored according to emerging individual and team requirements. The following diagram illustrates the ALE programme flow.

```
┌─────────────┐
│   Process   │
│  Overview   │
│   of ALE    │
│  Programme  │
└──────┬──────┘
       │
┌──────┴──────┐
│     Six     │
│ individual  │
│  and three  │
│  team ALE   │
│  sessions   │
└──────┬──────┘
```

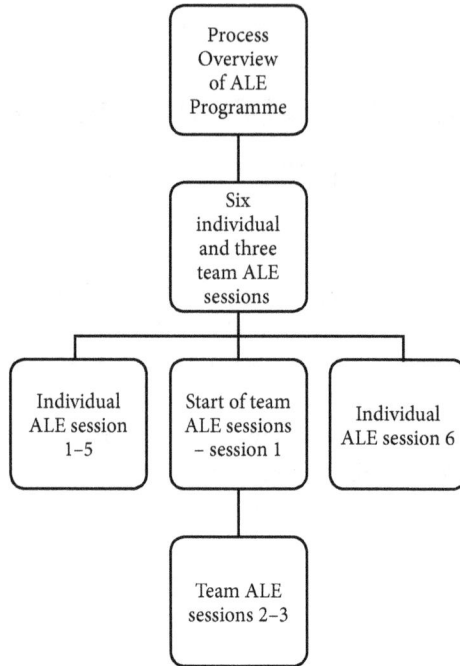

Figure 9: Process overview of leadership authenticity programme

The individual ALE programme aims to develop personal, followed by interpersonal and professional ALE at an individual level. The rationale that underpins my thinking is that if the development of authentic leadership could be equated to developing a garden, then the development of personal leadership could be equated to the preparation and fertilisation of the soil (therefore invisible), so that anything planted thereafter, as long as it is regularly watered, will grow and flourish. Once the personal leadership has been developed, it removes the limiting aspects of self, whilst enhancing a higher authentic potential of self. Leaders then become ready and willing to develop and enhance their interpersonal and professional leadership skills, allowing them to empower and influence others to deliver effectively towards achieving team or organisational goals (see Figure 10). However, a word of caution – maintaining and enhancing such leadership is an ongoing exercise, not unlike a gardener needing to continue with watering the garden.

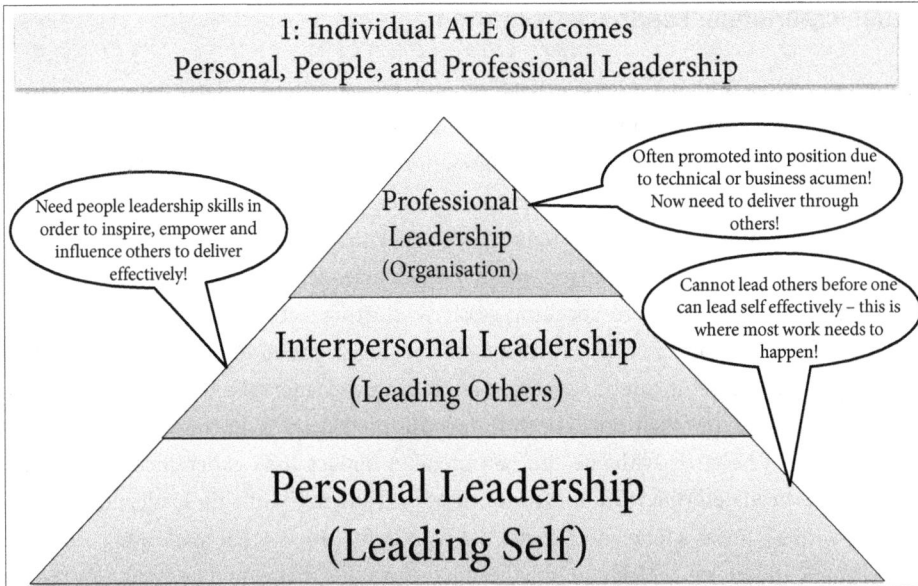

1: Individual ALE Outcomes
Personal, People, and Professional Leadership

Professional Leadership (Organisation)

Interpersonal Leadership (Leading Others)

Personal Leadership (Leading Self)

Need people leadership skills in order to inspire, empower and influence others to deliver effectively!

Often promoted into position due to technical or business acumen! Now need to deliver through others!

Cannot lead others before one can lead self effectively – this is where most work needs to happen!

Figure 10: Leadership areas for ALE outcomes

In both the individual and team aspects of the ALE programme, a systems approach, as reflected in Figure 8, is taken, where the participants need to understand what personal, interpersonal, and professional ALE outcomes they wish to achieve (output), who they currently are and who they need to be in order to achieve this (input). Finally, they need to understand what ALE tools they need to develop (thru'put) so that they can achieve their ALE outcomes, whilst being mindful of the systems in which they operate.

For various reasons a comprehensive programme such as this could be a challenge. The reference to individual leader developmental readiness also applies to organisational leadership development. Organisations often do not find it easy to admit that they need help, and they are accustomed to short leadership development training programmes that do not take up too much of their time and energy resources. Lencioni, a practitioner in developing organisational health, referred to the phenomenon of *stooping to greatness*, and once asked the CEO of a very healthy and successful organisation why their competitors did not invest in organisational health the way his organisation did. The CEO's sad response was "... I honestly believe they think it's beneath them"[88], and continued that these competitors quietly believed that they were too sophisticated, too busy, or too analytical to bother with it. This perception could be attributed to inappropriate invulnerability, where leaders are not prepared to admit their weaknesses. They might also lack the moral courage to deal with the issues that are preventing them from achieving greatness. Programmes such as these need to be facilitated by an experienced AL facilitator and are not for the faint-hearted. They do require investment in terms of time and internal resources.

Actual experience: Feedback from the field

The overall programme has a strong coaching underpinning, and it starts with determining the leader development readiness. I do this by asking participants to fill in a questionnaire (see Appendix 2) to determine leader development readiness, after which we have a coaching introductory conversation that helps to prepare participants for the journey that lies ahead.

The programme commences with six individual coaching sessions, which are usually about two to three weeks apart, during which individual leadership authenticity is developed. This is followed by three team-coaching sessions, starting with Team Session 1, between Individual Sessions 5 and 6, with each team session about one month apart. At the request of leaders, review sessions can be scheduled after an agreed interval after Team Session 3, to allow the team to review their ongoing shifts towards their desired outcomes.

Leaders have shared with me the considerable impact they experienced during this journey. It has been described as a "life transformational journey" with one leader commenting "the stuff works". It was a long and difficult but wonderful process that made a big individual and collective difference, which equipped leaders with skills that would be useful for the rest of their lives. Liam, the general manager, had the following to say:

> **Liam:** Look, it is a long process. It is a difficult process at times, but I think one can only look back at it and say it was a wonderful process in terms of what it has done for me as an individual; and what it's done for the team as a whole. I will recommend it to anybody to go through this. And even doing it just for an individual, the richness that comes out of that process alone is more than enough on its own. And if you want to do the team effectiveness, you've got to do the individual bit beforehand, otherwise you're not going to get there. I think you've made a mark on us as a team and on me as an individual, and I'll carry some of these things with me for the rest of my life.

I have found that once such a programme has been completed, clients usually agree that the time and energy spent was well worth it; however, at times it remains a challenge at the outset to convince the sponsors in an organisation that their investment, especially in the time it requires, is worth it.

DEVELOPMENT OF INDIVIDUAL ALE – PROCESS MODEL AND PROGRAMME COMPONENTS

The individual sessions allow for the development of intrapersonal/self-leadership. At the outset of the individual sessions I explain to each client that they will be working towards building a puzzle, but with two differences: 1) the puzzle pieces themselves still need to be developed, and 2) the resulting authentic picture is not available on the 'lid of any puzzle box'. This means that at the outset of the programme, each leader client needs to agree on a relationship of trust with the programme facilitator. Signing a programme commitment document (see Appendix 3) where both the facilitator and participant commit to the journey, goes a considerable way towards achieving this. It is usually by the fourth or fifth session that I hear clients making comments such as, "Oh, now I am getting it." This is usually a breakthrough moment in the journey. Until then, the leader has to work on a basis of total trust, not being entirely sure where this process will lead them.

During my Master's study on developing leadership authenticity, I asked my participant leaders for permission to record each session, which they granted. This resulted in an unexpected outcome; each leader then asked for an audio copy of each of their sessions for them to listen to again, often whilst travelling to and from work. The feedback I received afterwards was that the process of stepping back and listening to their sessions yielded further reflections, even meta-reflections (reflections about reflections), which increased the value of each session exponentially. Since then, I usually ask my leaders for permission to record the sessions and I offer these to those who wish to derive further value by listening to their sessions again.

As illustrated in Figure 11, the following describes at a high level how the individual ALE development journey usually unfolds, and links to each step of the journey, where applicable, the programme components employed in each phase, followed by a more detailed discussion of each component.

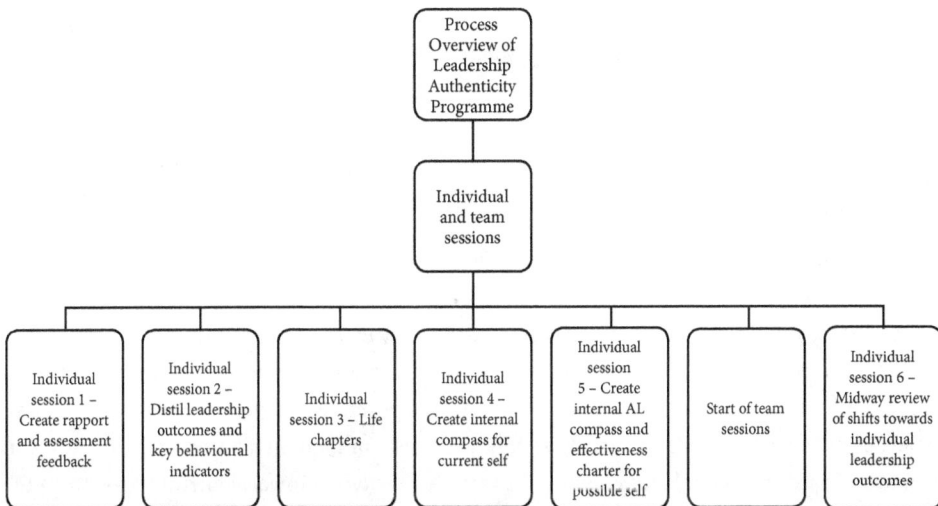

Figure 11: Process overview of the Individual ALE programme

The individual ALE programme comprises three two-hour sessions, followed by three 90-minute sessions. It commences with Individual Session 1, by creating more awareness of participants' perceptions of their inner landscapes and outer landscapes, and aspects of these that might work for or against them (Individual ALE step 1). At this point, they are introduced to adult experiential learning, which they use throughout the programme. The second session then allows them to set their intrapersonal, interpersonal, and professional leadership outcomes, with accompanying behavioural evidence of successful achievements of those (Individual ALE step 2). Assuming that each leader is a culmination of his/her life history, in the third session they explore how their life chapters have shaped who they currently are (Individual ALE step 3). In the fourth session, they use these themes to build an internal compass that informs the current self, and to determine the strength of the golden thread running through the various levels that make up this compass (Individual ALE step 4), using the structure of an internal AL Compass, as reflected in Figure 12.

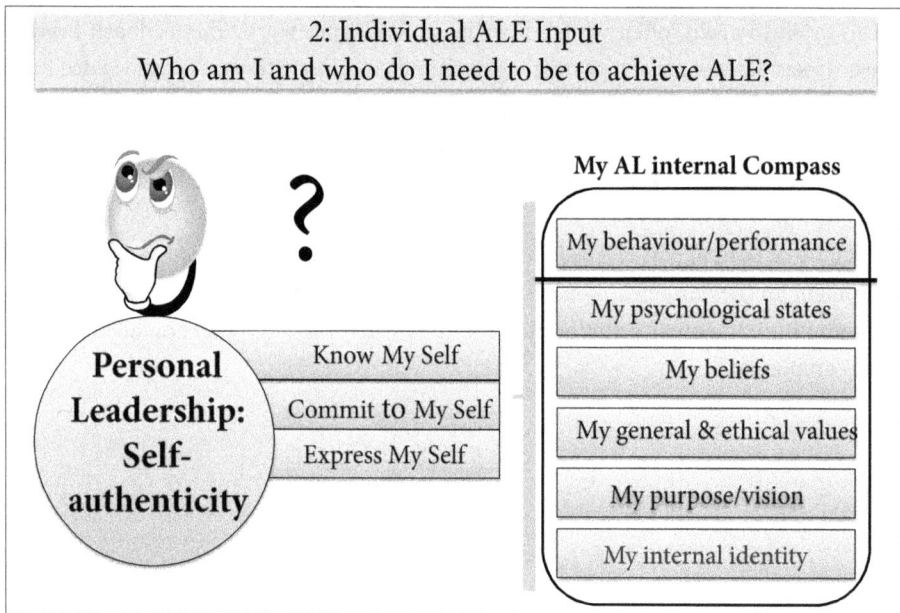

Figure 12: Who am I and who do I need to be to achieve ALE?

In Session 5, they refine that compass towards a next level of the possible self (Individual ALE step 5), completing the individual journey with a midway review of outcomes achieved thus far in Session 6 (Individual ALE step 6). At this point, leader participants will also have experienced some feedback from their followers, as outlined in Figure 13, and they can consider what further tools they require in their ALE toolbox towards further growth to the next level of leadership.

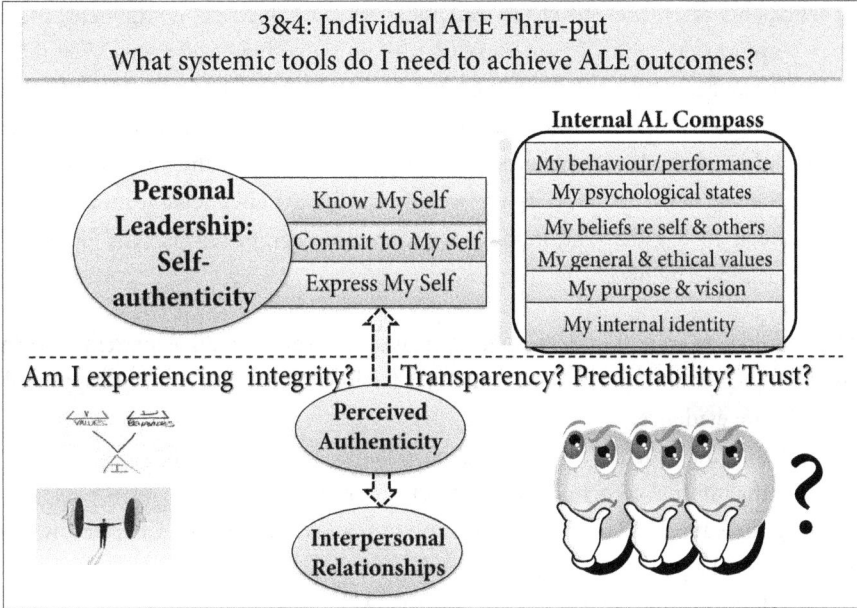

Figure 13: What systemic tools do I need to achieve my ALE outcomes?

Figure 14 illustrates the horizontal and vertical aspects of developing an internal AL Compass towards enhancing individual ALE. The horizontal and vertical aspects explore along our time-line how all our experiences have shaped our current self above and below the soil-line, so that we can consider what aspects require further work towards growing us to the next level of our possible selves.

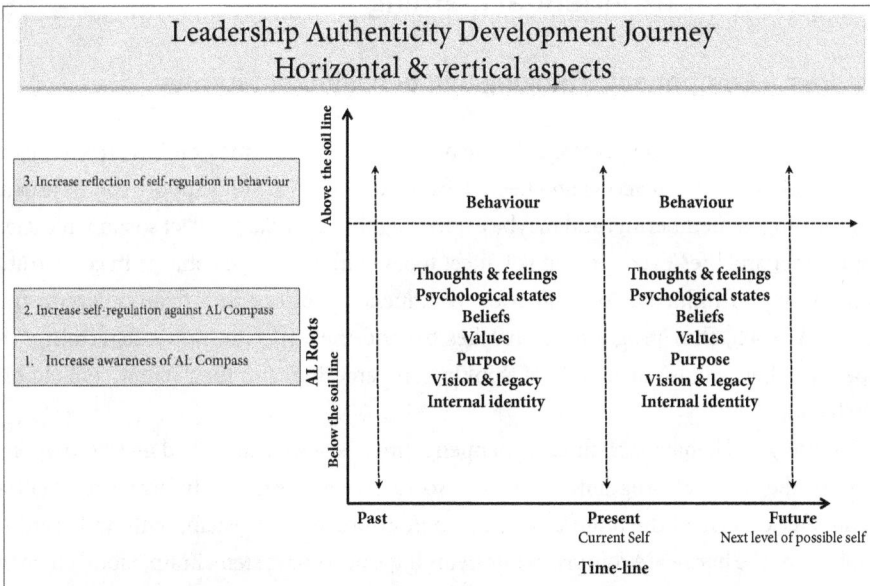

Figure 14. Horizontal and vertical aspects of ALD journey

Once participants reach the end of the individual ALE development component, there are usually two options available. If I am working with an individual leader only, then they can continue with their individual leadership coaching journey where I usually offer a further six coaching sessions during which they decide which outstanding outcomes still require work. If the journey has a team leadership aspect to it, then after session 5 the team is usually ready to continue the journey collectively as a team, towards further enhancing team interpersonal and professional ALE skills. The individual programme comprises six ALE development steps, summarised as follows:

1. Create initial awareness of development areas and introduce adult experiential learning.
2. Identify personal, interpersonal and professional ALE outcomes, supported by behavioural evidence.
3. Identify life and leadership themes that have shaped the current self.
4. Identify the internal compass that informs the current self.
5. Identify and strengthen the internal AL Compass and create an ALE Charter towards the next level of the possible self.
6. Consolidate towards the next level of systemic ALE.

Following is a detailed discussion of each step in the individual ALE programme. Within each step, I discuss both the theory behind the programme and process components employed, followed by actual experience, and feedback from the field.

Individual ALE Step 1 – Develop initial awareness and introduce adult experiential learning

Programme Component: Thinking and behavioural filtering

How we run our brain. Consider your frame of mind. In what frame of mind are you reading this book today? Did you access an effective frame of mind? Will it support you in learning, understanding, remembering, and maybe even using this material to effect sustainable change in your career and life? Every person you meet today, with whom you engage in conversation, whom you try to influence, or who tries to influence you, operates from a certain frame of mind. As such, that 'programme' that lies beyond their specific words determines their perspective, their values, their style of thinking and emoting, and their patterns of choosing and behaving.

Thinking and behavioural filtering happen by means of what are called *meta-programmes*, which are the internal programmes we use to receive and process information. Hall and Bodenhamer described the brain as an information-processing system, with both hardware and software. The hardware comprises our neurology, nervous system, brain, blood chemistry, Neuro-transmitters, and physiological organs, which all participate in inputting, processing, and outputting information. The software comprises our thinking and behavioural filters and preferences, which are informed by our beliefs, values, meanings, intentions, and our visions. Furthermore, beliefs, values, and thinking preferences all have a mutual influence on one another. These filters, like values and beliefs, are often informed by our life experiences and in the case of leaders, leadership episodes.

These thinking and behavioural patterns often, although not always, run along a continuum, for example, the thinking filter 'trusting...sceptic' operates along a continuum from *trusting* to *sceptic*. Being more trusting than sceptic would make 'trusting' the *driver* meta-programme or behavioural preference. Other examples might be *global* versus *detail*, or *task* versus *people* focused.

There are no outright *wrong* preferences; the value of each preference is context-specific. The question is whether any preference in any particular thinking or behaviour filter is serving or limiting desired outcomes at work and in relationships. Consider the example of *global* versus *detail* where it might be necessary to communicate at a very global (summarised or high) level with the CEO, whilst it might be necessary to communicate at a detailed level with new team members in order to orientate them. However, it is very important that there is sufficient flexibility in the way the leader uses any of the approximately 50 identified thinking and behavioural filters so that these always help rather than hinder the achievement of intended outcomes in any context or at any point in time. Being aware of these also assists in maintaining rapport with others and in all situations.

Arne Maus, the CEO of Identity Compass Internal, explains it as follows. "We focus on what is important to us. We generalise and distort what is outside of our focus. And we use generalisations and distortions to give meaning to our perceptions in order to understand the world"[90]. Understanding these filters helps a leader to understand how he or she currently filters input from the external environment, as well as the amount of flexibility in these filters, and it creates awareness of how the leader might be filtering differently to important others, and therefore might be breaking rapport with them. Understanding this helps the leader to understand what outcomes need to be focused on towards becoming a more effective leader.

Although there are numerous assessment tools that help leaders with understanding their inner landscapes, comprising their strengths, preferences, and development areas, I use Identity Compass®, a profiling tool that profiles approximately 25 of the most important thinking and behavioural filters that can either hinder or empower a leader. The following are the most frequent examples of thinking- and behavioural filters that leaders need to focus on, in order to enhance their personal, people, and professional leadership effectiveness.

- **Perspective:** *Own versus partner versus observer. Own* perspective (emotional – reflects what is important to them), *partner* perspective (empathic – reflects their tendency and ability to put themselves in the shoes of another), whilst an *observer* perspective (rational – can place themselves in the position of an observer and keep a cool and dissociated mind).

- **Reference:** *Internal versus external.* People with an *internal* preference provide their own internal motivation. Any external feedback or criticism is judged against an internal benchmark or compass. They can be judgmental or stubborn. People with an *external* referencing preference need other people's opinions and feedback to stay motivated. They judge themselves according to the feedback they get from others. They can be 'people-pleasers'.

- **Motive:** *Influence vs affiliation vs achievement.* The individual's behaviour is motivated either by *influence* (power over environment or result), *affiliation* (approval and acceptance from others), or *achievement* (performance excellence).

- **Work orientation:** *Relationship vs task focus. Relationally* oriented people primarily concentrate on the persons involved and are mainly concerned with the well-being of these persons. In case of a strong tendency towards this preference, the task gets out of focus. They put their attention on people and on the team spirit. They tend to care for other people. People with *task* orientation are mainly interested in getting the job done and reaching the goal. In the extreme, this can result in pushing others or themselves too hard. They focus their attention on the job to be done, and on the related dates and deadlines. They are attracted by tasks.

- **Direction:** *Away-from vs towards.* Problem oriented people move *away from* all sorts of problems. They follow an avoidance-strategy, they like to avoid problems or difficulties, and their attention is directed towards ensuring things do not happen. They can use this preference of caution positively to deliver high quality, to proceed in a safe manner and thus become very reliable. They can best be motivated by being shown negative consequences. People with a *towards* preference move towards a certain goal. They quickly leave the past behind and quickly address their tasks and goals. In extreme situations it can mean they want to get to the goal and overlook the problems on the way. Their motivation is the attractiveness of their goals.

- **Primary attention:** *Caring for self vs caring for others.* To people with the *caring for self* preference it is more important to first concentrate on oneself. Probably they would realise that they need something to drink before they see that others need something too before they go and get the drinks. This thinking preference is often used by athletes or in professions in which performance is very important. People with the *caring for others* preference take care of others first. They would, for example, notice that someone else needs something to drink and would go and get it. In this situation, they would likely get something to drink for themselves too. This thinking preference is often found in service and support jobs and in healing professions.

- **Working style:** *Individualist vs team player.* People with a *team player* preference want to be part of a team and prefer to contribute to the team performance. They like to share the workload and to work together. They care for the other team members and work faster and more efficiently in a team. People with the *individualist* preference work best when they are alone and independent and have full control over the project. They are well suited to finish jobs independently. They prefer to choose their individual working time and location. They want to avoid interference from others on their project. They care less about other team members and tend to work faster when they are left alone. The ideal profile for a leader is to be a group-player. This is applicable if the difference between team player and individualist is less than 15%. People with this preference like to have other people around but like to make an individual contribution to the team. They like to be responsible for their own area, where they work alone and make their own decisions but they care about their team members and outcomes.

- **Primary interest:** *people, information.* Someone with a *people* preference wants to mainly see, meet and interact with people. Generally, these people can keep names and faces in their memory. They are people oriented. People with an *information/knowledge* preference are mostly interested in what they can learn from the people, places, and activities around them. They are interested in the culture of a company, its history and the relevant facts and figures.

- **Convincer strategy:** *trustful vs sceptic.* People with a *sceptic* preference need to be convinced on an ongoing basis. They are sceptical and have a basic mistrust. It is very difficult to convince them. This thinking preference shows its value best in quality control jobs. People with a *trustful* preference need no demonstration to believe that something works or is true. They give trust in advance and check the details later. This is good for relationship-building, but they can sometimes be gullible.

- **Information size:** *global vs detail.* People with a *global* preference like to have an overview first. The chunks they focus on use a more global and abstract type of information. They concentrate on the general direction of a project. They can easily see relations and basic structures. They work best when they can delegate details to others. Their learning style is from the global to details (deductive). People using a *detail* preference concentrate on the details of a job. The chunks they use have a more detailed structure. They deal with the elements and components of a project. Preciseness and accuracy are important to them. Their learning style is from detail to global (inductive).

- **Thinking style:** *abstract vs concrete.* People with an *abstract* preference prefer to think in combinations, principles, and symbols. They would start such a project with drawings and plans before realising it. This is the search for an abstract solution. People with a *concrete* preference concentrate on clear facts and examples. A project would start with a concrete vision of how it can be started or of the final result. People with this thinking preference tend to take care of who is doing what and when, and how and where what can be done.

- **Time orientation:** *Past vs present vs future.* People with a *past* preference base their decisions on their experiences and find their orientation benchmarks in the past. In the extreme, they ignore the pleasant experiences in the present and may not plan for the future. This thinking preference is important for analysis and for solving problems. People with a *present* preference live in the here and now and they might ignore what has passed and ignore planning for the future. This thinking preference is important for immediate reactions, for service, and for improvisation. People with a *future* preference like to spend their time painting pictures of their future and making plans. If this preference is primarily used, they may not learn from the past and may not enjoy the results of their previous plans. This thinking preference is important for development of organisations, projects, or for the consideration of consequences.

- **Time frame:** *Long-term vs short-term.* People with a *long-term* preference put their emphasis on mid-term or long-term consequences and effects. They tend to overlook short-term consequences. They divide time globally. *Short-term* preference people's prime attention is focused on the immediate or short-term consequences. They tend to ignore the long-term aspects. This thinking preference is important for immediate reactions and for improvisation.

- **Management style:** *Managing vs self-reflective vs instructing vs not managing vs operational.* People with a *managing* preference know what they have to do, they know what others have to do and they are willing to tell them. They have the ability to reflect upon themselves as well as to observe others and to analyse them. People with a *self-reflective* preference do not care what others should do and it is not important to them to become a manager. They may have problems in observing others and in analysing them. They have the ability to reflect upon themselves. In any organisation, they are best placed in a position where they can be independent. People with an *instructing* preference are found quite often in administration and in middle management. They usually know what others should do and they do not hesitate to tell them. They may have problems in reflecting upon themselves. They have the ability to observe others and to analyse them. People with a *not-managing* preference know what to do to be successful. They also know what others should do but do not want to tell them. (Typical: "Who am I to tell you what to do?") They have the ability to reflect upon themselves as well as to observe others and to analyse them. They normally show very little interest in becoming managers but could, in case of such a promotion, change to *managing*. People with an *operational* preference usually spend no time reflecting on themselves or others. This could be interpreted to mean that this person may require or benefit from training, coaching and/or mentoring before assuming or maintaining a management or leadership role.

It is important to be mindful that the afore-mentioned states were described in cases where the drivers are very strong. Ideally, leaders need the flexibility to move from one driver towards another, as any situation requires. The following preferences are recommended for effective personal, people, and professional/organisational leadership effectiveness.

Personal leadership skills: To increase the ability to lead and manage self, leaders need to ensure competency in the following six most important patterns:

- Perspective: own
- Motive: achievement
- Direction: towards, away-from
- Reference: internal (with some external)
- Primary attention: caring for self
- Working style: individualist (with some team player)

People leadership skills: To increase the ability to lead and manage others, leaders need to ensure competency in the following six most important patterns:

- Primary interest: people
- Perspective: partner, observer
- Motive: influence, affiliation
- Working style: group-player
- Primary attention: caring for others
- Convincer strategy: trustful (empowerment) (with some sceptic)

Professional leadership skills: To increase the ability to lead and manage professionally, leaders need to ensure competency in the following five most important patterns:

- Information size: global (with some detail)
- Thinking style: abstract, concrete
- Time orientation: past, present, future
- Time frame: long-term, short-term
- Management style: managing

From the afore-mentioned, it can be deduced why flexibility is important as for the same thinking and behavioural filter one might need one driver for personal leadership, and another for people leadership. A good example is working style, where one needs to be able to work on one's own when required, as part of personal leadership, but this cannot be the driver for people leadership, where one needs to be able to work as a group-player.

Addressing the leader's outer landscapes, the Identity Compass® profiling tool also contains a section on job motivation, where the general theory on job motivation is underpinned by three general themes, those being:

1. *Autonomy vs. dependency:* Does the person's work make him/her feel powerful and in control?
2. *Security vs. absence of prospects:* Does the person feel that he/she is well accommodated in his/her current position and that he/she has found his/her niche?
3. *Challenge vs. pointless:* Does the person feel challenged by his/her work, and does it stimulate his/her faculties to the fullest?

These help leaders to understand their outer landscapes, by understanding what factors in their job environment they experience as motivating or de-motivating. When considering adult experiential learning and balanced processing required in AL, the afore-mentioned are good examples of where leaders might require flexibility in order to feel more motivated in their job environment.

Programme component: Adult experiential learning

Any changes in performance usually imply changes in the way we think and behave. Changes in thinking and behaviour usually involve learning. As adults, we learn experientially, and our learning is usually iterative in nature. Kolb included this *cycle of learning* as a central principle in his experiential learning theory, expressed as The Four-stage Cycle of Learning. He defined *learning* as "the process whereby knowledge is created through the transformation of experience. Knowledge results from the combination of grasping and transforming experience"[91]. David Kolb outlined a four-stage cycle of learning. The experiential learning theory model portrays two dialectically related modes of grasping experience – concrete experience (CE) and abstract conceptualisation (AC) – and two dialectically related modes of transforming experience – reflective observation (RO) and active experimentation (AE), as illustrated in the following figure.

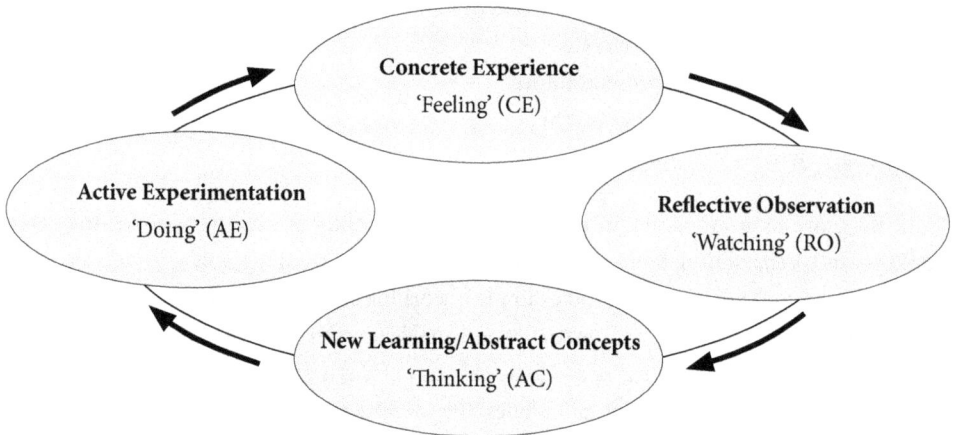

Figure 15: The four stages of Kolb's learning cycle

Kolb suggested that, ideally, individuals should include all four bases in an ideal learning process. For example, by continually reflectively observing (RO) what happened, what went well, what went less well during one's concrete experiences (CE), one can distil what new insights and abstract concepts can be learnt from that (AC). Finally, one can then actively experiment (AE) with these new insights, and create new concrete experiences to reflect upon and learn from, and so one becomes a continuous experiential learner.

This means that by engaging in adult experiential learning, we are mindful that our experiences allow us to observe and reflect on the outcomes of the activity. We then refine our ideas, which we once again put into practice. Unless we put learning into practice, learning is lost. It is only in the *doing* that knowledge and understanding are internalised in our minds and neurology. This style of learning, therefore, is more sustainable, in that it employs the body, mind, and emotions; therefore, our whole being. This is how adults do and should learn. Our learning is experiential, allowing for iterative cycles of learning and change, where we continually experiment and do new things. We reflect on how well we have done, and we learn how to refine on a continual basis what we do.

Kolb also stressed that individuals follow different approaches to learning, such as diverging, assimilating, converging, or accommodating styles. While individuals are often more dominant in one or two of the learning styles, leaders need to develop skills in all four learning styles in order to choose appropriate modes of behaviour for achieving specific outcomes. Having access to all four learning styles can help leaders to become more flexible and discerning in responding to organisational challenges. It is important for a facilitator or leader not to fall into the trap of relying too heavily on one's own preferred styles of learning when coaching others.

Similarly to requiring flexibility in the way we filter our thinking and behavioural preferences, I also encourage my leaders to work in all four modes of the learning style cycle. I introduce a self-reflective journaling technique that is based on Kolb's experiential learning theory (see Appendix 4). The purpose of reflective journaling is to develop a critical reflective ability, which holds a significant benefit for continual learners. The value of critical reflective thinking is not so much the content of what happens to leaders, but the meta-cognitive ability to allow double- and treble-loop learning processes contained in any experience, and how this learning is likely to inform the leaders in future. Reflective journaling therefore becomes a self-coaching tool that aids in self-learning and organisational learning processes.

Process component: Individual Session 1

In this two-hour session at the outset of the programme, I use the first 30 minutes to build rapport. I do so by learning more about the leader as a person, and invite them to share whatever they are comfortable sharing regarding both their work and their social life, and, in return, I do the same. I also offer them the gift of a book titled *A Guide to Coachees*[92], which outlines how to get the most out of any coaching journey. I ask them to read it, and in the following session to highlight the themes that had stood out for them. I introduce a coaching commitment document that they need to read, discuss and resolve any concerns that they might have, before it is signed both by the leader client and myself. This is an important process that encourages both parties to commit to giving their best during their partnership whilst on this AL coaching journey.

This is followed by each leader reviewing their feedback together with me on the Identity Compass® thinking and behavioural profiling and job motivation, completed prior to the outset of their coaching journey. This helps leaders to understand how they filter incoming information from the environment, and how this might differ from important others with whom they need to interact. It also helps them to understand where they experience insufficient flexibility in these filters, which might hinder them in achieving outcomes or experience a lack of job motivation.

The feedback is given in a tentative and respectful manner, bearing in mind that this is feedback on a self-assessment, and that leaders are the experts on their own content. It becomes an interactive session where the leaders attempt to make sense of the feedback, and it is usually a good way to break the ice between facilitator and leader; it also makes the leader aware of areas that might require further work. At the end of the session, I introduce the concept *self-reflective journaling* based on *adult experiential learning*, as postulated by David Kolb, and invite them to experiment with this to yield further learnings from each session.

Self-work activities after individual session 1: Leaders are required to:

1. Reflect on the Identity Compass® feedback, and to determine how this, if at all, informs the outcomes and value he/she wishes to derive from this programme;
2. Do reflective journaling on the session;
3. Consider the leadership outcomes to work towards, and the accompanying sensory-based behavioural evidence for each outcome;
4. Complete and sign the programme commitment document; and
5. Read the coachee guidebook, and distil the helpful themes towards a successful ALD journey.

Actual experience: Feedback from the field

The results of the *thinking- and behavioural filtering* self-profiling are usually discussed in the first individual session, so that participants can reflect on the areas where their thinking- and behavioural filtering might be limiting them in their work context. This contributes to preparing the participants for the following session, during which they identify the outcomes they wish to achieve in the programme, as it allows them to identify gaps and causes of those gaps in terms of the way that they filter objective realities. For instance, in the case of Andrea, her *internal referencing* preference, meaning the ability to check all incoming data against her internal barometer rather than the opinions of others, was not high enough, which impacted on her belief in herself. Once she understood this better, she knew what outcomes to work towards, explained as follows.

Andrea: The internal/external was extremely helpful, from the perspective that I knew from a self-belief point of view I needed to work on that... in order to improve my self-belief. So that whole upping the internal reference! Checking within yourself what it is you believe, as opposed to just listening to others...

In terms of the *impact* of self-profiling of thinking- and behavioural thinking, feedback was discussed in the first session, and then immediately used in Session 2 to determine desired outcomes. Leaders do this feedback to start the process of introspection in order to increase their awareness of their current self. This allows them to determine what shifts they wish to make, and how they can recognise those shifts when they happen.

Dobek: Through this whole thing [profiling feedback] I've done a lot of reflection, and I think I was more innovative a few years ago than I am now, and I think that's also because of just being comfortable and complacent where I am. So I need to shake up!

The actual experience in the field indicates that discussing the feedback of thinking and behavioural profiling is a helpful process with which to commence the ALD journey.

Adult experiential learning, in the form of reflective journaling, is usually introduced to the leaders at the outset of the programme, and they are encouraged to use it throughout the programme, after every session, to yield further reflections and learnings from each session. The idea is that, as a form of adult experiential learning, they would eventually do this in their head after any important concrete experience from which they could and should learn.

In terms of the *role* of journaling, leaders find that it assists them in developing sustainable adult experiential learning. Reflective journaling allows them to reflect, a pattern that they can maintain on their own. After a while, they can reflect without doing so in writing, and they often start to do so whilst travelling to and from work. They realise that they need to focus, not only on their gaps, but also on the positive aspects, so that they can see themselves in a balanced way. Leaders initially find it hard to be so self-honest. However, it helps them to solidify their learnings, and the sooner they do it after any relevant experience, the fresher the details are in their minds. Although it requires effort, it is actually very useful in terms of on-going self-learning. Darren and Justin shared their experience as follows.

Darren: I did my own, in my own way, every day, in my car on the way to work and back. It just became a pattern for me, and I'll continue to do it. I think that was probably the hardest work because that's where you've got to be honest with yourself because it's almost the What?, and the So what?, and the Now what? And you've got to be very, very honest with yourself.

Justin: When you reflect, you've got to reflect on the good, and I think that's what you brought out as well. Reflect on everything, see yourself as a whole person, understand where you are in totality.

In terms of the *impact* of journaling, although not all leaders are equally willing, most leaders experience considerable value in engaging in reflective journaling. For those who do engage, it helps them to overcome challenges, and they can use this outside of the programme as well. In this instance, it helped them to attain new insights and, for some, the process of reflection was a new skill that they had not engaged in before. It further helped them to reflect on what had happened during their day, how they responded, how they could have done it differently, and what to bear in mind for the next occasion, as Vanya shared.

> **Vanya:** *It was helpful... just to understand what reflecting was about, it was good, but now I can do it in my head. So, now, when I reflect on the day, it's more around: How could I have done it differently? What would I have done differently? And knowing that, if that situation or a similar situation arose, this is how I must react to it.*

It therefore becomes a most important self-coaching tool. Ideally, reflection-*on*-action can become reflection-*in*-action, where leaders can reflect and self-correct in the moment. Having a sense now of what the gaps are helps leaders to identify leadership outcomes to work towards, as follows in individual ALE Step 2.

Individual ALE Step 2 – Identify personal, interpersonal and professional ALE outcomes

Programme component: Outcomes and key behavioural indicators

Once leaders understand their gaps in effectiveness, during ALE step 2, they are usually in a position to distil their leadership outcomes to work towards in this journey. On occasions when this is not yet the case, leaders might ask me to obtain further 360° feedback on them to help them understand their development gaps. The following outlines the theory on ALE outcomes, and on how the evidence of success is measured by means of key behavioural indicators (KBIs).

ALE outcomes

> "If you don't know where you are going, any road will get you there."
> Lewis Carroll, author of *Alice in Wonderland*

The outcome of the programme is to develop enhanced ALE, broken down into: 1) intrapersonal- (self-) leadership, in order to support 2) interpersonal (people) leadership, and 3) organisational leadership outcomes, which need to manifest uniquely in the case of each leader within an organisation. Once gaps have been established, the next aspect I usually explore with the leader is what outcomes they need to achieve in each of these categories. Once these outcomes have been identified, it is important to establish evidence of success, that is, how the achievement of these outcomes will be measured in concrete, leader-specific sensory and behavioural indicators.

Systems thinking implies that if we know what outcomes to work towards, it focuses us in getting there, and this is especially so in the case of AL, where leaders have to align their true self to the goals or outcomes that need to be achieved. It is important that these outcomes are stated in positive terms; in other words, rather than focus on the negative outcomes they wish to avoid, leaders need to identify and understand what outcomes they wish to achieve. For instance in personal leadership, the outcome might be, "To develop and present a confident sense of self when presenting to the Board". In people leadership, a typical outcome might be, "To inspire my team to perform to the best of their ability". In organisational leadership, a typical outcome might be "To ensure that my division meets and exceeds all its Balanced Scorecard targets".

Evidence of successful outcomes: Key behavioural indicators (KBIs)

These could be somewhat compared to key performance indicators (KPIs), as they are called in the organisational context. I prefer to think of my clients as whole human beings rather than just human resources, and human beings behave so that they can perform, hence my use of the term *key behavioural indicators* (KBIs). When my clients identify the leadership outcomes that they wish to work towards, these are usually quite abstract, and therefore not easy to measure. How does one, for instance, measure whether someone is confident or not, and would one measure this in the same way for everyone? For a journey such as this to produce positive and sustainable well-formed outcomes, these outcomes need to be expressed in concrete behavioural terms, specific to that leader in a specific context. It is therefore important that sensory-based KBIs support an outcome. This helps to solidify potentially abstract outcomes into sensory-based concrete evidence that can help determine the progress in achieving desired outcomes.

Especially in the case of personal and interpersonal leadership, the ipsative method of measuring progress is appropriate when measuring progress towards achieving desired results. Each individual identifies the sensory-based self-evidence that is appropriate to measure progress towards achieving his/her leadership outcomes. These KBIs usually need to be positively stated, and in the present tense, so that at any moment in time it is very easy to ask, for instance, out of a rating of 10, how closely the leader's behaviour aligns with a particular KBI. For example, in order to support the aforementioned outcome (To develop a confident sense of self when presenting to the Board), an accompanying KBI might be: "My heart rate remains normal while I present to the Board" or "I hear my voice being calm and relaxed as I present to the Board." How true this is, is then rated out of a possible score of 10, where 0 is "*not at all*", and 10 is "*completely achieved*".

In my experience, my clients often find it extremely challenging to identify these KBIs, as this is not something they usually engage in. In order to assist them, I then ask them what the current indicators are that indicate to them that they need to work towards a specific outcome. These are then used in an 'instead of' statement, as follows: "Instead of feeling my throat close up and being unable to speak normally, I now feel my throat relax, and I hear my voice being calm when I present to the Board." It is therefore about what I and others notice as different in my behaviour, which tells me that I am achieving my outcome.

An unexpected finding in my Master's research was that these KBIs became a self-coaching tool for my clients, as they started to monitor in their everyday life whether they were moving closer to or away from these positively stated behavioural indicators. Furthermore, bearing in mind that KBIs were normally identified and decided upon by themselves, I found that, whilst on this journey towards developing leadership authenticity, my clients came to know themselves extremely well and that they had no desire to delude themselves in terms of the shifts that they were achieving towards their outcomes. The implication of this is that my clients usually start to take ownership of achieving their outcomes as identified by their KBIs. Whenever we do a midway review to determine their progress, I usually ask the following regarding each KBI: "Out of 10, where 0 represents *not achieved* and 10 represents *fully achieved*, where do you believe you were when you started, and where are you now?" I repeat this exercise in the final review, and have found that, in the final session, leaders assess themselves without hesitation, having become more self-aware and committed to their growth, and they give qualitative behavioural examples to support their assessments. I furthermore find that often my client's sense and my sense of the client's shifts coincide, and the client's final assessment review often supported and built on his/her midway assessment review. I regard this as an indication of authenticity.

During my Masters research, when I asked my research clients about this phenomenon, I was given two main reasons for the reliability of the results using this ipsative approach, these being: 1) they were much more aware of self, and 2) they no longer had a need to mislead themselves or others. Their need for social desirability had lessened, and this in itself confirmed the development of leadership authenticity, as self-regulation had replaced self-monitoring.

Process component: Individual Session 2

This two-hour session is often quite gruelling. Not only do leaders need to explore what outcomes they need to work towards and state these in positive terms, they also need to identify the sensory-based KBIs that are to be used throughout this journey to measure the shifts made towards the outcomes. Leaders are not accustomed to such an exercise and it is easier to identify what behaviours they no longer want rather than what behaviours need to replace these. However, until the indicators of successful outcomes are stated in positive and in present-tense terms, they are of limited value. These often require iterations of further refinement. At the end of the session, I introduce a template for writing their *life chapters* in order to distil the themes that had shaped them, in preparation for individual ALE step 3.

> *Self-work activities after individual session 2:* Leaders are required to:
>
> 1. Complete the exercise on overall outcomes and KBIs;
> 2. Engage in some reflective journaling on the session; and
> 3. Complete the life chapters' exercise in preparation for the next session.

Actual experience: Feedback from the field

In terms of the *role of identifying outcomes*, usually determined in Individual Session 2, client leaders find that it helps to start the programme with the end in mind as it focuses them on what they want to achieve in terms of intrapersonal, interpersonal, and professional leadership outcomes. Even when leaders are not sure what they wish to work towards, this component provides a foundation. It helps them to become focused on the future they desire, and it guides them in their behaviours during their day-to-day activities. This foundation therefore provides cohesion in their journey towards developing ALE. This is how Darren described it:

> **Darren:** *That [outcomes] pulled the thing together for me. Because that almost underpins everything as a starting point of how I think, or of how I do my day-to-day business. So it was almost the glue that keeps it together.*

Leaders realise the importance of doing this hard work at the outset of the programme as it allows them to monitor their own behaviour on a daily basis against the outcomes that they have identified, as is the intention. Whereas the outcomes help leaders to become future-focused, they find that the role of the KBIs is to help them to bring their outcomes down from an abstract to a leader-specific, concrete level. This is a very challenging process, not often found in development programmes. Through questioning, a critical coaching skill, I often encourage leaders to look within themselves to determine the specific sensory-based concrete evidence that allows them to determine shifts they wish to make towards achieving those outcomes. It forces these leaders to be honest, genuine, and precise, and they often find this experience draining. I encourage them to identify as many KBIs as they can for each outcome, allowing them to determine not only the behaviours that needed to be in place but also, for instance, the thoughts and feelings that will need to accompany those behaviours. This is what the following two leaders had to say:

> **Gugu:** *Firstly, it was a nightmare (laughs). Oh my word! I think that was the hardest part of the programme. I think the way that whole system is structured to distil to the KBI's, it's done so well, you have to force yourself to be genuine, to be honest, and to be precise. So, for me, that's why it was a very hard process. It forces you to look within. It forces you to speak out loud outside your own head in terms of what you want, what your future must look like, and what you aim to do.*

Andrea: It was very helpful in the sense that you got to the core of what we wanted to see, how we should behave. I think it was very helpful to the point that it wasn't just the one thing that you would say – you needed to give a couple of ways that you would see that, and you would need to give situations. And then also unpacking how you would feel. ... So you're almost double-checking ... does your behaviour change? But also, how you feel in that situation if you relate that back to uneasiness, in a sense, from the outcomes that you were going to decide on, you need to have seen a change in how you feel as well.

Distilling the KBIs for every outcome was especially helpful as it became a self-coaching tool, which allowed them to review on a daily basis whether they were stepping into new behaviours or slipping back into old habits of thinking and behaving. It allowed them to review their shifts from time to time, to determine what had already been achieved, and where further work was required. This was how Liam experienced it.

Liam: ...it gave you the understanding, the clarity in terms of who you are, what you do and how you react. And then, obviously, knowing what you look like there, it's easier for you than to say, "What do I want to look like?" I suppose it just created the awareness in terms of this in the way that you do behave and, in some cases – or in the cases where it was negative – it just sort of jumps front-of-mind in terms of, "Watch out for this, watch out for that!" And that helps you, as I said, to create the possible self.

Once the intrapersonal, interpersonal, and professional leadership outcomes with accompanying KBIs have been identified, leaders understand the end-states they wish to achieve. The next question then is, 'Who am I currently, and how have I become who I am today?' In ALE step 3, leaders consider life events and leadership episodes that have shaped them thus far.

Individual ALE Step 3 – Identifying life and leadership themes that have shaped current self

Programme component: Life chapters

Leadership authenticity requires that leaders have knowledge and clarity regarding who they are, what they believe in, and what they value as important. The internal compass of the current self can be regarded as shaped by a culmination of all our life and leadership experiences, and more importantly, our responses to those. A life-story approach to developing AL suggests that self-knowledge and clarity can be obtained through the re-construction of life stories, which then allows the leader's concept of self to become apparent. Rather than the usual training or workshop programmes that develop new *doing* skills, it is about the *being* aspect, in that the leaders can start understanding how their life stories have shaped who they are and how they behave. Telling their life stories and distilling the once-off or repeated themes that emerge help leaders to understand which of these themes might be hindering them and which could empower them further. Combining this with reflective thinking allows leaders to create more meaning out of their experiences that have been and still are definitive in terms of who they are.

A guided life review process can be done by asking the leader to draw a lifeline with valleys and peaks, or alternatively to populate life chapters, which is also very effective. In the case of this ALE programme, the life chapter template (see Appendix 5) is based on a template offered by Cox[93]. For each life chapter the leader is asked to describe memorable events, important people, places, challenges, and themes that inform who they are today, concluding with what transitioned them to the next chapter. This allows the leader to tell his or her story, and then to reflect critically, at a meta-level, on once-off or recurring themes that might have shaped the self and the course of their lives. This often leads to considerable transformative learning.

I have found that this allows the leader the opportunity to put time aside to reflect in a unique and valuable way on the self as a continuum, rather than a snapshot of the present moment in time. It allows the leader to ask the self what past 'baggage' they might no longer need to carry and can let go of, once learning or meaning has been extracted from that experience. It further helps to remind the leader how great they have already been throughout their lives, which can be very valuable, especially when they are currently feeling challenged. It is almost as if aspects of the *past self* of the leader can become a role model and inspiration for the *current self*. In my experience, especially when the life history has been a challenging one, this exercise often becomes a very liberating and transformational experience.

Process component: Individual Session 3

During this two-hour session, leaders start the process of sharing their life chapters in a narrative style. Once again, this can be a very challenging exercise, as some individuals have had very challenging life histories. For instance in South Africa, some might have experienced the apartheid years, where, as young Black individuals, they might have been on the *wrong* side of the colour line, or else, as young White males, were forced to enter into military conscription, and had to engage in warfare activities that went against their value systems. Whereas it might not have been as dramatic as that, many individuals still carry *baggage* with them that hampers their development, without necessarily realising this. Others might experience current challenges, where they might feel that life or organisations tend to *squeeze the self out of the self*, resulting in them not knowing whom they really are any more. Consequently, they might feel like imposters or fakes, fearing the thought of being *found out*.

We need to remember that we are a culmination of all our life experiences rather than a snapshot of the now. What is important though, is to remember one of Frankl's often-quoted comments, originating whilst being a prisoner in the Nazi camps during World War II, which refs to the fact that the quality of life is determined not so much by what happens to us but rather by how we choose to respond to it[94]. This becomes useful when distilling the themes from any life history, where we ask what we can learn from any experience, realise which of those can empower us further than it has to date, and let go of those that might still limit us or be of no use to us. I have noticed that, although it often takes considerable courage for any leader to start this process, or it might even be the first time ever that this life history is shared with someone else that they can trust, it becomes an immensely liberating and empowering experience for the leader.

At this point, it is important to note that I am mindful of emerging themes that are out of the bounds of leadership coaching, which might need to be dealt with in psychotherapy. It is therefore important to get a sense of the ego strength of the individual in this process, and to agree on what can be dealt with in the coaching, and what needs to be dealt with outside of this process. However, in my experience, leaders at a senior or executive level with traumatic themes in their life history often do have the ego strength required to deal with these themes in this process. In doing so, they manage to take the limiting self-aspects out of the way of the self.

Self-work activities after individual session 3: Leaders are required to:

1. Distil the limiting and empowering themes across the life chapters that have culminated in the values, beliefs, and psychological states of the current self; and
2. Engage in some reflective journaling on the session.

Actual experience: Feedback from the field

Once the gaps have been identified through self-profiling, followed by introspection, and outcomes with accompanying KBIs have been identified, Session 3 focuses on exploring life chapters. This starts the process of leaders better understanding the self who wishes to achieve the outcomes. Using the rationale that we are a culmination of all our life experiences, the life chapters' exercise allows leaders to better understand themselves by understanding how their past experiences have shaped their current selves.

In terms of the *role* of the life chapters' exercise, leaders have shared that it affirms the importance of knowing their values and beliefs developed throughout their life experiences (of which work plays a part). It also explains and affirms the value of self and life, as they look back at everything they have already achieved, and it allows them to be more comfortable within and true to themselves. It is almost like building a puzzle, putting all the puzzle pieces where they fit, so that they can see a more complete picture of who they are. During this process, they also remember life episodes that allow them to become proud of themselves.

Justin: Going through this process, it's almost like building a big puzzle where you're putting pieces all over, and at the end you see the whole picture, and that's exactly what it was like. It was almost like I was doing these piecemeal bits of work that eventually fell into place.

Gugu: I am the only matriculant and university graduate in my family's history. I passed matric, and I did so with an exemption and some A's, staying in a shack without electricity and studying by candlelight, while holding a part-time job.

Furthermore, it allows leaders to become role models to themselves, knowing that if they could have achieved what they had before, they can do it again. It allows them to understand themselves better and to become more honest about their current selves, which is necessary before they can consider who they can possibly become. Whilst it is not therapy, it is thought provoking for each leader to understand their life themes before moving forward, allowing them to become more self-aware of trends in their behaviour, also, in terms of how they were contributing to the negative dynamics within their team. This is what leaders had to say.

Peter: Learning through this to become more self-aware of my contribution to the problem...

Andrea: I think that was useful, because you could see the trend... So looking at the different chapters and saying, "Is there a trend of certain things that always happen...?"

Once leaders realised how they were still embracing behaviours that might have been helpful in earlier life chapters, but were currently limiting them, they could start transforming the self. The next ALE step is to identify the internal compass that has guided their current selves to date.

Individual ALE Step 4 – Identify the internal compass that informs the current self

Programme component: AL Compass

A human being's *internal compass* could be thought of and divided into logical levels of human processing. I developed an internal AL Compass template, which, over the years, I adapted from the original model for neurological levels of change developed by Dilts[95], used in Neuro-Linguistic Programming (NLP). These original neurological levels of change comprise 1) environment, 2) behaviour, 3) competencies, 4) values and beliefs, and 5) purpose. Simplistically explained, one could then ask the following questions:

- *Environment:* In what environment do you wish to explore your behaviour?
- *Behaviour:* Which behaviour do you wish to explore?
- *Competencies*: What skills support you in this behaviour?
- *Values and beliefs:* What do you believe about this, and what values are important in this behaviour?

- *Identity:* Who are you when you engage in this behaviour? What does this say about your identity?
- *Purpose:* How does this behaviour fit with your purpose?

I found it useful to expand this model, now called the internal AL Compass (see Appendix 6), to suit the development of leadership authenticity. Firstly, the leader needs to explore the internal compass for the *current self* using the AL Compass template. Once an understanding of the compass for current self has been gained, the leader can develop an internal AL Compass towards the next level of a *possible self*, based on how the leader wishes to grow into the future. My rationale in this instance was that we first need to understand who we currently are *(current self)* before we can explore our next level of *possible self* towards attaining our *highest authentic self*. As human beings, leaders operate in at least two contexts, those being at work, and outside work. This template therefore allows for multiple contexts, or working internal compasses, within the leader's internal AL Compass. The original neurological levels have been adapted further to suit the development of AL. Referred to as AL levels, it is important to note that whilst the first three AL levels need to be considered at the overarching AL Compass level, the remaining four AL levels need to be considered more specifically at a working compass level within the AL Compass, as follows.

AL Level 1: **Internal self-identity:** Internal or self-identity is often a new concept for leaders to grasp. This is not to be confused with the construct of social identity which is based on who we are in terms of the groups of whom we form part. In the case of AL, it is about who we understand ourselves to be at a very deep level, whether at work or elsewhere. What is the internal identity that drives us and our behaviour, whether we realise it or not? Might it be *people-pleaser* or *doormat*, or could it be a *powerhouse* or *captain of my ship*? I often encourage leaders to consider a metaphor of one or two words that describe their internal identity. For instance, when I worked with one particular client, what came to mind for him was *Jumbo Jet*. When he considered what this might mean to him, he realised that he often carried numerous others and their baggage. Once he realised this, he could start exploring what beliefs supported this internal identity, and start setting firmer boundaries. A good question to reflect on once we have identified our internal identity is: *How well does my current internal identity support my leadership purpose and vision?*

AL Level 2: **Leadership purpose, linked to vision/legacy:** Most often, leaders do not specifically consider their overarching leadership purpose. This might include their purpose as a leader not only at work but also in life. A strong sense of purpose helps leaders to set goals in line with their purpose, and to persist when situations become challenging. Purpose can be linked to vision, as it helps us to visualise where our purpose will take us and what legacy (the result of realising that vision) it will allow us to leave behind once we leave a job or even life itself.

AL Level 3: **Values, ethical and general:** People often talk about values, without truly knowing what this means. Barrett defined values as: "the universal guidance system of the soul"[96]. For me, it simply means those things that are important to us; that we will fight for, persist for, and sacrifice other things for, which aligns with Demartini's[97] statement that values are: "what you truly value most, what truly inspires you, who you truly are, and what your true purpose is..." Oftentimes, when my clients first start thinking about their values, they might list honesty, integrity, or hard work, without considering the value of, for instance, their family, friends, kindness, or health. We need to consider what aspects we need to reflect in our behaviour that will indicate how true we are to our values, as this will indicate whether our values are enacted or merely espoused values. Values are hierarchical, and our purpose could be regarded as our highest value. The two further questions that then need to be asked in the context of enhancing leadership authenticity are: 1) *How ethical are my values?* and 2) *How well do my values support my identity and my purpose?*

AL Level 4: **Beliefs:** Beliefs could be thought of as assumptions or committed thoughts that we hold to be true, based on our experiences from the past. Put differently, our thoughts are informed by and filtered through our belief systems. Beliefs can be limiting or empowering and can therefore hinder or help us in living true to our purpose, both at work and in life. We furthermore hold beliefs about those beliefs, which we also run through filters, such as generalisation, deletion, or personalisation, and it is therefore important for us to understand what we believe; furthermore, to examine our belief system, and to let go of those beliefs which no longer serve us. I divide beliefs into beliefs about 1) *self* and 2) *and others.*

- *Beliefs about self.* What are all the beliefs we hold about ourselves that drive our behaviour? Do we believe that we can do anything we set our minds to, or do we believe that we are failures? What further do we believe about those beliefs? How do those impact on our daily thoughts about ourselves, our abilities, and our behaviours?
- *Beliefs about important others.* I divide *others* up into *others at work* and *others outside work,* and then I encourage leaders to consider the beliefs about each of the *others,* both individually and systemically, in the leader's various contexts. Furthermore, the leader has to consider which of those beliefs could be more empowering, or might still be hindering the outcomes that need to be achieved, both in life and at work.

AL Level 5: **Psychological states:** These comprise emotional and mind states that result in thoughts and feelings. It is important to note that I do not prescribe to my leaders which psychological states they should develop in order to be regarded as an authentic leader. Instead, leaders are encouraged to identify which states currently drive their behaviour, both in life and at work, whether these are helpful or hindering, and if necessary, what empowering states these need to be replaced with.

- *Thoughts.* These are the internal conversations that often occupy the leader's mind, and which influence the states of mind and emotions of the leader. The questions that can then be asked are how these thoughts are informed by the leader's beliefs, and whether these thoughts create empowering or limiting mind states. For instance, do these thoughts create states of transparency, resilience, agility, and creativity, or do they create states of wanting to give up? Questions that could be asked are: *How do these thoughts impact on any feelings or emotional states I experience, and are these thoughts helpful or a hindrance?*
- *Feelings.* Feelings, impacted by thoughts, result in emotional states that can either limit or enhance the leader's performance. What are the feelings that the leader experiences? Are these, for instance, feelings of excitement, optimism, passion, and hope, or feelings of frustration and despair? Questions that could be asked are: *How do these feelings impact on any emotional states and behaviour that I experience, and are these feelings helpful or a hindrance?*

AL Level 6: **Skills/Competencies:** Skills or competencies are gained through training or experience, and assist leaders to perform better. However, competencies need to be applied, and how well they are applied, depends on the preceding AL Levels 1 – 5, and whether those are empowering or limiting the leader.

AL Level 7: **Behaviours:** Behaviour is the result of all of the aforementioned levels. Whereas Levels 1 – 6 exist below the soil-line, and are therefore invisible, this is the only level that exists above the soil-line, therefore visible to others, both at work and outside work, and for everyone to experience via their sensory channels. Behaviours can both be seen and heard, and are either empowering or limiting to self and others. At work, behaviour translates into performance.

Once awareness has been created at each of the aforementioned levels in terms of the compass of the current self, it can be determined how well those levels support one another to allow for a congruent presentation of self. I refer to this as the *golden thread*. Often the golden thread is not as strong as it should be, as the leader does not understand what is truly important to him/her, whilst it might also explain why a leader is not as effective as he/she could be. At this point, the leader can start asking what needs to change at each level in order to create a more congruent and a more authentic *possible self*, this time, starting with identity, purpose, and vision. This process allows us to develop, amongst others, those attributes, such as resilience, hope, self-efficacy, and optimism, that, together, create the positive psychological capital required in AL. Furthermore, the process encourages self-awareness, transparency, ethical/moral capacities, and balanced processing that AL thought leaders such as Avolio, Gardner, Walumbwa[98] refer to. In fact, for me this is what balanced processing is all about, and this is what allows us to create an internal AL Compass that allows us to remain "*True North*".

Once an understanding exists of the AL levels, it is useful for the leader to understand the notion of his/her *internal power zone*, which below the soil-line comprises thoughts and feelings, manifesting above the soil-line into speech and behaviour. Self-empowerment happens by consciously taking accountability for one's own internal power zone, whilst resisting the temptation to take accountability for those of others.

Process component: Individual Session 4

By now, we have created some rapport, the leader has a sense of how the sessions work, and we reduce the duration of our further sessions to 90 minutes. In session 4, I introduce the notion of an internal compass, which in the case of an AL becomes an internal AL Compass, and facilitate the process of populating the various AL levels for the current self, starting at AL Level 7 with specific behaviours at a sensory level. Again, this is an unusual exercise for the leader to participate in, and it often requires an experienced facilitator to 'loosen' the thinking of the leader somewhat, so that he/she can reach these levels below the soil-line that inform his/her current behaviour. Whilst this process is initiated within the facilitated session, it often requires further reflections after the session for it to become more meaningful to the leader. The leader is thereafter encouraged to determine how strong the golden thread is that runs through all the AL Levels of the internal compass of the current self.

Self-work activities after individual session 4: Leaders are required to:

1. Complete the *AL Levels* exercise for the current self by populating their internal compass, and determine the strength of the golden thread, if it existed at all, throughout all the levels; and
2. Engage in some reflective journaling on the session.

Actual experience: Feedback from the field

Once participants have completed their life chapters' exercise, the exercise for identifying AL levels for the *current self* in Individual Session 4 allows them to explore their current purpose, vision, and the legacy they wish to create. It further allows them to explore their internal identity, values, and beliefs about self and others, and finally, it allows them to distil their thoughts and feelings, culminating in psychological states that underpin their current behaviour and form part of their working internal compass within their internal AL Compass.

This is the start of creating a full picture of who they currently are, both at and outside work, above and below the soil-line. What is important, from a developmental and pragmatic AL measuring perspective, is that the leaders are not prescribed how, and to what they need to shift in order to increase their AL. Leaders decide for themselves what shifts are required from them in order to become more effective as authentic leaders.

In terms of the *role* of AL levels, leaders shared that exploring these allows them to develop awareness of their current internal compass and mental models, and in terms of the alignment of the various levels, they can, for instance, ask whether their behaviours reflect their values. It also allows them to question their purpose, and what legacy they wish to leave behind. I have found that they struggle with this exercise, as they have never before been encouraged to engage in such reflections. Hannah and Andrea experienced this exercise as follows.

> **Hannah:** *Again, I think it forces you to be more aware of your current thinking, which sometimes we just sort of do without really realising that is the mental model that you work through. So some you might be aware of, but others you're not quite aware of, and I think it's bringing that to the surface.*

> **Andrea:** *I think it was helpful because your behaviours needed to reflect your values and, a lot of the times, it may have been in conflict... And then, the last aspect I found very useful, because it's one of the questions I was asking myself in terms of: Why am I here? What purpose do I want? What legacy do I want to leave? Those questions were quite important for me in terms of the programme.*

This process does not always leave leaders feeling comfortable, and this is exactly what might be required in order to prepare them for the change they might require. I worked with Justin, and after session 4 with him, I had written the following in my reflective journaling on his session.

> **My reflections on Justin:** *He shared that he had more questions than answers at the moment, and that, in the synagogue, the Rabbi had suggested that everything is pre-destined, and that we need to accept that what will be, will be. The more we try to move away from it, the more we move towards. So his question was really where it left him with this. He admitted that he found himself in a very uncomfortable and frustrated state now, and I was delighted, as this prepared him for change.*

> **My further reflections on Justin:** *We then moved to Justin's AL levels, and from his current to his possible self. We explored his suggested internal identities, and, at first, he thought he could keep those, until we start unpacking the possibility of being 'the perfect one.' It was not surprising that he had a fear of failure. We then discussed the notions of appropriate and inappropriate vulnerability and invulnerability, and how he could be more influential.*

In terms of the *impact* of AL levels, leaders find that going through the exercise and putting it on paper is very helpful in obtaining a better self-understanding. Once they have completed the internal compass exercise for the current self, they can use the same model in Individual Session 5 to create a more congruent internal AL Compass for the possible self towards which they wish to grow. Leaders have shared that once they have a better understanding of any incongruence within their current self they can start exploring what the levels in their AL Compass for their possible self need to contain, so that they can commit to that. It helps them to understand what is important to them, what their values are, and the vision and legacy they wish to create. It also helps them to formulate what shifts they wish to make, and what identity they need to step into in order to support the changes they want to effect in their leadership. This is how Gugu and Vanya experienced it.

> **Gugu:** *Understanding what's important to me, understanding what my values are, understanding some of the aspects around legacy and vision, I think that helped formulate the shifts that I wanted to make. It helped to shape the new identity I wanted to take up and some of the shifts I wanted to make around my leadership.*

> **Vanya:** *I think... if I had to go back to the possible self, I'm very close to where I currently need to be, but I think some of it may change in terms of the future. I've grown to where the possible self may actually change some more. So, in terms of where I am on the possible self, I would say I'm overall about 80 percent there, but I'm happy to be 80 percent there and to update my possible self.*

The following specific AL levels below the soil line experienced by leaders participating in this ALE programme are discussed further: 1) purpose, vision and legacy, 2) internal identity, 3) beliefs about self and others, 4) values and ethics, and 5) psychological states. Skills, such as business and technical skills, are usually already in place and can be obtained elsewhere, and are not specifically discussed in the following.

AL Level 1: **Internal identity.** In this programme, leaders are encouraged to find two- or three-word metaphors to describe their internal identity, as these could be easily remembered. In terms of the *role* of this component, leaders have shared that it allows them to develop awareness of the internal identity that drives them, both for the current self and the possible self. It helped them to understand how their history had shaped them; for instance, in the case of Gugu, the internal identity of *Band-Aid* (a first-aid plaster) and *fixer-upper* had come about because of her hardships in her earlier life. However, in her current leadership role, this had become a limiting identity, and she moved to being a *leader as coach*, which she explained as follows.

> **Gugu:** *The identity I entered in the programme with, which was a **fixer-upper/Band-Aid** one, was shaped a lot by my history and what I've been through, but to some degree, it was limiting in terms of the new identity I wanted to step into. So, it helped in understanding why I'm in this fix-everything-up mode. It made me understand it and where it comes from, and what's limiting about it.*

Some leaders, like Justin, realised that they had unrealistic internal identities, such as *the perfect one*. Andrea realised that her current internal identity was *rollercoaster*, which was also a limiting internal identity, and stepping into the identity of *tree of life* helped her to stabilise, as the roots would keep her stable, whilst the growth at the top of her tree would trigger growth in self and others. This was how she described it.

Andrea: I said "**tree of life**." … it was the tree, specifically the deep roots to keep me stable, especially in view of the roller coaster, and the growth in terms of the top of the tree, in terms of the growth that I want to trigger in others and myself.

At times, leaders find that they initially have multiple internal identities that drive them. For instance, Liam discovered that he had two underpinning internal identities in his current self. His authentic self tended to be kind, wanting to rescue others (internal identity *Mother Teresa)*, but his life and especially his work history, had also taught him how to fight to survive, so he had embraced that fighter, aggressor, pusher, dictator identity to get to the top (internal identity *Honey Badger*). The result of vacillating between those two identities created considerable confusion in his team, and they were very cautious of him, as they never knew who was walking into the boardroom, *Mother Teresa* or *Honey Badger*.

In terms of *impact* of internal identity, leaders find that identifying their internal identities has a considerable impact on them, as they can determine whether these are limiting or empowering them. They can also check how well their internal identities are supporting their purpose and vision. In the case of Liam, realising that his multiple internal identities were limiting him and creating distrust between himself and his team, allowed him to identify a more helpful internal identity. Moving into his possible self, he wished to become the wise leader whom others felt comfortable to approach for guidance (internal identity *Mufasa* from the film *The Lion King*). Although he wished to keep certain aspects of his previous internal identity, those being a fighter, a driver, and a winner, he now wished to be display those in a calm, compassionate, respectful, and fair but tough leader who achieved success through others. This was how he explained it.

Liam: The **Mother Teresa** one is probably the more natural one that is within me, the way that I was developed through my life and my life history, and sort of got me to be a bit like that. It was natural, but it came natural to the people that it came natural to, so – people that I love, people that I care for, people that I took interest in. It was very overpowering that I wanted to help, and support, and coach, and guide, and get them to there. I didn't have that with everybody. It was very special, dedicated people that I thought I would help that way.

The **honey badger** one, I mean, that was just the way that I had to survive through my life. It was as simple as that. Right from the beginning, from early days, I had to fight to survive. I had to rise above the rest, I had to find tricky ways to get to the top, and I used that in every aspect of my life to get where I was. I suppose that is in some way … a successful mechanism, in my case, to compensate for my gaps and my weaknesses, is just to be the fighter, to be the aggressor, to be the pusher, the dictator, all of those sort of things. The confusion, I can see that, no doubt about it.

…**Mufasa** was the king of Pride Rock (Lion King) and Simba's father. Mufasa's role is as an omniscient leader whose wisdom and judgment are always correct, and to whom every character looks for guidance. He is a wise king who commands respect from the other animals. He is always calm, but is prepared to fight to save his pride and his family. Even after his death, his spirit *remained, to guide his kingdom. I like to continue to be the fighter, a driver, and the winner. I want to be known and respected as the calm, compassionate, thoughtful, fair-but-tough leader – achieving success through others.*

AL Level 2: Purpose, vision, and legacy. In terms of the *role* of purpose, vision, and legacy, leaders shared that exploring their current purpose, vision, and the legacy they wished to create, allowed them to develop awareness of these aspects within themselves, only to find that for most these either were non-existent, quite abstract, not well-defined, or misdirected in terms of what they wished to achieve.

> **Darren:** *It was difficult. I didn't have purpose. I thought I had one. ....there was no vision.*

Exploring and creating awareness of their purpose, vision, and legacy for their possible selves made them more purposeful about their purpose and vision. Those leaders who are already questioning themselves about the legacy they wish to create, and why they are doing what they are doing, find that the programme helps them to answer those questions.

> **Liam:** *At the end of the day, when you got to what you want to get to, it was a lot wider, it's a lot more deeper, it's a lot more real – and because you now know yourself, and you know what you would like to be, it's a lot easier to distil the truth out of a real, meaningful vision.*
>
> **Andrea:** *And then, the last aspect I found very useful, because it's one of the questions I was asking myself in terms of: Why am I here? What purpose do I want? What legacy do I want to leave? Those questions were quite important for me in terms of the programme. ....what I'm doing in my MBA team as well, it's to say: We need to grow the team, we're here to learn. We have disagreements, and we have feedback, we have openness, and honesty, and trust.*

In terms of the *impact* of purpose, vision, and legacy, leaders shared that increasing their focus on both their purpose and vision helped to them refocus and revive their energy.

> **Nikhil:** *I've never really thought about: What is my vision? and, hence, What legacy do I want to leave behind? but I know about it. I never followed a structured approach to understand who I am, who my team members are, and what our focus is. I think the programme brought a lot of structure to maybe haphazard thought and ideas. It's brought more alignment from that perspective. So, I think it clarifies to a certain degree what is already subconsciously something I'm working towards.*
>
> **Andrea:** *It was very useful, because it's things you probably are doing, but now you've framed it in a way that you can say that that's what you always seek in situations – if you look at your future self, that's why you have the values that you have, that's [sic] the behaviours you show...*

AL Level 3: Values and ethics. In terms of the *role* of values and ethics, leaders have shared how the programme has assisted them in creating awareness of their general and ethical values. Of all the AL Levels, these seemed to be the most important to leaders across the board. Whereas *values* refer to anything that leaders value, *ethics* refer to the moral and ethical aspects that leaders value. As a result of the programme, leaders realise that the values and ethics that they have always regarded as important are not necessarily that important after all, as these are not reflected in their behaviour. The programme allows them to reflect on the importance of their values and on how they can re-align their behaviours to their values.

> **Darren:** *I think a lot of the values that I thought were values were not values. They were just run-of-the-mill stuff. There were a lot of the values that I thought I had which I actually didn't have... when I put here in the beginning "family," that was – you say that, but it was nonsense. I wasn't putting in what I should've been putting in. It was a value, but I wasn't living it.*

> **Andrea:** *I think it was very valuable to look at the values from a point of view that we reflected on what drives you, and what are those things that are core to who you are, and that you really find valuable. It helps you to build the full picture of your future self; so it was incredibly important in terms of to say, "Does my behaviour show my values?"*

In terms of the *impact* of values and ethics, a number of leaders feel they are already values-driven in their behaviour. Even so, most leaders experience considerable value in distilling their values and ethics. In this case, they felt that these provided them with an internal moral compass as it allowed them to confirm what was truly important to them, such as their family. They also realised the importance of aligning their values and ethics with their purpose, vision, and legacy.

> **Hannah:** *It's like something like an anchor... when you go through the process, there's [sic] a lot of things that you almost get confused about, and going back to those values, anchors you.*

Some realised that their values were not supported by their psychological states, and that they needed to ensure that these became more aligned, and others realised that their values were not reflected in their behaviour.

> **Andrea:** *In terms of looking at them, where it was important was to really say, ... "I have these values" and "Is it what I'm seeing in terms of how I'm thinking?" "Is it in conflict with how I'm thinking, and is that why I'm as frustrated in certain things as I am?" I remember "**passive**" ... So, if **challenge** is one of my values ... and yet you're passive simply because the job bores you; you're going to get frustrated. So, that whole conflict between values, behaviours, thoughts, and feelings, that was interesting.*

They realised that a golden thread needed to run through all of the afore-mentioned levels for them to feel and come across as congruent and authentic.

Level 4: **Beliefs about self and others.** In terms of the *role* of beliefs, leaders shared how the programme had assisted them in creating awareness of their limiting and empowering current beliefs about themselves and others. Leaders realise that, although it is a challenging exercise, it is very helpful to better understand their beliefs about themselves and important others, at work and in life. In this case, increased awareness of beliefs about the self allowed them to increase their belief in themselves, whilst increased awareness of beliefs about others made them realise that they had not really known important others as well as they had thought, and that they needed to make more effort in getting to know others. The programme allows leaders to adopt more empowering beliefs, and this is how Darren explained it:

> **Darren:** ... *if you don't believe in yourself, you're not happy... I found it extremely challenging, but again, it was exciting at the same time. If you don't believe in anyone else; you make them unhappy. I didn't know some of the people as well as I should've. So, it challenged me to think deeper, and maybe even to go out there and get to know them a bit more.*

The *impact* of unpacking their beliefs about self and others is that leaders realise how they treat others according to how they wish to see them, and not as others really are. This exercise helps leaders to accept others as they are, resulting in more flexibility in the leaders themselves, as Justin explained.

> **Justin:** *What I did find, was that when I looked at the beliefs that I had of others, I realised that I was treating them as I wanted to see them, not as they really were. It's certainly helped me with my family; I have better relationships, and not try and change them for who I want them to be, but rather: They are who they are; how can I work around who they are? The same at work. I've looked at the beliefs around myself and I said: "Are these real beliefs, and how do I overcome them?"*

It also helps leaders to reflect regularly on assumptions they might have been making, resulting in valuable introspection. Leaders also realised that their beliefs about others needed to change, because others were changing. Conversely, at times others also changed, due to the leaders changing their beliefs about those others. An important aspect of the value of exploring beliefs is to ask whether these beliefs are limiting or empowering the leader.

> **Darren:** *The current versus the reframed beliefs for other people, if I were to write it again right now, it would be very different from what it started at, for most people. An example is the way Liam has changed... and he's incredible as a leader. I thought, "Okay, well, maybe it's going to happen once or twice." No, it's happening continuously. It's difficult for him; I can see it, but it's happening.*

This confirms that examining and regulating our beliefs is extremely important for further growth towards our next level of our possible self.

AL Level 5: **Positive psychological states.** In terms of the *role* of positive psychological states, leaders shared how the programme had assisted them in creating awareness of their current psychological states, and whether these were helping or hindering them in achieving their leadership outcomes. Once they realised that their psychological states were hindering them, they could address this by selecting more empowering states with which to replace those. They needed to manage their states, rather than have their states manage them.

Darren: *...you know what that did for me? It made me realise that I was in a rut, and I was unhappy in many ways but just living with it, doing nothing about it.*

Justin: *Well, one of the things – and I said it before – is when I looked at those emotional states and how they were, I wasn't being proactive in how I was driving them, I was letting them drive me.*

In terms of the *impact* of positive psychological states, leaders usually experience considerable value in distilling their current and possible psychological states. In the case of Justin, previously embracing the identity of *the perfect one* caused him to experience fear of failure. He learnt to overcome it by becoming more proactive and driving results, rather than doubting himself and fearing failure. Liam found that, once he became aware of the changes he needed to make and he found the courage to *cross his Rubicon*, it was quite easy to change his psychological states. The following is how Justin and Liam explained it.

Justin: *So, if I look back at this stuff I did, so – fear of failure. How do I change it from a fear of failure? I need to become more proactive in around driving the results outcome rather than fearing the failure itself. Doubting abilities – what do I doubt and why do I doubt it? So, a lot of them I wanted to change, actually, and I wanted to become more positive and take ownership of it, instead of it taking ownership of me. And I think that was the important part.*

Liam: *Although it was painful to see some of the gaps, it was actually quite easy to change. I didn't find it very difficult. It was just like you had to flick the switch in your mind and then you go. It's not a difficult thing to – I suppose sometimes you'll fall back into it, but I think once you've crossed the Rubicon, as they say, it's easy enough to carry on with it.*

This concludes the discussion on the actual experience in the field on becoming aware of, and self-regulating the AL levels in order to develop an internal AL Compass that will take the leader to the next level of the possible AL self, which follows next.

Individual ALE Step 5 –Strengthen internal AL Compass towards next level of possible self

Programme component: Authentic Leadership Effectiveness Charter

The aforementioned underpinning work allows the leader to start creating individual puzzle pieces, without having the benefit of seeing what the final picture of the self will look like. The Authentic Leadership Effectiveness Charter (ALEC) (see Appendix 7) allows the leader to put all the puzzle pieces in place, allowing for a systemic picture of the self to emerge, which acknowledges the multiple contexts in which the leader operates. This framework, initially designed during my Masters research, and subsequently refined, is divided into output, input, and thru'put, allowing the leader to reflect on a systemic story of the self, as follows.

Output: *Leadership outcomes.* Leaders need to identify and understand what outcomes they wish to achieve and need to work towards, and the accompanying KBIs of each of these that will allow the leader to measure progress towards achieving these outcomes. In this case, this was identified in ALE step 2, and can now be used to populate the leader's outcome in their ALEC, as follows:

- *Personal – leading self.* One cannot lead others before one has mastered the ability to lead self. This requires both significant self-awareness and self-regulation, so that one's behaviour reflects one's true self, together with alignment and commitment to one's role as a leader.
- *Interpersonal – leading others.* At this point, a leader is often required to deliver through others. Over and above the content expertise, such as technical and business acumen, the leader is required to have the ability to communicate and interact with others in a way that is influential, motivating, and empowering. These 'others' include all stakeholders, which might comprise the team, peers, and, interestingly enough, also superiors.
- *Professional – leading within the organisation.* This builds further on *leading others*. At this point, the skills a leader is required to have are cognitive abilities, such as strategic expertise and being able to communicate and interact with all stakeholders, both within and outside of the organisation, in a way that is influential, motivating, and empowering.
- *Societal –* leading beyond the organisation (at home, in society, if applicable). A veritable leader is able to lead wherever and whenever required.

Input: *Meaningful drivers that underpin and inform the individual's leadership.* The leader is now able to start populating the input section of the ALEC with the themes from the life chapters, and levels from the internal AL Compass that were identified during the exercises in ALE steps 3, 4 and 5.

- *Themes from life and work history.* These are the themes that limit or empower the self, which are distilled from the *life chapters' exercise*.
- *Training and development.* These are aspects of training and development that have allowed the leaders to obtain the skills that they have in their leadership toolbox.
- *Theoretical perspectives.* These might be well-known sayings from others that stand out and inform the leader's worldview. It is important to be specific. For instance, these theories might be Mahatma Gandhi's encouragement to be the change you wish to see in the world, or Victor Frankl's thoughts that the quality of life is determined not so much by what happens to us, but rather by how we choose to respond to it.
- *Internal identity.* A two- or three-word metaphor is used to describe the internal identity that drives the leader. I have come across metaphors such as *victim, power-house,* or *alchemist.*
- *Leadership purpose.* This refers to the leader's belief about why he or she was placed on this earth, or as a leader in the organisation.

- *Leadership vision (or legacy).* What is the legacy the leader wishes to leave behind when leaving this organisation or life, which informs the vision to work towards?
- *Values and ethics.* What are the important and non-negotiable principles and guidelines that inform the leader's beliefs and behaviours?
- *Beliefs about self and others:* What are the limiting or empowering beliefs about self and others that inform the leader's behaviour?
- *Mind and emotional (psychological) states.* These are the limiting or empowering states of mind and emotions that drive the leader's thoughts, feelings, and behaviour.

Thru'put: *Leadership toolbox.* In order to achieve intended outcomes, informed by the leader's underpinnings, what is required in the leader's toolbox in terms of leadership skills/processes/models? These have to be very specific. For example, if one needs to hit a nail in the wall, one needs a hammer, and not a saw. The same applies here. This is divided as follows:

- *Personal – leading self.* What tools does the leader need to have in place, in order to achieve his or her personal leadership outcomes? Could it, for instance, be one's values or one's internal identity, or could it be the skill of setting boundaries? If so, what aspects of the leader's underpinnings helped, or could help, to develop this skill?
- *Interpersonal – leading others.* In order to deliver through others, over and above the content expertise such as technical and business acumen, what does the leader require in his or her toolbox in order to achieve his or her people leadership outcomes? Could it, for instance, be coaching communication or influencing skills? If so, what aspects of the leader's underpinnings helped to develop these skills? Could it be more empowering beliefs, or leader as coach training?
- *Professional – leading within the organisation.* Building on *leading others,* what cognitive skills does the leader require in order to achieve his or her organisational leadership outcomes? Would it be, for instance, strategic expertise, financial expertise, or the skill to negotiate with all stakeholders, both within and outside the organisation? If so, what aspects of the leader's underpinnings helped to develop these skills?
- *Societal – leading beyond the organisation, for example, at home or in society.* What additional tools might the leader require to achieve leadership outcomes in the broader context?

Once the output, input, and thru'put of the ALEC have been populated, it is important to establish how strong the golden thread is that runs between those three main elements. In other words, how well do the tools in the leader's internal toolbox (thru'put) support the achievement of intended outcomes (output), and, furthermore, how well has the leader ensured that he or she has yielded as many tools as possible from his or her underpinnings (input)? This process of checking the alignment between the elements in the output, input and thru-put sections of the ALEC allows for the development of congruency in the story that explains who the authentic leader is at any point in time. This template can become a living document that can be used continually to support the process of balanced processing that allows a leader to maintain and grow authenticity as the leader's outcomes or contexts change.

Process component: Individual Session 5

In this session, the *AL Levels* exercise is repeated in order to strengthen the internal compass towards a more powerful AL Compass for the *possible self*, this time starting at the level of internal identity, purpose, vision, and legacy. At this point, it becomes important to ensure that a golden thread runs throughout, from identity, purpose, vision/legacy, reflecting in behaviour.

The ALEC for the possible self is then created, incorporating all the AL levels for the possible self in the input section. The leader then needs to determine the strength of the golden thread between the output, input, and thru'put sections.

Self-work activities after individual session 5: Leaders are required to:

1. Complete the AL Levels exercise to create a strengthened internal AL Compass for the possible self, and ensure that there is a strong the golden thread that runs throughout all the levels;
2. Create an ALEC for the possible self, and ensure that there is a strong golden thread that runs through the output, input, and thru'put sections, which might well highlight what puzzle pieces are still missing in order to complete the picture of the authentic possible self; and
3. Engage in some reflective journaling on the session.

Actual experience: Feedback from the field

Once leaders have completed their AL Compass for their next level towards their possible self, they are ready to create a systemic view of themselves, as by now they have their outputs (outcomes and accompanying KBIs they wished to achieve) and most of their inputs (their underpinnings from their life chapters and AL Levels). Next, they need to establish what they need in their *internal toolboxes* (thru'put) to achieve their outcomes, and which of those tools they have already sourced from their input section.

In terms of the *role* of the ALEC, leaders find that this component assists them in creating systemic self-awareness, which is a requirement in the development of ALE. It helps them to strengthen the golden thread between what they want to achieve, who they are, and what tools they have in their toolbox. They often discover that, initially, there is no golden thread, as they have not been true to themselves or any vision they may have. Looking at how to strengthen that golden thread allows them to establish those aspects that they need to strengthen in order to achieve what they wish to achieve, as explained by Vanya and Andrea.

> **Vanya:** ... there wasn't that [golden thread] for me. And that's why, when we spoke about golden threads, I just couldn't find the golden thread. It was difficult for me, and I almost made it up. And now I'm starting to realise that there isn't a golden thread because I'm not being true to myself as a person that has a vision.

> **Andrea:** It was helpful in terms of that I could say what kind of things I needed to be stronger at, to achieve what I needed to do, and I think discipline was one of those.

They realise that it is hard work, and that they therefore need to want to change. It helps them to understand for the first time that they do not necessarily have the tools in their toolbox that they require in order to achieve what they wish to achieve. It allows them to determine the gaps, and what they need in place in the input section (for instance, is it more training, or improved psychological states?) to allow them to add new tools in their toolbox.

> **Darren:** ...no successful people have gotten there without hard work. First of all, you've got to make the decision you want to change. So, some people might say, "I'm happy being like this and I'm just going to carry on," and they can carry on being miserable or whatever the case may be. But, if you want to change your life and become a more effective leader and individual, it's going to take hard work. And it's going to take a bit of hurt. You've got to deal with things that you are not doing well, that you're maybe not even good at, that people don't like, that you'd have to go and change. But there's also the stuff that'll make you happy and you can celebrate that you're good at.

> **Vanya:** Initially it was very painful, and I couldn't see the picture. I really couldn't, all these things in terms of key behavioural indicators and then going to the AL levels, considering the possible self. I suppose it came through in the final ALEC framework, where we started putting tools into the whole system, and I started to realise my tools are not talking to who I want to be in the future. And my future is constantly changing in terms of my vision and purpose, but I still have the wrong tools.

In terms of the *impact of* the ALEC, leaders find it helpful as it pulls together everything they have done until now, and it provides some clarity and a sense of the way forward. Leaders can use this tool on an on-going basis, and once this framework is in place, it incorporates all prior components, like pieces of a puzzle, allowing leaders one systemic framework and picture with which to continue, as explained by Hannah and Liam.

> **Hannah:** I think, at some point, you almost get a little bit confused during the process, and how this step helps, is to bring back clarity. That then just pulls it all together, and gives you the way forward.

> **Liam:** I suppose it is still developing; it's still working. I mean it's something that we work on every day. For me, the outcome – after that exercise, the outcomes were a lot clearer, and it was a lot easier to say: "I want to do that, and this is the way I'm going to get there." So, the whole journey became clear at that point, and that is probably the one document that you must not walk away from. You've got the total package in one document. It takes you through the whole process, where you want to go and how you want to get there.

I usually do warn my leader clients that they will be somewhat confused until this point, and then, if they have worked well, the penny will drop, and all will fall into place. It is about being on that edge of chaos and discomfort that allows deep transformation to happen. This takes the leader to the final step of consolidating a systemic framework towards individual ALE.

Individual ALE Step 6 – Consolidate towards the next level of systemic ALE

Process component: Individual Session 6

This 90-minute individual session is held after the first team session. In this session, previous work is reviewed, and a first review is performed in order to determine the shifts already made towards achieving the overall leadership outcomes supported by their KBIs. The review also determines what aspects require further attention. We do this by reviewing each KBI, and by asking that if 0 is not at all achieved, and 10 is completely achieved, what they believe their scores out of 10 were at the outset of the journey, and what they might be at this point.

It is interesting to note that at no point until now have the leaders worked specifically on their leadership outcomes. Yet, so often, shifts towards those outcomes have occurred. It is also interesting to note that the leaders very seldom give themselves full marks for achieving those outcomes, as they are comfortable in the knowledge that they have gained the inner resources to continue the work that they have started.

Once we have reached this point, we have completed the creation of the foundation for the development of individual ALE. In a one-on-one ALE programme, individual leaders will continue with further individual leadership coaching sessions, while in an individual and team ALE programme, we will continue to work collectively to develop further team ALE.

Actual experience: Feedback from the field

Leaders have shared that they find these sessions valuable, even enjoyable, as these allow them the time and safe space to talk to someone and to reflect upon themselves, their work, and life; a luxury not often afforded to those in the organisational world. They realise that even when they felt challenged to go below the surface, it benefited them as it allowed them to grow.

> *Vanya: So, what went well in the individual sessions was, although it was difficult at the start, because you're actually getting information out of us and going below the surface line. It was difficult, it was confusing, but it went well, because it started to bring up stuff that I wasn't really ready to see or hear. And everything we've done throughout the process really helped me as an individual.*

During their last individual session, each leader does a midway review, comparing their shifts against their outcomes and accompanying KBIs identified in Session 2. Although they have not specifically worked towards achieving their outcomes, these are usually back-of-mind, and to their surprise and delight, they had actually shifted.

More specifically, although leaders are usually asked to give feedback on how the programme can be refined, they do generally experience the programme as well designed and appropriate, confirming that the programme itself is authentic, one of the criteria highlighted in AL theory on AL programme requirements. The processes are clear and methodical, and every process builds onto the previous one. Leaders notice their own progress every time they meet with me. They also experience the theory underpinning the programme as good, both in the individual and the team sessions. Although the workload is considerable, they realise that it helps them to process their thoughts, and to do the introspection required to develop more self-awareness and commitment to their internal AL Compasses and development towards increased leadership authenticity.

> **Gugu:** *So, the prep-work leading up to the sessions helped, because you got into the space of thinking about the things you need to think about related to the programme.*

> **Liam:** *I really think the process is well designed; the process was very clear, methodical, one built on the other one, and we progressed every time we met. I think the programme worked out very well.*

It is always surprising how quickly the time is used up in these sessions. Although leaders often mention that they would have liked more time for each session, they realise that time is a precious commodity, and that sufficient time is allocated. They do not feel rushed during the individual sessions, and, at the same time, they do not feel at any stage as if they are wasting time.

> **Peter:** *There was actually a good amount of time allocated. Time was always, as we said, a precious commodity, and we actually gave the time for it, and we needed that time. In fact, you normally came out of there thinking, I wish I'd had a bit more time. So that was good. And it's [programme venue] just quiet and out of the way and a different environment.*

I have learnt that the travelling to and from their place of work to my coaching office often allows my leaders to transition from *work* to *reflective mode*, and helps them to get the most out of their programme. It is therefore preferable to have these sessions away from their place of work.

The aforementioned steps are required in individual ALD, in order to learn from the past, so that the current self can be understood. Once that self-awareness has been gained, leaders can explore what further is required to move to the next level of the possible self, and apply self-regulation to achieve that. Crossing that Rubicon to a higher level requires intent, commitment, and moral courage, and often leaders experience that once they have crossed, there is no turning back. This encourages them to sustain growth towards that higher level of the possible self.

DEVELOPMENT OF TEAM ALE – PROCESS MODEL AND PROGRAMME COMPONENTS

The team sessions allow for the collective development of interpersonal and organisational leadership. The first of the three sessions is usually scheduled to take place towards the end of the individual sessions, before the sixth and final individual session. The rationale for this is that, by this time, each leader should be well on their way towards developing individual ALE. Any fear and trepidation in anticipation of such a team session, combined with inappropriate invulnerability, which often accompanies any team with challenging team dynamics, will by this time have been replaced with cautious optimism, and appropriate vulnerability. The following diagram highlights the structure of the team ALE programme, comprising three team sessions.

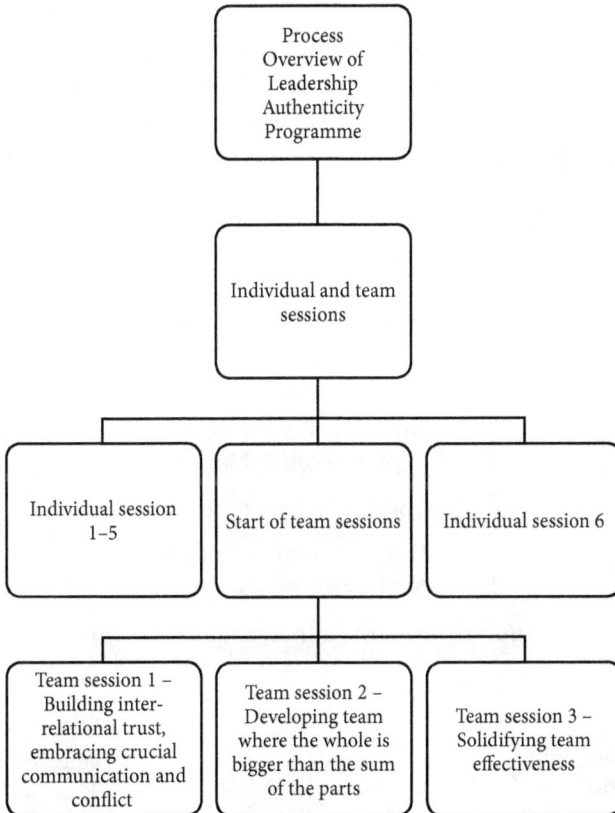

Figure 16: Process overview of the Team ALE programme

Each of the three two-day team sessions is usually scheduled a month apart, with self-work activities between each session. As reflected in figure 16, in the first team session, the leadership team members start the process of building a foundation of inter-relational trust, and are introduced to leader as coach skills (Team ALE step 1), which they practise and use throughout the programme. They are gradually introduced to the five levels of team ALE throughout the team sessions (Team ALE step 2), and, by the third team session, they normally have an Authentic Leadership Effectiveness Charter (team ALEC) in place (Team ALE step 3).

Following is a detailed discussion of each step in the team ALE programme. Within each step, I discuss both the programme and process components employed, followed by actual experience, and feedback from the field.

Team ALE Step 1 – Building a foundation of trust

Programme Component: Five levels team ALE

Whilst the value of individual ALE is unquestionable, it needs to translate into team ALE in order to yield the ultimate positive impact for any organisation. A lack of inter-relational trust is often the cause of team ineffectiveness (see Figure 5), and effective AL at the helm goes a long way to help a team to become authentically effective. Figure 17 reminds us of the link between the development of individual AL, allowing for perceived AL and interpersonal relationships of trust to develop, which in turn forms the foundation of team ALE.

Figure 17. Link between AL and team effectiveness

The five building blocks of team ALE that underpin this programme start with solidifying inter-relational trust, upon which the effectiveness of the team relies. The importance of trust and its link with AL and team effectiveness has already been explored in the review on the impact of leadership authenticity, and I believe that interpersonal trust always needs to be preceded by intrapersonal trust. By this what is meant is that it is very difficult to trust others until one can trust oneself. Once trust in self is in place, it allows for strength-based vulnerability and relational transparency, which can lead to the development and increase of interpersonal trust. Such trust allows for healthy conflict, increased commitment, self- and peer-to-peer accountability, and an increased focus on results. This theory is deployed as follows in the development of team ALE.

Team ALE Level 1: **Interpersonal/inter-relational trust.** One of my leaders, who previously never trusted anyone, shared an epiphany during her journey of developing leadership authenticity, that it was impossible for her to trust unknown entities, and prior to the development of her leadership authenticity, the biggest unknown entity had been her own *self*. As a result, she was never able to trust her own instincts about anything or anyone else. It was only once she got to understand herself at all her AL Levels that she could start trusting her own inner voice and, in doing so, start developing inter-relational trust with others.

This vignette confirms the notion that inter-relational trust needs to begin with trusting the self, which can only start once a leader has developed both awareness and regulation of the self. Whilst learning to trust the self begins with the development of self-leadership, it needs to translate into inter-relational trust within the team. At this point in the programme, it is important that each member of the team allows vulnerability and a willingness to share with others the themes from their life histories that have shaped who they currently are (current self) and who they wish to become (possible self). Furthermore, it becomes important to have the skill of interacting with others in a way that builds rather than breaks relationships and inter-relational trust, which illustrates the rationale for developing coaching skills for the leader as coach.

Team ALE Level 2: **Healthy conflict.** Once inter-relational trust is being developed amongst team members, and team members know what they need to achieve collectively as a team, it becomes possible to be appropriately vulnerable and willing to engage in passionate dialogue and positive conflict around issues and decisions that are key to the team and organisation's success. Not everyone is equally comfortable in dealing with conflict, and this discomfort is highlighted and dealt with in the development of self-leadership in the individual coaching sessions. Several filters, reviewed in the profiling feedback in individual session 1, can shed more light on how comfortable an individual is in dealing with conflict. Consider, for instance, the reaction filter of *consensus versus polar*. An individual who scores high on *consensus* usually prefers agreement, which is good for communication, teams, and relationship-building, but in the case of healthy conflict, it is better to have flexibility towards *polar*, where we can play the role of devil's advocate, and comfortably deal with confrontation when necessary.

Other thinking/behavioural filters that may affect an individual's response when dealing with conflict are *referencing* (internal versus external), *motive* (influence, affiliation, or achievement), and *perspective* (own, partner, or observer). It is important for the team to understand each member's profile in terms of these thinking- and behaviour filters, so that everyone can adjust to one another, and strengthen the inter-relational rapport that would allow healthy conflict to occur.

Team ALE Level 3: **Commitment to team outcomes.** Lencioni pointed out that achieving collective commitment towards the achievement of agreed outcomes requires two components: buy-in and clarity, even when there is no consensus yet on how best to achieve these outcomes. Commitment requires that team members know that their ideas have been heard and considered with open minds. Furthermore, it is about extracting every possible idea, opinion, and perspective from the team, considering each of these, and then having the courage and wisdom to make a commitment to adopting the best of these in order to achieve the outcomes.

For the sake of clarity, once this has been achieved, the decisions need to be summarised, and communicated to the rest of the staff, preferably in an interactive forum. This gives employees a chance to ask questions, and seek further clarification. Finally, it is important to remind the team that, beyond the behavioural commitment, there needs to be commitment to principles, such as purpose, values, mission, strategy, and outcomes. With the positive influence of an authentic leader at the helm, each member then needs to take collective ownership of these commitments.

Team ALE Level 4: **Accountability.** Regarding teamwork, Lencioni defined accountability in teams as "the willingness of the team members to remind one another when they are not living up to the performance standards of the group"[99]. Rather than teamwork requiring the participation of the team leader at all times, firstly self-accountability and thereafter direct peer-to-peer accountability is required. Self- and peer-to-peer accountability should become part of the team's culture, and it is important that this behaviour is modelled by the leader. I have found that it becomes easier for peers to hold one another accountable when they know that, if they do not, the leader will. However, it is far easier to hold people accountable for their results rather than their behaviours, but behaviour usually precedes results. Therefore, the secret is to hold self and peers accountable for behaviours, in this case insufficient performance towards achieving the results the team have committed to achieve, so that behaviours can be modified and become more effective.

This means that leaders need to overcome the hesitance to give critical feedback to one another, and this is where the art of giving and receiving feedback in the form of a coaching conversation becomes important. It is imperative to master the skills of giving and receiving constructive feedback; by holding back, team members are hurting not only the team, but also their peers.

Team ALE Level 5: **Focus on results.** Once the building of the foundation of inter-relational trust is in place, it is important to ensure that everyone agrees and commits to the collective outcomes the team needs to achieve. A team ALE charter and a Balanced Scorecard can assist towards monitoring the behavioural indicators of success that need to be in place towards the successful achievements of those outcomes. Authentic leaders are often willing to be the first mover, whether it is to embrace strength-based vulnerability and relational transparency that allows for further development, or to commit to an action towards achieving team outcomes.

Programme component: Leader as coach skills

I usually introduce this component into the programme during ALE team session 1 when leaders need to develop empowering interaction skills. There is a business case for creating a coaching culture in organisations that comprises external professional coaches, internal coaches, and also leaders as coaches. This is because coaches encourage those that they coach to think for themselves and to develop an awareness of conscious and unconscious behaviours which may impact on performance in the workplace. I often introduce coaching skills to my leader clients, as these can be extremely valuable when there is, for instance, a requirement for the following:

1. Crucial conversations – difficult conversations with important others regarding behaviours and outcomes, within and outside the workplace;
2. Giving and receiving feedback – especially during performance review conversations, especially the more difficult ones; and
3. Developing people through tasks – giving them a challenging task, and then, at the outset, coaching them through it, so that both leader and direct report feel comfortable that the requirements of the task, from beginning to end, have been considered and understood.

The third point is especially important. I find that leaders are often good at tasking their team members, but come the delivery deadline they are disappointed when either the tasks have not been completed, or else have not been completed to the standard required by the leader. The leader might then suspend delegation and rather do the work themselves, or else start micromanaging those who have been tasked. In both instances, rather than empowering those who report to them, they themselves are working below their level of work. This is when I introduce Gillian Stamp's[100] concept of the *Tripod of Work*. Gillian Stamp, a long-time researcher who co-authored several papers with Dr Elliott Jaques, including key work on Stratified Systems Theory, developed some models that bring humanism to levels of work. One of these is the *Tripod of Work*, which identifies tensions that most managers feel when managing, as follows:

- **Tasking** – We have to get things done and so require *tasking* our subordinates.
- **Trusting** – Yet subordinates need to feel that they have freedom to do their jobs which requires *trusting*. However, bearing in mind *earned trust*, it is important for the leader to "trust but verify".
- **Tending** – People need *tending* to ensure that they are on the right path, getting the right growth opportunities, feeling connected. As we do this we provide review of their abilities to complete their tasks, including any issues and roadblocks that arise. These are the conversations that benefit from a coaching underpinning.

I often tell my clients that *tending* by a leader could be somewhat likened to a gardener tending a garden. Rather than planting a seed, then tasking it to grow and trusting that in a month's time it will be a fully-grown shrub, a gardener understands that first he/she needs to fertilise the soil, then plant the seed, and finally remember to water it on a regular basis. Only then is trust earned.

In the same vein, operational excellence occurs when all three of these aspects are optimally balanced by engaging in coaching conversations. However, not all coaching conversations need to be done in a formal setting. One can even have an informal exchange in passing. For instance, employees might ask the leader, regarded by them as the expert, what his or her thoughts might be on a matter. At such a time the leader, by remembering to stay out of *expert mode* for as long as possible, can ask them what *their* thoughts are, and continue to ask them further questions to stimulate thought. In order to be effective as leader as coach, I introduce leaders to concepts such as coaching states of mind, coaching skills, and a structure for a typical coaching conversation.

Important considerations for the leader or leader as coach

I outline Ting's[101] six coaching principles, supplemented by my reflections, which apply to external coaches, and can apply to the leader as coach as well.

1. *Principle 1: Create a safe and challenging environment.* It is the leader as coach's responsibility to create a safe environment in which the coachee, meaning the person being coached, can take risks and learn. This means that the leader needs to be able to both challenge and support the coachee in order for the coachee to achieve the coaching outcomes.
2. *Principle 2: Work with the coachee's agenda.* Although this is strictly speaking not always the case for a leader as coach, the learning experience needs to belong to the coachee being coached.
3. *Principle 3: Facilitate and collaborate.* Although this can be a challenge, the leader as coach needs to play a facilitative and collaborative role rather than the role of the expert who makes recommendations and gives answers. The leader should focus on the coachee's needs, and avoid personal reactions.

4. *Principle 4: Advocate self-awareness.* Often, in organisations, we witness value statements in writing, but not in behaviour. However, every behaviour and attitude is linked to values and beliefs, and it is important that our behaviours reflect the values we wish to embrace as this makes us congruent. One of the most powerful outcomes of coaching, therefore, is increased self-awareness as it is only then that the coachee can start experimenting with chosen actions in order to achieve desired outcomes.

5. *Principle 5: Promote sustainable learning from experience.* Most individuals have the capacity to learn, grow, and change, once they encounter the right set of experiences and are ready to learn. Allowing opportunities to reflect on those experiences is a powerful method of identifying personal strengths and development needs as well as opportunities and obstacles.

6. *Principle 6: Model what you coach.* The leader needs to exhibit those leadership- and emotional competencies, such as self-awareness, self-management, social awareness, and social skills, which the coachee needs to develop.

Coaching states of mind

In my ALE practitioner experience, in order to be effective as a coach, the following states of mind facilitate more empowering coaching conversations:

- A *know-nothing* state. This entails stepping out of expert mode and suspending all assumptions about another or a situation, also called *bracketing*, combined with
- A *sense of authentic curiosity*. This is a desire to really understand what the other person is saying. Rather than being inquisitive, it is about being deeply interested in what the other person believes, and how he/she has come to believe this. Empowering and exploratory questions from a leader not only help the leader to understand the coachee better, but more importantly, they allow the coachee to develop a deeper understanding of self.

Coaching skills for the leader as coach

The most important skills required in order to facilitate a powerful coaching conversation are listening, supporting, questioning, and feedback. These are described below.

- **Listening so that the other feels heard**: Discerning listening is not simply about being quiet and attentive to what others are saying, it is about continually developing an awareness of our own listening. Our listening is a powerful and ever-present part of our daily lives, and we often do not listen to everything others say. We often are biased and prejudiced in our listening. We listen from a particular mind-set (including emotions and body posture), paying attention to what best suits our needs, interests, and concerns at the moment. We then make our own sense of what others are saying and, much of the time, this is not correct. We listen, and then we generate our own meaning about what others said. Covey, in his book *The Seven Habits of Highly Effective People* stated under the fifth habit, "Seek first to understand, then to be understood"[102]. We typically seek first to be understood. We listen with the intent to reply. We filter everything through our own paradigms, reading our autobiography into other people's lives. Instead discerning listening enables the other to *feel heard*, and so facilitates discovery.

- *Support: How do we support one another?*: What are the sensory-specific aspects that convey support? Support involves empathy, and we empathise by acknowledging emotions, such as "that must feel X" (some feeling words). Support is holding the other's outcomes and agenda throughout the conversation, being able to hold the other's outcomes as the frame and purpose of the coaching conversation. Support in coaching is about creating a safe and supportive space, a place where transformation can occur, and where the other can access the courage to speak his or her truths.

- *Questioning to elicit creative thinking in others*: Quality questioning is about the ability to ask powerful questions that get to the heart of things, that open up new possibilities, open doors into their worldview, influence the direction of thinking in a profound way, and that focus on being solution-oriented. This refers to non-judgmental exploration that explores, asks, and responds without judgment. Powerful questioning uses open-ended questions, and relentlessly explores meaning, possibilities, and solutions in the coachee's worldview. Precision questioning involves using intensely focused questions that make explicit another's inner world.

- *The art of giving and receiving feedback*: To give feedback is not to give a judgment or opinion about another, but to accurately mirror, using as precise sensory-based language as possible, what we saw, heard, and felt from the other. Sensory-based feedback needs to be tentative and invite the other to offer an even fuller expression. Using our mirror, we feed back what we experienced, pointing to the specific behavioural evidence that triggered that impression. Given in a non-judgmental way, it offers a corrective reflection. Summarising is one way to give feedback, and to get to the point succinctly. When we receive feedback, we do so best when we listen to it carefully, acknowledge what it means to the speaker, seek sensory-based referents, explore it fully to understand it, and then use the parts of it that seem useful for refining our skills and presentation of self. By embracing the process of receiving feedback, we welcome the evaluation, so that we can monitor and manage our self, which is an expression of emotional intelligence (EQ).

Structure of a leader coaching conversation

In order to help my leaders, I usually introduce a structure for a coaching conversation that is underpinned by the coaching steps outlined in the GROW (goals, reality, options, way forward) coaching model, as outlined by Clutterbuck and Megginson[103], merged with the Axes of Change coaching model[104]. The resulting coaching model that can easily be followed by any leader as coach is as follows.

1. *Phase 1: Identify the need for the conversation.* Give concrete/sensory-based, specific feedback to demonstrate the need for a conversation. The need for coaching may arise for various reasons. Usually, the coachee would need to be coached, as there is evidence flowing from the concrete experience of the coachee that a current situation needs to change.

2. *Phase 2: Determine outcomes for the conversation and identify the accompanying KBIs –* concrete examples that will illustrate outcomes. The coach and coachee should attempt to establish behavioural evidence, or KBIs, that will indicate successful achievement of coaching outcomes (what the coachee or others will hear, see, or feel that will indicate successful outcomes). Stated positively this has the ability to create a collaborative, solution-focused dynamic to the conversation.

3. *Phase 3: Explore current reality, and uncover real issues.* Once the outcome has been identified, it is important to uncover what the coachee is currently experiencing, believing, thinking, and feeling about the current situation. Understanding the reality of the issues presented is essential, so that any resultant planned action may be well founded. Although it is tempting to move straight to the solution phase in any conversation, often, the bulk of time in coaching time should be spent on this phase. The use of open-ended and insightful questions is the primary tool that enables the coachees' current reality to be understood. In the majority of cases, the options for finding a solution become clearer as a direct consequence of having invested in this phase.

4. *Phase 4: Increase the motivation for change,* When others are unwilling to change, it helps to ask about the consequences (and further consequences of those consequences) should they not achieve their outcome, followed by questions about opportunities that will open up (and as a result present further opportunities) once they achieve the outcome. A coachee usually does not commit to change unless there is a sufficient level of motivation to change.

Now start moving towards solutions/outcomes:

5. *Phase 5: Facilitate exploration of all possible options, and select preferred solution.* Explore possibilities, strategies, ideas, bearing in mind that the first idea is not always the best. Once the coachee has described his or her reality in rich detail, the coach's role is to help the coachee generate some options with which to move forward. Here the leader coach needs to be reminded of the inherent capability of coachees to see their way through issues, problems, and development needs. In the majority of cases, it is not necessary for the leader to intrude into a natural process of self-discovery.

6. *Phase 6: Planning and actualising. Actualise and identify a plan of action.* The coaching session now arrives at the action phase, and if the leader coach was rigorous with the previous stages, appropriate actions may have become obvious. The coachee is now ready to drill down to his or her final action plan, and this is the one time where a challenging approach can be supportive. Select the best way forward, and check the first step, then all steps, followed by deadline dates and researches required. What contingency plans

need to be in place should plans get derailed? Using a variety of closed (yes/no) questions can ensure that a coachee has fully checked his or her position, which will increase commitment, and ensure that a coachee feels accountable for any outcome.

7. *Phase 7: Check coaching goals achieved, and provide support.* Arrange a follow-up conversation, if necessary. In this final phase, the leader coach plays the role of providing reinforcements or rewards for the actions that are going well, through supporting, celebrating, nurturing, validating, and cheerleading. This reinforcing can occur through the coachee's own acknowledgments, or through the systems, such as accountability structures or the community.

Coaching is an iterative process. Coaching is completed when the coachee has integrated the new behaviour so well that it has become part of his or her way of being in the world. Although this process might seem time-consuming, what can be more so than when others do not take ownership of self-development and improved work performance? This process is an effective way for leaders to motivate and empower others.

Leader as coach in team meetings

More recently, I have learnt that this coaching process can also be used in team meetings in order to ignite collective minds and create a thinking team, and when combined with some of Nancy Kline's suggestions for creating a *thinking environment*, it increases team effectiveness. She explains, "Giving everyone a turn increased the intelligence of the group. Knowing they won't be interrupted frees people to think faster and say less"[105]. Meetings form the heartbeat of organisations. However, too many leaders spend all day in meetings, and considering the quality of those meetings, one can't help wondering whether they don't feel bored throughout and brain-dead when they leave those meetings at the end of the day. Kline offers the following guidelines that, aligned with coaching principles, are important for effective group work in that it allows everyone to contribute and receive value from the group in a non-threatening and relaxed way:

1. **Confidentiality:** Whatever is said in this session remains with us and in this session.
2. **Attention:** Listen with respect and curiosity. Listening of this calibre ignites the human mind. The quality of your attention determines the quality of other people's thinking.
3. **Incisive questions:** Remove assumptions that limit ideas, freeing the mind to think afresh.
4. **Equality:** Treat each other's ideas and questions as valuable, giving equal turns and attention.
5. **Keep agreements and boundaries.** Knowing you will have your turn improves the quality of your listening.
6. **Appreciation:** Practise a five-to-one ratio of appreciation to criticism in order to help people to think for themselves. Change takes place best in a large context of genuine praise.

7.   **Ease:** Offer freedom from rush or urgency. Ease creates. Urgency destroys.

It is important for the leader to give everyone a turn to speak without being interrupted, and to follow the guidelines learnt in one-on-one coaching conversations. At times, the team can be divided into thinking partnerships, especially when the team as a collective becomes stuck. It is important to allow team members to share their truths and information, and to allow members to express their feelings. This is what is required to build a foundation of trust in a team.

Process component: Team Session 1

During this two-day session, the focus is on 1) building inter-relational trust, 2) introducing coaching conversations, and 3) embracing conflict. This session builds further on individual work that was done on *life stories*, as leaders share their most empowering and limiting themes and stories with one another on the programme. Whenever conversations of this nature are conducted, I usually get the leaders into a circle around a '*potjie*' (a special SA three-legged cast iron cooking pot used to cook on a fireplace) that represents the container of their collective thoughts. I then offer them a talking stick, which is not unlike an Indian prayer stick. The idea is that the only one allowed to speak and to share is the one holding the talking stick, whilst others are encouraged to listen with the intent of getting a better appreciation of the one who is speaking. Once the speaker has finished sharing, the talking stick is passed onto the next participant. This helps leaders to appreciate one another at a human level, and it often creates the breakthrough required to start developing a foundation of inter-relational trust.

This is followed by the introduction of a coaching style of conversation, and leaders start practising these skills in their interactions with one another by using, for instance, listening and questioning skills to better understand the thinking and behavioural filters that limit or empower others, and in so doing, learn to engage in, and embrace healthy conflict. Between team sessions 1 and 2, individuals are encouraged to do some final individual work, together with some teamwork.

Self-work activities after team session 1: Leaders are required to:

1.   Review and update AL Levels in the individual internal AL Compass for the possible self;
2.   Review and update individual ALEC for the individual possible self;
3.   Coach at least one peer or direct report per week;
4.   Receive peer-coaching at least once every second week;
5.   Use a coaching style when running meetings; and
6.   Continue with reflective journaling as a self-coaching tool.

Actual experience: Feedback from the field

The team ALE levels programme component is usually introduced in session 1, and used to develop team ALE over three team sessions, starting with the foundational aspect, inter-relational trust. Ideally, by now the leaders have engaged in their individual authentic self-leadership exercises and, through continual introspection have increased their awareness of their internal AL Compasses. They have also committed to developing and refining those towards the next level of their possible self, and are reflecting that in their behaviour. As a result, their trust in self should have improved and by the end of Individual Session 5, they are ready to engage in their first interpersonal team session, where the intrapersonal trust can be extended to interpersonal trust.

In terms of the team ALE levels, two additional aspects are discussed, those being 'initial versus current' team reality. An interesting finding is that the development of the five levels of team effectiveness is not a linear process. It is an iterative process, as inter-relational trust needs to be in place for healthy disagreements and crucial conversations to take place, and as those take place, it allows for a further increase in inter-relational trust. The following illustrates feedback from the field on the development of each of the ALE levels leading to team effectiveness, starting with inter-relational trust, the foundation required for team effectiveness.

Team ALE Level 1: **Inter-relational trust within the team.** During my doctoral study on evaluating this individual and team AL programme, programme participants had to score simultaneously themselves as being trustworthy, and the level of inter-relational trust that existed in their team. Interestingly, leaders scored their own trustworthiness higher than they scored the inter-relational trust within the team. Of special interest were the scores of Gugu, who initially scored herself quite highly, and although this improved, indicated that she initially did not trust her peers. Most leaders indicated that inter-relational trust within the team had grown, with the highest shifts indicated by three leaders who also indicated big shifts in their own trustworthiness. This shows that there might be a link between developing trust in self and interpersonal trust, where interpersonal trust might well be the lagging factor that requires trust in self to be in place first.

Leaders have shared with me that often the desire to engage in a programme such as this one is due to a lack of trust within the team. They have found that participating in an ALE programme builds trust. When there is a lack of trust, they tend to focus on what is wrong outside of the team rather than what is wrong in the team itself. Justin explained it as follows.

> **Justin:** *So, what happened before is that, when there's no trust, you tend to focus on everybody outside of your team, instead of within your team, and it doesn't focus you on what you need to do.*

During their participation in the programme leaders usually realise the importance of trusting one another. They realise that there needs to be better teamwork, and that they need to trust one another that commitments will be kept so that each one can focus on their own contributions towards the deliverables.

> *Justin: Trust is quite important. If you're going to work together, you've got to trust one another. The importance of teamwork is that the team has got to work together as a whole. You've got to trust that your teammate is going do his side of the work and commit to what he's going to do. Once you have that trust, then you can focus on what you need to focus on to drive the team forward.*

Also of interest is the fact that sometimes one has to put the cart before the horse and create *conditional trust* in order to create the space for others to deliver. Real trust can follow once there is a successful delivery of goals. Psychological state management is important at this point as team members need to allow themselves to be open and honest with one another, despite the fear and anxiety that initially exists, and this requires courage. Managing these psychological states allows the team to build the inter-relational trust required to engage in healthy conflict.

> *Liam: ...I was quite amazed around how honest and open people were at that point in time, despite the fear and the anxiety of where we are and what this team is going to do. I mean, it was critical for us to be able to get the effectiveness of the team right. That was a fundamental part of any team environment. ...healthy conflict is always good, but you've got to have a little bit of courage, you've got to have the trust to be able to do that. ...There was a lot of conflict in the team. We built trust and therefore, putting it in as part of the programme was great.*

The trust-building process is aided by the exercises in *storytelling*, as it is described by participants. These are vulnerability-based trust-building exercises that are introduced at the start of Team Session 1, a session that team members can sometimes be extremely nervous of due to the lack of trust in the team. These exercises encourage strength-based vulnerability and more openness in revealing self-referential information with one another, further allowing team members to bond with one another. This is an important requirement when developing team effectiveness.

Leadership coaching skills are usually transferred to the leaders in the first team session. In terms of the *role* of this component, it allows a coaching style to underpin empowering communication, especially helpful when conducting challenging crucial conversations. Leaders do not find it easy to stay in this mode, as they are accustomed to *telling*. Now they have to learn to listen, be curious, and ask meaningful questions.

> *Vanya: It is actually difficult to be in that mode, because you've got to learn the skill. It's not something that comes naturally. What comes naturally is you're going to tell people what can be done and what can't be done.*

Team ALE Level 2: Healthy conflict within the team. Oftentimes, conflict is avoided because it is uncomfortable, and the outcome is usually negative. Alternatively, leaders do experience conflict, though it is unhealthy conflict. It can be described as *immature conflict*. Leaders have indicated to me that before they participated in the programme there had been very little healthy conflict within the team, explained as follows by Justin and Nikhil.

> **Justin:** *So, conflict was something that we avoided, because it was uncomfortable and there wasn't an outcome and it was more negative.*

> **Nikhil:** *Aah. Yes. If I can put it lightly, it's immature conflict.*

Leaders have shared that during the programme they realised that conflict did not have to equate to arguments; rather, if used appropriately, it could become a collaborative, solution-focused discussion. Whilst there could still be disagreement regarding the way forward, it did not need to be destructive. Team members now became much more willing to engage in conflict. Because of the trust being built, team members could now start to become more deliberate about focusing their crucial conversations on business issues. Andrea understood it as follows.

> **Andrea:** *Because we've … in a sense, centred the trust side, and we've made conflict one of our values or behaviours we want to see, it's become a lot more deliberate around that we need to do this in order to continue and move forward. So, in terms of conflict specifically, the trust has helped us do that. It's about the business issues. And also because you have the trust and conflict at a higher level, you can almost have those conversations, whereas before you couldn't; it was very personal attacks in a sense, where now it's more objective.*

This focus was strengthened by the additional tools of coaching- and feedback skills passed on to them during the team sessions. Although, on an individual level, the extent of shifts in inter-relational trust and healthy conflict differed, there was a correlation between the average team improvement in inter-relational trust and healthy conflict in the team.

In terms of *impact*, most leaders experience considerable value in engaging in a coaching style of communication. When dealing with difficult situations, it allows them to communicate in a structured manner that does good rather than harm. Rather than telling others how something should be done, coaching others encourages them to find solutions for themselves.

> **Liam:** *It's been very helpful in terms of me dealing with difficult situations, it just gave me the tools to tackle these difficult things in a structured manner, in a manner that can do good rather than harm.*

> **Andrea:** *The coaching is useful, especially if you see the change in how you coaching someone else can allow them to think of solutions for themselves. I think that was particularly useful in terms of seeing someone being completely stuck, to seeing like little gems coming out such as, "I could do that!", rather than telling someone something: "This is how you should do it."*

Many years ago, I was involved in an organisation that had a values-driven leadership model, which stipulated which values needed to be avoided, and which values they needed to focus on instead. One example was that they needed to move from being *task-focused* to *task and people-focused*. The leaders in my group were uncomfortable with this preferred behavioural value, as they felt that this still implied a sugar-coated focus on tasks. When I asked them what value they would prefer in its place, they responded, "To grow people through tasks". This created a win-win situation, as people came first, but if managed correctly, would not compromise the completion of tasks. When I asked them how they envisaged doing that, they suggested that once they had tasked their team members with challenging tasks to help them learn and grow, they would use a coaching approach, such as I have outlined, to future-pace them through those tasks. Following the Tripod of Work approach, this allowed both the leader and the team member, at the outset of embarking on a challenging task, to feel comfortable with what needed to be done. Therefore, the *tasking* is about the "what" that needs to be achieved and the *tending* is about "how" this can be achieved, which allows the element of *inter-relational trust* to be earned between the leader and the team member. Earning trust is as much the responsibility of the leader as the team member.

Team ALE Step 2 – Further alignment of the five levels of team ALE

Process component: Team Session 2

Whereas the individual sessions are aimed at individuals enhancing their intrapersonal leadership, i.e. the leadership of self, Team Session 1 builds on this by further enhancing interpersonal leadership skills, allowing leaders to strengthen their relationships with their peers. The two-day team session 2 moves the team towards enhancing their professional leadership by leading the team members towards a whole that was bigger than the sum of its parts. This team coaching session builds on Team Session 1, and continuing with the team ALE levels programme component, also allows for further strengthening of inter-relational trust, embracing healthy conflict, commitment to action, and individual and mutual accountability.

More specifically, this session reviews progress on the outcomes of Session 1, and builds further on individual work done on *life stories* and the limiting and empowering themes that were distilled from these, using a coaching style of conversation to distil a collective outcome and worldview to guide the team to work as one. During this session, the team starts to explore individually and collectively what they would deem important in a team ALEC, which they then need to reflect upon further, so that their team ALEC can be completed in their following team session.

> **Self-work activities after team session 2:** Leaders are required to:
>
> 1. Consider and strengthen the five team ALE elements of trust, healthy disagreements, commitment, and self- and peer accountability in the team;
> 2. Reflect upon the beliefs and behaviours linked to the five team ALE elements, so that their team ALEC can be completed during their following team session.

Actual experience: Feedback from the field

The leaders realised that, initially, they had been in denial about the health of the team. They were not honest with one another as they were not communicating, which resulted in strained team dynamics. Even though not everyone had shifted equally within the team and there was still work to be done, the team had come a long way in terms of becoming more effective as a team, and each member had a better understanding of the role that they needed to play within the team.

Of particular importance was improved individual psychological state management of individual team members. One of the states required to increase the level of effectiveness in the team was moral courage, an important AL quality. They engaged more in crucial conversations with one another, which included giving and receiving feedback, in terms of what each could do better. In particular, they had the following to say about the improvement of commitment and accountability in the team, concluding with an increased focus on the results that needed to be achieved.

Team ALE Level 3: **Commitment within the team.** Leaders shared with me that initially they experienced a lack of commitment within the team. They found that team members drove their own agendas, so no one was prepared to commit to what the team collectively required. The desire for everyone to talk the same language, drive the same things, and commit to the same outputs was often lacking.

> **Nikhil:** *...but nothing there as a collective to say: The brewery is battling here, let's all of us get involved in this thing, let's make a real positive change, and all of us must be talking the same language, driving the same things, and be committed to the same sort of outputs. That was lacking.*

During the programme, the whole process that leads up to building a collective team ALEC helps to develop commitment within the team. Leaders commit to the team ALE stipulations in their charter, to be finalised in Session 3, and they are prepared to hold one another accountable for it. That is what made the commitment real. It focuses team members, and together with a different and more empowering leadership style from the team leader, allows the team to develop further inter-relational trust and transparency.

> *Gugu: ...the whole process of preparing for for a charter, putting a charter together, writing stuff down you're going to do, I think that helped with commitment. People have said, "I'm going to do it," and now there's something to hold them accountable to doing it. Here's the document, you read it, you made notes on it, it's real. It makes commitment real.*

> *Vanya: The commitment came with us being more focused, and I think it really came from Liam rethinking his approach to the team in terms of what he wants out of us, and how he wants us to work as a team, rather than each of us drive our own KPIs. So, I think the commitment is there now, with a different type of leadership style. And ... having inter-relational trust has improved; however, it can improve some more to get more commitment and delivery.*

This led to increased clarity about their vision, and it improved team commitment towards achieving the team outcomes.

***Team ALE Level 4*: Accountability within the team.** Leaders often experience a lack of self- and peer-to-peer accountability within the team. They experience a false sense of security about the effectiveness of the team as they are not always honest with one another, and they do not communicate sufficiently with one another. Team members do not hold themselves accountable either; instead, often the leader has to hold everyone accountable for their behaviours and for achieving their outcomes. It is not surprising that the leader might then become more autocratic.

> *Darren: We had a false sense of security in some ways, I think. We were not being honest with each other, we were not communicating properly with each other, no one was taking accountability – or no, some people were taking accountability.*

Leaders have found that during the programme the average level of self- and peer-to-peer accountability improves, but sometimes not as much as the average levels of healthy conflict or commitment. At times, this is because the leader needs to learn to step back and allow team members to engage in lateral leadership. This means that they are now starting to hold one another accountable, without having to go through the leader.

> *Peter: Again, I've got to give Liam credit for this. With him stepping back to an extent there's been less fear, so people are now, instead of just covering their own stuff, – it's a much more open debate, and people feel much more okay with saying to someone: "But, hang on, you said this," and whatever. Liam was the prime mover in this change.*

However, whilst lateral peer-to-peer challenging and leadership is being developed within the team, there might still be a concern that team members are getting away with too much, and that reins might need to be pulled in somewhat, which Liam was trying to avoid. He felt that one of the main culprits was Nikhil, who simply ignored requirements that he personally did not deem important, just like he did whilst participating in the AL programme.

Liam: There's [sic] more people doing their lateral challenging and lateral leadership. We still allow as a team people to get away with a lack of accountability at the moment. I'm worried that if I let it go, at some stage, I'm going to have to pull in the reins, and then people are going to tell me that I'm going back to my old ways. I've asked guys to do stuff for me, ...The normal culprits are there. Nikhil, he just ignores. It's a bit like he dealt with your AL programme requirements as well.

This illustrates that patterns that manifest whilst participating in the programme can reflect real-life patterns, and it is then possible to explore this further with programme participants.

Team ALE Level 5: **Focus on results.** Contrary to what we might wish to see, experience in the field has shown that the team focus on achieving results takes the longest to improve, which could be due to it being a lagging factor. It is therefore important that the prior team ALE levels have been achieved in order to allow for an increase in a focus on achieving results.

Justin: I think, in the past, we were focusing on everything but the results. The results aren't as high yet, because, as I said before, it's a lagging indicator. But I think the drive, the accountability, the commitment.... I think we're already seeing good results.

Leaders have shared that they experienced an increased focus on results, but warned that yet more work needed to be done on increasing the level of commitment and accountability within the team. The team members need to continue their focus on achieving the results, not only in terms of *what* they needed to achieve, but also in terms of *how* they would achieve it, as that ultimately was what would pull the team together. In the case of the team under discussion, previously they tended to focus on too many smaller result areas, and during their participation in the programme, they selected five focus areas, which proved very useful.

Liam: It's just probably the thing that is pulling the team together at the moment. I think we're reasonably clear around what it is we want to achieve. Everybody has bought into that, everybody is in agreement with that, everybody has given their commitment to that.

Nikhil: I think, initially, very focused on results, but not on how we're getting the results. So now it's more on how we're getting to the results, as opposed to just the numbers.

Andrea: The five focus areas that came out of there that was useful, and how we're going to do that.

However, there was a need to pull all of the ALE elements under discussion together so that it could be front of the team members' minds on a daily basis, and finalising a team ALEC accommodates this.

Team ALE Step 3 – Building a Team Authentic Leadership Effectiveness Charter

Programme Component: Team Authentic Leadership Effectiveness Charter

In order for a team to be effective, the team needs to focus on achieving their organisational goals, as that, ultimately, is why any organisation creates teams. Not only do teams need to be committed to achieving those outcomes, members need to hold one another accountable for achieving those outcomes. In terms of skills requirement, team members need not only technical and problem-solving skills, but need to extend these to include interpersonal skills. In the same way that individual leaders need to understand their internal identity, their leadership purpose, vision, and legacy, so does the collective team as a whole. It is extremely important that the team members collectively agree on the team values that they will hold dear and to which they wish to align their behaviour. They need to understand what it is that they wish to believe about their team and organisation, and how this will reflect in their behaviour.

Finally, the five team ALE levels need to become part of their everyday beings and doings. Trust, as a foundation, builds sufficiently strong interpersonal dynamics to allow for healthy disagreements at times in order to develop strong commitment. Commitment encourages the willingness to hold self and peers accountable, so that the desired team results can be achieved. It is therefore important for the team to identify and agree on the beliefs they wish to hold about each of the five elements, and how they intend to reflect those beliefs in their behaviour.

Building a team Authentic Leadership Effectiveness Charter (team ALEC): Every team needs to agree on the rules of team member engagement, as having clear guidelines gives any team a significant advantage when it comes to ensuring the exchange of good ideas. Towards this end, I developed a team ALEC (see Appendix 8) by enhancing the individual AL Compass (see Appendix 7) with required five team ALE elements. The team ALEC includes the element of a scorecard, and commences with the identification of the organisational goals or results that the team needs to achieve. This should be followed by agreeing on the collective hard and soft skills required to achieve those goals, in order to ensure that the team has the requisite skills in place, in order to be effective. Understanding the team internal identity, purpose, vision and legacy, and values are very important, as the purpose, for instance, of especially a leadership team can extend beyond the role assigned to them. It is about what inspires that specific team to reach their collective goals in the most inspirational and moral way (if that is important to them). It is not only about what makes them not sleep at night, but also about what makes them jump out of bed in the morning. Those two factors are very different. Finally, the team ALEC needs to reflect the team members' empowering beliefs about the team and organisation, and more specifically about the role that the team ALE levels will play towards their team ALE.

Once these factors have been identified in the team ALEC, they need to be accompanied by how their beliefs will reflect in their behaviours as a leadership team. It is important for the team to consider what makes up the current team by considering their behaviours (above the soil-line, that are observable by others), underpinned by numerous factors below the soil-line. Once they understand this, they can collectively decide what aspects of their team they need to change to allow for a more effective team. Finally, once again it important to consider the strength of the golden thread running through all the team ALE levels.

This allows the team members to consider how well their individual AL Compasses support their team ALEC; for instance, they could determine whether there was any conflict between their individual values and the team values. This affords the team the opportunity to create a team worldview, which further allows them to determine the level of alignment between themselves as individuals, the team as a collective, and the organisation, in a way that is congruent and effective. Every team member can then sign the team ALEC, and have it posted on individual office walls, in strategic spaces, and even in the meeting rooms for all in the organisation to witness.

Process component: Team Session 3

This two-day team coaching session builds on Team Session 2, and focuses specifically on finalising a team ALEC, which records the results that the team needs to achieve. More specifically, this session focuses on:

1. Reviewing progress since Team Session 2;
2. Focusing on the results achieved thus far;
3. Solidifying peer-to-peer accountability;
4. Finalising a team ALEC, and
5. Solidifying individual and team authentic leadership effectiveness.

This session reviews progress on the outcomes of Team Session 2, and builds further on team ALE by adding the various team ALE elements into a team ALEC. Furthermore, this session focuses on progress in peer-to-peer accountability, attention to team results against goals, and adhering to the team ALEC.

A very important exercise during this team session is the *team-on-one* exercise, where leaders are asked to prepare and give feedback to each other regarding their most empowering and derailing behaviours in adhering to the team ALEC. This is a very powerful exercise, as this is the first time that the team is ready to both give and receive feedback from their peers in a way that is helpful to them as a team moving forward. During this team session, the team decides on the *how* of remaining aligned to the team ALEC so that they can remain authentically effective, and for the first time I usually notice how the team members are taking ownership of their own effectiveness. The process no longer relies solely on the facilitator.

Actual experience: Feedback from the field

The team ALEC is the main framework used to guide and sustain team ALE. Leaders have shared that development of the charter is an experiential journey, which forms the basis of how a team needs to behave in order to attain the desired results What makes it successful, is the process leading up to the development of the team ALEC. Instead of it being a window-dressing exercise, it becomes a process, which evolves as the individuals and interpersonal dynamics within the team evolve. This is not an easy process, and team members have to be very honest and open with one another. They also realise that they need to develop the moral courage to hold one another accountable, have healthy disagreements, and trust one another, in line with the team ALEC. For instance, one of the guidelines in the charter for the team under discussion was *silence is consent*, so whenever necessary, they needed to speak up for the good of the team.

> **Hannah:** *Certainly, I think it's the whole process that leads up to that. Because you almost don't jump into it in the middle. You start at the beginning of the process, and the process can evolve as the people evolve and the dynamics evolve.*

> **Vanya:** *It was actually quite painful putting it together, because one had to be very honest … and what came out in terms of the future team, which is in the team ALEC, firstly helps you realise that lots of other people feel the same way, firstly. The second thing is that, to be able to … achieve the ultimate goals, we need to live by that, and that's going to take a lot of courage to be able to hold each other accountable, have healthy disagreements, trust each other, and it is a process.*

Leaders experience considerable value in creating and adhering to this team AL Compass as it gives them a common language and a guide in terms of measuring the each member's engagement towards achieving a collective outcome. It allows them to hold one another accountable in terms of trustworthiness and commitment within the team, and it focuses the individual minds on how they wish to operate in achieving their results. It allows co-operation within the team so that they can all *row in the same direction*, as Nikhil described it. This was corroborated by Liam, who had the following to say.

> **Liam:** *I think it concentrated the minds. It got everybody's agreement around how we would like to operate, how we would like to be seen by the rest of the business, how do we hold each other accountable, for what things we hold each other accountable, and then finishing it off with these are the targets we want to achieve at the end of the day. And I've seen it being used a few times over the last while – and people will say: "That's not according to our team compass."*

The creation of the compass concludes the processes that need to be in place to create sustainable individual and team ALE. Once this is in place, it is a matter of constantly ensuring that values, beliefs, and behaviours adhere to what has been collectively agreed to in the team ALEC.

The three team workshops are run about a month apart, starting with Team Workshop 1, after Individual Session 5, aligning with the AL intervention guidelines, which refers to nested sessions. This allows individual leaders to meet with the facilitator one more time after their first team workshop, to allow for reflections. The team sessions contain theory, tools, and techniques, and theory is interwoven with practical exercises, allowing leaders to start practising with one another during and in between the sessions. Examples of these are crucial conversations using coaching techniques and feedback sessions on a one-on-one or team-on-one basis. These team sessions are usually held off-site, preferably at a venue with peaceful surroundings and numerous breakaway nooks.

Leaders have shared that the workshop design, and, more specifically, models, techniques and tools, peer-to-peer coaching, and interpersonal sharing exercises are valuable. They enjoy getting to know one another, and being able to practise using tools and techniques learnt. They feel that there was a good balance between theory and practice, and they enjoy tools like the talking stick as it allows only the leader with the talking stick in his/her hand to talk, whilst others have to listen. More specifically, the vulnerability-based trust exercise, the team-on-one feedback session, and the development of the charter have been highlighted as being valuable. The peer-to-peer coaching exercises are valuable, as is the coaching buddy system that is created to allow leaders to continue with the coaching when they return to work.

> **Liam:** *What stood out for me was that first trust session where people sort of opened up for themselves. The team-on-one feedback was very constructive and good. The creation of the compass, I think, was done very well. In that last session, I quite enjoyed that last hour or so that we spent time working on a physical something that we want to go and do in the workplace.*

Leaders have referred to the duration of the workshop, experiencing the pace as measured. The workshops need to be well facilitated, considering that teams can be challenging with strong-willed individuals. The venue also needs to lend itself to the purpose of this work.

> **Dobek:** *One of the things that I think has been also very good is the venue – just going up onto that hill, I think, it put us in a different frame. And just to be out there just sort of had that, like, step back and say: "Wow, look at this! How nice is that?" It just puts you in a different frame to start with.*

Leaders, especially members of challenging leadership teams have shared with me that whilst they might sometimes fear the first team session, they start looking forward to the following ones.

Justin: I think, towards the end, we looked forward to the sessions, to the coaching, we looked forward to the interactions we had with one another to understand each other's reality: How do you see it, and how is it that I can guide you or coach you into a different mind-set? Getting to know the individuals in the team better, and, ultimately, coming up with that, you know, we all want the same thing. And what was interesting – we all want to win, we all want to do well, we want to do well individually. Previously we were all like that, but we had a different way and a different method of getting it. It was getting us, in all the different directions, to all work in the same direction. It was difficult to get us here, but we got here.

The workshop and programme is closed by doing a final review of the shifts towards each individual's own leadership outcomes, and determining what would further reduce the gap. A final exercise of adult experiential learning can then be completed to consider principal learnings about AL, inter-relational trust, and individual and team ALE throughout the programme.

Follow-up sessions. These can usually be arranged, if desired, once it becomes clear after the Team Session 3 that the team members want more time to solidify their outcomes.

This concludes the systemic overview of the usual structure of the authentic leadership programme. However, a programme such as this one needs to be tailorable to suit the needs of an organisation, as each organisation usually has different needs that need to be addressed.

TAILORABILITY OF THE AUTHENTIC LEADERSHIP EFFECTIVENESS PROGRAMME

AL has been equated to the highest form of leadership effectiveness, and if developed in a sustainable manner, it requires more work than a silver bullet can offer. The development of individual and team authentic leadership effectiveness is suitable for:

- An individual leader that needs to increase authentic leadership effectiveness;
- New leadership teams that need to gel quickly and effectively;
- Any existing leadership team that is not yet gelling as a coherent team;
- Leadership where the leader might not yet have an empowering leadership style, which has impacted on the foundation of trust and the effectiveness of the team he/she leads; and
- Any leadership team that needs to lead effectively during challenging or uncertain times.

However, whilst it is ideal for the whole team to participate in the full ALE programme, time and financial resource constraints do not always allow such. I have found that the individual and team ALE programme to some extent can be tailored to the needs of the organisation concerned. Before an organisation invests in the full team ALE programme, it is advisable to commence with a half-day introductory programme, during which AL, and the impact and development thereof is introduced, and the leadership developmental readiness of the leadership team can be determined. Once that has been done, decisions can be taken, such as whether all team members, or only some, need to participate in the initial individual sessions of the ALE programme.

In my experience, it is imperative that the leader of the team participates in an individual ALE programme before commencing with the team development, as the leader needs to model the change that is required in all. In the case where it is not possible for the whole team to participate in the individual sessions, I do amend the team sessions to allow team members to catch up on their individual ALE development first. At times, the team sessions will highlight members who might need some further individual support, which can then be discussed and agreed upon with the organisational sponsors.

SUSTAINABILITY OF INDIVIDUAL AND TEAM AUTHENTIC LEADERSHIP EFFECTIVENESS

Whilst I have found that individual leaders are more likely to sustain the ALE gained during their ALD journeys, further measurements need to be in place for organisational teams and cultures to sustain ALE, otherwise all the good work done might yield temporary benefits at best. This is because organisational structures constantly change. Leaders are further promoted, find more senior positions elsewhere, companies merge, and restructuring takes place.

I usually address this with leadership team participants towards the end of their ALE journeys. There are various ways in which to sustain ALE, and it is important to co-create strategies to ensure that this happens. Following are some ideas that may be considered.

1. At what level should buy-in be obtained for the creation of organisational ALE?
2. To what extent, both horizontally and vertically, should the development of ALE be rolled out in the organisation?
3. Do all levels require the same extent of ALE development initiatives?
4. At senior levels, bearing in mind that a team ALEC is in place, the following needs to be considered:
   a. What is the responsibility of any outgoing leader in terms of introducing the team ALEC, and what underpins it, when handing over to the incoming leader?
   b. What are the responsibilities of the remaining team members in terms of introducing the team ALEC and its underpinnings, when new members, including a new leader, might join the team?

My personal belief is that it is important that individual and team ALE ideally be developed at senior levels first. Thereafter these leaders need to become the change they wish to see in the organisation. They need to be transparent about what they stand for as individual and collective leadership, and have their team ALEC displayed for everyone to see. They need to be prepared to have others hold them accountable to remain true to their AL Compass.

At lower levels, I would encourage that all those who have reporting teams below them should at least have leader as coach skills to allow them to empower, inspire, and ignite the minds of those through whom they need to deliver. Such a culture can best be sustained when the initiative is supported at executive or board level of an organisation.

CONCLUSION

Recent organisational scandals, highlighted earlier, suggest that organisations cannot afford to wait years for the development of this type of leadership. It is for this reason that an understanding and evaluation of this ALE programme is so important, both in terms of its effectiveness and the purpose of its steps and components, so that years of development may be fast-tracked into a journey of no longer than three to six months.

INDIVIDUAL ALE EXERCISE: YOUR INTERNAL AL COMPASS

1.	Populate your AL Compass (template in Appendix 7), and identify your AL internal identity, purpose, vision, legacy, values, beliefs, and psychological states for your current self.
2.	Now repeat this exercise for your next level of your possible self.
3.	How easy was this exercise for you? How well do you really know yourself?
4.	How strong is the golden thread across the AL levels in your internal AL Compass?
5.	How helpful could a well-developed AL Compass be to you, especially in challenging times?

TEAM ALE EXERCISE: YOUR TEAM ALE CHARTER

1.	As a team, populate the team ALEC (template in Appendix 8), and identify your team scorecard, internal identity, purpose, vision, legacy, values and beliefs, and behaviours with a specific focus on the five AL levels of team effectiveness.
2.	How did you fare? What is this saying about your team's AL effectiveness?
3.	How helpful could a well-developed team ALEC be to your team, especially during challenging times?

Chapter 8

AUTHENTIC LEADERSHIP PROGRAMME EFFECT – DETAILED CASE STUDY

This chapter focuses on a detailed case study of the effect of an ALE programme such as this one. It outlines systematically the development of individual and team ALE, and the effect thereof on building intrapersonal and inter-relational trust, and individual and team leadership effectiveness. Feedback will once again be provided by the same ten-member leadership team that participated and provided feedback on the programme and process components in Chapter 7. The programme ran over six months during 2012 and 2013, with a final review session three months later, after which each participating leader was interviewed.

This discussion commences with the findings of the direct programme effect on leadership authenticity, followed by the further programme effect on inter-relational trust, and individual and team leadership effectiveness.

DIRECT PROGRAMME EFFECT ON LEADERSHIP AUTHENTICITY

Feedback indicated that the programme had a considerable direct effect on the enhancement of personal (intrapersonal), interpersonal, and professional authentic leadership. The following figure illustrates, at a meta-level, the programme effect on the development of ALE.

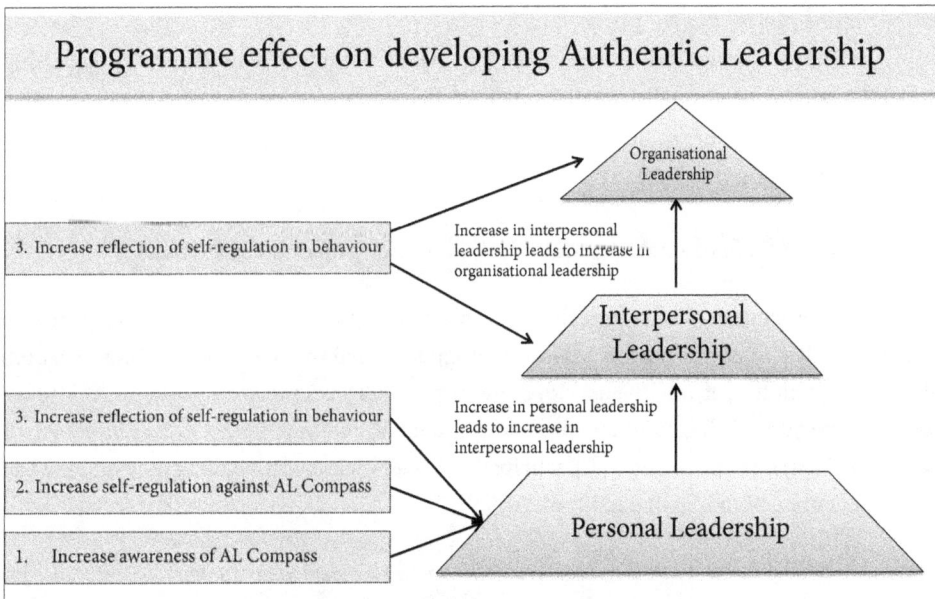

Figure 18. Programme effect on development of AL

From an **intrapersonal perspective** it became clear that the enhancement of personal AL required all three ALD processes. These comprised 1) developing more self-awareness and clarity of the elements within one's internal AL Compass, 2) self-regulating those internal AL Compass elements towards increased authenticity and 3) reflecting the self-regulation in authentic behaviour.

From an **interpersonal and professional leadership** perspective, once personal leadership had been developed, interpersonal and professional leadership required mostly only the third ALD process, which was to reflect the self-regulation against the AL Compass in behaviour. Aspects such as relational transparency and consistency in behaviour became noticeable, and participating leaders became much more relation-orientated. The growth in personal and interpersonal leadership allowed them to develop further inter-relational trust, and to become much more effective in their individual and team professional leadership capacities. Interestingly, a process such as this is not one-directional. Whilst it might start with the development of AL, once it further impacted on the afore-mentioned, the links become two-directional and iterative, meaning, for instance, that whilst AL allows for increased inter-relational trust, inter-relational trust then also impacts on further solidification of AL, to be clarified in more detail in the discussions on the further effects of the AL.

The following discussion of the findings is grouped, wherever possible, into the development of personal, interpersonal, and professional AL. Within those, supported by feedback from the leaders, the focus is on the following three ALD processes:

- **ALD1:** Self-awareness: awareness of elements within the internal AL Compass,
- **ALD2:** Self-regulation: regulating elements in order to strengthen the internal AL Compass, and
- **ALD3:** Behavioural reflection: reflecting this self-regulation in authentic leadership behaviour.

Effect on personal AL

The enhancement of personal AL required all three ALD processes, as follows.

ALD1: **Self-awareness**: Authentic leading starts with being able to lead oneself before one can lead others. The findings indicated that the programme led to a considerable increase, both in the understanding of, and the development in personal leadership. For instance, before the commencement of the programme, there was limited or no awareness of the notion of AL or personal leadership, and in general, participating leaders acknowledged that they initially had insufficient understanding of good leadership.

> *Andrea on lack of understanding AL: I don't know if I had an understanding of what leadership authenticity was before.*

Leadership, as the participants understood it, usually did not acknowledge the self; instead, it was prescriptive and came with a one-fit-for-all formula.

> **Gugu on previous understanding of leadership:** *...like your 10-day MBA. They'll put in a section there, some extracts about what good leadership is. .... I think it was very prescriptive before; it always comes with a formula... it always put up an ideal identity that you need to live up to.*

> **Liam on limited understanding of leadership:** *I mean I've always regarded myself as a good leader, and I probably wouldn't have achieved what I have in life if I didn't have the basic make-up of a good leader. What I didn't realise is that you do have ways and means that actually inhibit other people's performance, inhibit your own performance, and it's that realisation that can take me from where I was to where I'm hoping I'm going to at the moment.*

Most leadership styles do not necessarily acknowledge the authentic self, rather prescribing a one-fit-for-all skills set that is transactional in nature and pertains to social and cognitive organisational outcomes only. Rather than prescribing only the organisational requirements of leadership, AL describes more the personal aspects of being, regardless of context.

Previously participants also experienced mostly a lack of self-awareness/knowledge of their own internal AL Compasses. Not only did they not realise how they contributed to the toxic dynamics within their team, they also did not realise their potential value-add to the team.

> **Gugu on lack of self-awareness:** *We all think we're not the problem when we start with these things (laughs).... I thought I was not the problem and I thought there was very little room to change or improve on anything.*

> **Andrea on not knowing potential:** *I did not know what my potential could be in a sense. Knowing that there's probably a lot more growth that I could get out of me...*

Self-awareness is usually gained through the practice of continuous introspection. During the programme, participating leaders realised the importance of, and started the process of continuous introspection in order to increase self-awareness of the elements of their internal AL Compasses.

> **Darren on continuous introspection:** *...actually doing a lot of introspection continuously. The thing is to be honest with yourself and recognise what your flaws are and where you need to work hard, what your strengths are and to make them even stronger.*

> **Gugu on knowing AL Compass drivers:** *...know what's true to me as a person, know what drives me, understand how I see the world and how I see other people. I think once I understood that, it became easier to interact with others around me in a much more real and meaningful way.*

> **Liam on knowing self better:** *I think it's had a huge effect on me. It gave me the opportunity to get to know myself much better. It gave me the time to become comfortable with myself, understand myself, understand the values that I have, and being able to be comfortable to articulate that...*

Gaining self-knowledge about one's potential, one's purpose, vision, and self-identity, and especially one's core values, which one needs to adhere to, usually results in increased self-confidence, all requirements for the development of AL. During the programme, the participants' self-knowledge increased. The increased self-awareness also extended to what they believed about self, others, and even what leadership really could entail.

> *Justin on gaining knowledge of self and others: What it's done is, it's giving me a lot more scope to understand other people not just myself. Part of that learning to understand yourself better, is to understand others better. Once you understand others better then you respond to them differently, and you'll treat them differently. Work is around relationships. At the end of the day everybody works and lives in a world where relationships are important.*

> *Vanya on purpose, vision and identity: I've learnt to see the value in what I really want out of life. Purpose talks to the vision, so that's changed a lot for me. Identity has changed in terms of me being more authentic and true to myself.*

> *Nikhil on values and beliefs: I think in terms of being true to yourself at the end of the day and standing up to what you believe in, your beliefs internally and also the value system that you grew up with, and aligning that to the organisational values and principles, I think that's core to what leadership authenticity is.*

> *Andrea on purpose: ... purposeful – I think that's quite important because if you don't know what your purpose is, you're like a reed in the wind.*

> *Andrea on own potential: In a sense you always know what you're able to do but do you live it out, do you live up to what your potential is? Now you know what you can do without doubting some of the things. And sometimes you get smacked on the head, get pushed down, and you get up quicker and you move on, knowing that it doesn't have to hold you back in life.*

A programme such as this can never be evaluated in isolation. It needs to be cognisant of and use trigger events to test and further develop leadership authenticity. Participating leaders were able to identify specific work episodes and life events that had tested and further developed their awareness of self and others towards increased leadership authenticity. Particularly when at work, increased introspection and remembering who they wanted to be rather than how they had behaved before, helped them to focus on and solidify new behaviours towards increased leadership authenticity.

> *Liam on being tested during leadership episodes: There's been a couple of conflict situations that arose with some of the more difficult people where all the good intents I had were really tested. I had to talk to myself and say, "don't fall back to your old self, and don't fall back to the way that you're comfortable with, go back to what you want to be". Every attempt that you try to do that proves that it works. It built up a bit of momentum and the next time it happened, it was a little bit easier.*

In terms of life events, introspection allowed them to increase their self-belief, which helped them to deal with traumatic episodes. It assisted them in appreciating the uniqueness of important others, allowing them to develop more flexibility towards increased motivational and influential relationships with those others.

> **Justin on introspection during life events:** *And one of the things I've realised is that I have three children who are exceptionally different. What you learn is that what drives the one doesn't drive the other and I've got to change myself in order to motivate them differently. Not everybody is the same and you have to deal with that. This programme has brought that out a lot more I think.*

> **Andrea on being tested by life events:** *I think in terms of the break up with my partner – that was quite hard. I think going through this programme at that time was very beneficial because I was working on the self-belief aspect as well, and I did a lot of writing and actually managed to get through it in quite a decent space. I'm proud of the way I was acting, and proud of the way I was dealing with the break up issues.*

ALD2: **Self-regulation:** Participant leaders felt that previously, they were simply deluding themselves in terms of who they were and the skills they possessed, and that, in fact, they experienced psychological states such as anger and stress, self-doubt, and being too trusting.

> **Darren on deluding himself:** *Almost an inflated sense of self... maybe I was fooling myself in that I thought I was good. If I ignore this thing, I'll just live with it. I'll just file it at the back of my mind but oh, I'm okay. I think I was fooling myself. ...I think it's about not wanting to deal with it.*

> **Gugu on emotional states such as stress and anger:** *...initially my emotional state was such that I was in such a negative place. I think it was a combination of, there's little problem with me, the problem is everyone else plus the fact that I was stressed and very angry.*

> **Andrea on self-doubt:** *If I look back at when we first started, I was very much at a high in terms of getting really good results, but then still questioning what I wanted to do, and where I was going. There was a lot of self-doubt about what I could do and what my value was to the company...*

> **Dobek on being too trusting:** *... during the early sessions, I went back and I said I'll go and get feedback from my team, only to find that maybe I was too trusting and maybe I accepted more than what I should've. That sort of thing was a bit of a shock to me because I then went and explored what was being said and found some of it to be true.*

Increased awareness could lead to increased internal management of psychological states such as accountability (psychological ownership), commitment, consistency, honesty, trust, truthfulness, and respect, all requirements of AL. In terms of commitment to being true to one's self and to one's core values, participants felt that once an awareness of the drivers of the leader's behaviour was in place, self-regulation towards being true to the leader's internal AL Compass could follow.

> **Vanya on psychological state management:** *If somebody says something that I totally disagree with, don't bang the table and say "You're wrong." Rather absorb the information, hear what the person is saying, and try to understand what the person is saying. Then respond in a manner that*

allows the person to hear me rather than having a defensive approach because I am being abrasive.

Darren on accountability: *I thought before that to make an unpopular decision, well I'd rather shy away from it. That's not good leadership. You sometimes have to do that, but it's how you communicate it and how you control that situation.*

Gugu on commitment to be the best true self: *I think that's where authentic leadership is different because it looks at what you bring to the table and what your identity is and it formulates a solution around that, versus just some standard set of points that you have to adhere to, to be a good leader. I think it connects the two, who you are and how you behave.*

Dobek on inter-relational trust: *How much do you trust the team that you're in and how much do you think the team trusts you? This is followed by "what are the decisions that we're making, can we make those decisions without actually having to analyse them?" We know it's been made for the good of the company and us as a team. I think it's really about that trust and being true to our values.*

Appropriate vulnerability increases intrapersonal and interpersonal trust. Because of the programme, participants felt that increased self-awareness of one's AL Compass led to increased commitment to the further development of one's self. For example, they experienced increased psychological state management, particularly in terms of developing states such as being hopeful.

Gugu on increased psychological state management: *Some time ago I felt "That's it, I'm giving this job three more months and then I'm out of here." And now, I probably haven't thought about that in a couple of months…Yes, there's difficult days but it's not as bad. It's bearable. My first solution is not to jump ship …. I think every ship has a difficult day but there's some that you'd rather go to the shark in the water than stay on the ship. Either way you're going to see your demise but there's hope for the future versus surviving every day.*

From a practitioner's perspective, it is important to elaborate more on the concept of *appropriate vulnerability*, also referred to as *balanced- or strength-based vulnerability*. Numerous psychological states can be used appropriately and inappropriately. For instance, appropriate vulnerability would be a strength-based vulnerability, used appropriately and with a positive intent. In fact, one can step into such a state only once one feels sufficiently congruent within. On the other hand, the psychological state of invulnerability, in particular *inappropriate invulnerability*, is often applied as a coping mechanism by those who do not feel strong enough to show balanced vulnerability. The programme helped participants to develop appropriate strength-based vulnerability so that they could accept and grow from feedback from others.

Gugu on appropriate vulnerability: *I think I have shifted in the way I approach the team. The trust has improved; I've opened up a little bit more. The programme also forced me to do some things that I really was not planning to do. Like consider the feedback from other people.*

Very valuable also was the development of their *internal power zone*, a notion introduced to them during the programme, which comprised their internal thoughts and feelings, manifesting externally in speech and behaviour, with the understanding that they could be accountable only for their own internal power zone, not that of another. Understanding the difference between reacting (not taking ownership) and responding (taking ownership and remaining true to self), allowed them to develop self-accountability, also called *psychological ownership*.

> *Gugu: There's some things for you to own and there's some things for other people to own. I generally just used to find myself upset and angry and not getting results but I've learnt, for example, I can now sit and assess – instead of getting angry about that person's response, I must just accept they responded that way. They can own that response; it's not mine to own. There are tools that help me deal with that stuff on a day-to-day basis.*

The programme led to increased consistency, self-belief, self-confidence, self-discipline, self-honesty, and being true to self.

> ***Hannah on consistency:*** *I think [previously] the desire to be a good leader led to me being inconsistent, negatively affecting others. So that had the opposite effect of being a good leader ... being more true to myself means that I'm more consistent ...Knowing why you're doing things and what you believe in and then having your actions be consistent with that.*

> ***Andrea on self-belief:*** *I think that aspect, that whole self-belief aspect, has grown immensely in terms of my value, whether it's to my family, or to my organisation.*

> ***Darren on self-discipline:*** *...the most important is self-discipline; not to procrastinate. Now what this programme has taught me, is the value of doing the things that you sometimes think are not going to add value for you, and how much value it actually did add. It was the self-discipline, not procrastinating, the consistency, and the biggest of all my self-belief.*

> ***Darren on self-honesty:*** *It requires knowing yourself. Sometimes you don't like it, and you just file it in the back of your mind and you think it's going to go away, it's not. This programme draws these things out of you; that's what it does.*

> ***Hannah on being true to self:*** *Being more true to myself means that I'm more consistent. If what I do has a negative consequence but I can reflect back on it and say that my motivation, my reasons, or my actions, were pure and aligned to what I believe in, then I feel comfortable with those actions.*

In terms of trigger events, participants referred to specific work episodes that had tested the effect of increased management of psychological states such as resilience, self-belief, and self-confidence. Interestingly, participants also referred to the fact that they had developed the ability of self-coaching, which indicated that they were committed to further positive self-development.

Hannah on general state management: *I suppose I do have my moments when I allow emotions to get the better of me and feel sorry for myself. I interpreted a specific example as a rejection and I became uptight about it and left work. As I was driving away, I said "Well, you know, what people project to you is what you project." So, if people project rejection to me it's because I do that and I'm pulling myself out of the team. I was able to, quite a lot quicker, just to come to the point to say it's my issue not their issue and they're just reflecting it.*

Hannah on self-coaching: *I think I've always been fairly good in talking myself through a process and getting to the point of the realisation, but I think the difference is that it was a lot quicker. It's very difficult to do that in a particularly emotionally intense period. Given the stressful and emotional circumstances that I'm in, I think the difference is the fact that I could so quickly get to that point.*

Darren on resilience: *It assisted me in being a lot more resilient whilst adjusting to a new and very different environment.*

Dobek on self-confidence: *It's standing up for what I believe is right, which made me feel better about myself, and I have more confidence now.*

Enhancing their awareness/knowledge of the reality of others allowed for relationship-building that led to better delivery.

Justin on relationship-building: *It's not just about me; another individual could have something that's important to them and I can't discount it. If it's important to them I need to take it seriously, have the discussion but ultimately it is important to them, so deliver on it.*

Increased positive psychological states allow leaders to use trigger events that further help them to develop themselves, an important aspect of AL. In terms of allowing life events to test and further develop them, participating leaders found that they had developed the ability to be more present; for instance, despite what was happening at work, when at home with their children, their focus was on their children. They had also become more resilient in the face of challenging situations, had developed self-accountability, had learnt to respond rather than react when challenged by their teenagers, and they experienced more self-belief when faced with daunting tasks.

Vanya on being present in the moment: *I suppose with my kids as well. I used to bath the kids and then feed them but I'd be constantly thinking about work because I left things undone, unsaid, or un-dealt with. Now that I deal with situations as they arise in the most appropriate manner, I'm able to actually enjoy bath time with the kids. Sometimes I lie in bed, and I look at the trees and I think, "Wow, look at those beautiful colours." I'm able to have those conversations with my kids around the colour of the leaves.*

Darren on responding versus reacting:... relationship with my son and that I think I was just judging him before that. I'd just go fly off the handle. I'd get stuck in, and we'd argue with each other.

Lately, knowing myself better, having the tools available to me, I actually just sat back, listened, thought about things before I responded. I didn't react; I responded. I listened to his point of view because before I was never in the wrong, he was always in the wrong.

ALD3: Behavioural reflection: The lack of self-regulation previously manifested in, amongst others, participants not dealing with issues, and at times, having no work/life balance.

Nikhil on work/life balance: (my reflective journaling): I asked Nikhil how happy he currently was at work, and he admitted that he was frustrated and unhappy, and he realised this often when he went home. He also was starting to ask how he was adding to the problem, and what he needed to do to be part of the solution. He realised that he had stopped doing certain things. He was not leading a balanced life; it seemed to be all about his work. This was creating a tension in him...

Participants started to use the self-development tools introduced during the programme.

Darren on using self-development tools: The biggest thing this programme has taught me, were the tools. You don't often get those tools. I call it my toolbox, and I can really use it. The nice thing is it can be at work, it can be at home, it can be with friends. It's not limited – it's a life thing.

Participating leaders gave examples of leadership episodes where they had been tested in terms of their behavioural shifts, such as the positive effect of being able to conduct crucial conversations and relationship-building, which led to better team delivery. They were better able to hold team members, and on occasion, even their seniors accountable for their behaviour and for delivery.

Vanya on impact on crucial conversations with Liam: ...I've given feedback to Liam in our sessions where I've seen him change a lot. At the same time I've actually given him feedback saying, "Liam, don't change too much because you're going to lose yourself in the process." Sometimes he tries very hard and I was able to give him on-the-level feedback. I'm also able to give him feedback about where I believe peers can improve, at the same giving the peers feedback.

Thought leaders on AL often refer to the effect of AL on followers without necessarily limiting those to subordinates. In this case, authentic leaders could even, at times, lead those senior to them (previous example of Vanya and Liam), illustrating that they lead by presence rather than position.

When referring to being tested by life events, leaders referred to three categories, namely the ability to have crucial conversations, leading by presence rather than position, and a positive regard for the uniqueness of others. They were better able to have difficult but meaningful conversations with their families (especially their spouses), and they were better able to deal with conflict at home. Finally, they had developed an increased positive regard for the uniqueness of others, which allowed them to build better relationships with members of the workers' unions. This indicates the overlap of lessons learnt across different contexts of life and work.

> *Peter on crucial conversations outside work:* I've learnt about the communication issues I have – I mean my wife and I know we have issues in that arena, mainly on my side. I've been working at those as well, which is great.

> *Darren on leading by presence rather than position:* ...it's about leading yourself. It begins at home and I'm calling myself home (chuckling). It begins with me, and how I believe in myself, what I believe about others, how I respond versus react, and how I deal with conflict. It's a package.

> *Andrea on positive regard for the uniqueness of others:* I think of how I deal with the union members as well. I respect them completely in terms of where they've come from, how they run their own homes, and I try to find out about what's behind the people rather than just saying it's a group of people that we have to deal with.

I do believe that developing authenticity needs to reflect an element of psychological ownership in one's behaviour and the way we speak about ourselves. I often challenge my participant leaders when talking about themselves in second or third person, and encourage them to refer to themselves in first person ("I" instead of "you" or "one"), as this indicates psychological ownership of what we say. The following highlights the AL programme effect on developing or enhancing interpersonal leadership, also called people leadership.

Effect on interpersonal AL

However, whereas all three ALD processes were required in developing personal leadership, only the third process was required in the development of interpersonal AL.

ALD3: **Behavioural reflection:** The findings indicated the programme had a considerable effect in terms of an increase in both the understanding of and development of interpersonal AL.

In terms of the participants' original perspectives on interpersonal leadership, participants had previously been introduced to the notion of *engaging leadership*. However, there was a sense that, even if leaders are encouraged to engage with others, they were not necessarily authentically doing so; rather than showing their true selves, they would create an impression that they were truly engaging with others.

> *Andrea on engaging leadership:* Previous understanding of leadership was very much based on engagement, more the aspect of what a leader should look after or possibly behave in a certain way. I mean in terms of leadership it would be an engagement style, inspiring people, it's more around those individual aspects, being able to drive performance, and drive results.

> *Vanya on creating an impression:* ...general leadership, I always believed that it was something where you had to put on a facade, behave a certain way, and not show your true self.

This is called impression management, which does not constitute AL. During the programme, participants realised the importance of leaders reflecting appropriate vulnerability, also called *balanced* vulnerability, by being prepared to be open to others.

Peter: Taking people into your confidence, I suppose that's part of openness really. Appropriate vulnerability!

They realised the importance of consistently holding others accountable, as others would then know what the leader expected of them. They referred to understanding and adhering to increased states of interpersonal respect, interpersonal trust, and realised the importance of truly knowing themselves. This reflected in their behaviour as it allowed them to engage in meaningful and empowering communication with others.

Darren on interpersonal accountability: They've got to know that is exactly what Darren wants, ...that I know he's going to react that way, I know he's going to hold me accountable and that's that.

Gugu on meaningful and empowering communication: ...know what's true to me as a person, know what drives me, understand how I see the world, understand how I see other people. I think once I understood that it became easier to interact with others around me in a much more real and meaningful way. For me it's really about understanding myself within the context of the world to be able to live up to the best vision of who I want to be.

Leaders also received feedback regarding their increased recognition and positive regard of others. However, participating leaders still sensed that one of their peers adhered to impression management, which they did not regard as true authenticity.

Effect on organisational AL

The findings on the effect on developing organisational AL yielded the following.

Additional *ALD3*: AL forms the foundation of positive leadership: The findings indicated a considerable increase in both the understanding and development of organisational AL. In terms of the leaders' original perspectives on organisational leadership, they considered this restricted to mainly positional leadership and driving results.

Peter on positional leadership: Before, I just worked on downward leadership, I didn't really think of working on upward or peer leadership.

Liam on driving results: It was about the hard numbers and I suppose it still is about the hard numbers. I suppose in retrospect, if I'd changed my approach I might've been able to turn it quicker by not just focusing on the task or maybe give a little bit more of a balanced approach to it.

During the programme, participants realised that leadership authenticity forms the foundation of positive leadership. It is a type of leadership that goes beyond position, and it is a balanced situational leadership that allows one to be true both to oneself and to the organisational environment. This, in turn, allows the leader to create a culture worth following, which is conducive to the achievement of results. AL differs from other forms of leadership in that it could be regarded as an influential leadership by, for instance, using a coaching style of leading.

Justin on leadership beyond position: Now I realise that leadership authenticity is a lot broader. It's about looking at yourself in totality, and how you are within different environments, how you are in the work environment, at home, how you live your life. Leadership authenticity is how you live your life whilst being real to yourself.

Peter on leadership beyond position: … It's opened my eyes to the 360 – I wouldn't have used that phrase but that's the right phrase – to be able to have a total view of upwards, sideways as well as downwards.

Dobek on being to true to self and organisational environment: It's how true you are both to yourself and to the environment or the people that you're working with. How we as a team gel when everybody has different values. It does talk to both your internal values and I think we relate to the company values that they publish. I wouldn't be able to work in a company where I couldn't subscribe to those values and I think that's part of it. It is about being true to those.

Gugu on coaching style of leading: The coaching aspect of it for me was quite critical. There's some things that I've taken through to, for example, the guys who report to me – one of my employees that I had to coach through something. It helped in dealing with those things to say – versus just telling or instructing or doing the usual day to day, take a different approach, the coaching approach… That also helped.

Dobek on creating a culture worth following: We as leaders have to get our people to follow us. You can't do that if you're not true to yourself and true to the values.

Liam on achieving results: It was about the hard numbers and I suppose it still is about the hard numbers.

Those close to the leaders, such as their manager, noticed how developing leadership authenticity in the leaders had enhanced effectiveness and commitment within the team, and that these leaders had developed a more empowering style of leadership.

Manager on Gugu's effectiveness and commitment within the team: I have seen her willingness to make the team a more effective and coherent group. She supports every team initiative and demonstrated a real need to improve brewing's overall performance.

In summary, once awareness of one's internal AL Compass has increased, self-regulation in terms of commitment to the further development of personal leadership can follow. It was only once self-regulation of the elements in the AL Compass was in place that the development of personal AL could start leading onto the development of interpersonal and organisational AL.

FURTHER PROGRAMME EFFECT ON INTER-RELATIONAL TRUST

In terms of the effect of developing AL on inter-relational trust, findings indicated that there was a noticeable increase of inter-relational trust during the programme, as illustrated in Figure 19.

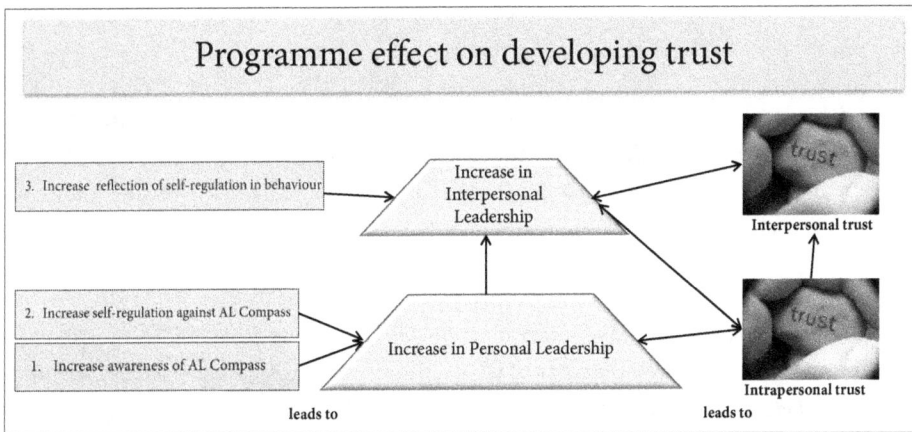

Figure 19. Programme effect on developing trust

Whereas the findings on the AL effect on building trust under personal AL supported the first two below-the-soil-line ALD processes (awareness of and self-regulation against AL Compass), under interpersonal AL, the focus was more on the third ALD process, the above-the-soil-line reflection in behaviour, that others could notice. This creates a symbiotic link between enhancing AL and enhancing inter-relational trust.

Effect of development of personal AL on building trust

The enhancement of personal AL on building trust required the first two ALD processes.

ALD1: **Self-awareness:** In terms of the effect of development of personal AL on inter-relational trust, when asked about developing trust, participants stated the importance of continuous introspection and an intrapersonal feedback loop, as that helped them to understand their values, strengths, and weaknesses better. Not only did it allow them to be proud of what they had already achieved, they could then address emerging gaps that needed attention.

> *Liam on continuous introspection: I suppose the issues you understand by doing the introspection, by getting to understand yourself is that you understand what you're doing to cause mistrust or distrust and you then try and eliminate those. You understand your gaps, you fix your gaps and that creates the trust within the team.*

Nikhil on intra- and interpersonal awareness: Each person was getting to know themselves better within the team and being more cognisant of the fact that there are differences between individuals and that we also have a single objective that we want to drive collectively.

Andrea on intrapersonal feedback loop: I think the trust in myself is to say now that you've done certain things you can see the benefit of that, and it's like a cycle you go through in terms of looking after yourself, getting to the potential, showing that drive, and you just gather your self-belief.... It's definitely about the results and being able to trust that you're on the right path and being able to trust that you can do anything you put your mind to.

It was for this reason that they believed that it was imperative for the programme to commence with individual sessions as it allowed them to understand themselves and how they had contributed to any destructive dynamics that had previously existed in the team. They could introspect and allow feedback from others to reflect upon; a requirement for the emergence of AL.

Hannah on importance of starting with individual sessions: ... the individual sessions allowed everyone to understand themselves and how they were contributing to any dynamics that might've existed previously in the team.

Andrea on importance of starting with individual sessions: Yes, it was incredibly important because you needed to stop first to look at yourself and what you struggle with. Actually be real to yourself, be honest enough, so that when people gave you feedback on certain stuff you either knew it, or if it surprised you, you needed to say, "Now why did that surprise me, why didn't I know that, what is it about me that I didn't know that?"

Increasing awareness and understanding not only of the various self-aspects, but also those of others, translated into increased self-efficacy and intrapersonal trust. One of the participants explained that, if you do not have trust in self, it affects other people's ability to trust you.

Hannah on trust in self: Well I think if you don't have trust in yourself, it affects other people's ability to trust you.

Furthermore, one cannot pretend to be authentic, as people easily see through it. If people do not feel that you are authentic, you will not have their trust, and you will not be able to lead them.

ALD2: **Self-regulation:** Once they had developed an increased awareness of their AL Compass, participants found that this could lead to increased emotional state management.

Gugu on being calmer: I think I behave in a much calmer way, which probably means the people around me are calm and it's easy to approach me, it's easy to interact with me, and it's easy to come ask for help now because I'm less stressed and there's more time to engage. It's a bit more relaxed,

I can start investigating or exploring solutions with the person versus dishing them out and just making sure that they get out of my office, so I can get onto my next thing.

Liam on knowledge and understanding of self: *I now know where my buttons are, so that if people get close to that I know that I need to be careful in terms of how I react to that. It just gave that knowledge and understanding, just made me trust myself and my behaviour much better. When you know how you will respond and you know how you should respond, and you try and achieve that most of the time, you do trust yourself and you'll behave a lot better.*

They had developed more self-awareness of the triggers that elicited unhelpful responses, and self-confidence in managing their responses during disagreements on contentious issues. They felt that they now experienced an *understandable* trust, rather than an arrogant trust; it was a more genuine trust, a more authentic trust in self, based on a better understanding of self.

Justin on authentic trust: *It's different because it's an understandable trust. In the past, it could've been arrogance. I could've thought I trusted myself because I felt I was intelligent enough, I knew what I was doing. I think once you've unpacked it and you've understood it better, then I think you've got a more genuine trust in yourself, a more authentic trust.*

They were more conscious of remaining calm and consistent, even if the situations were challenging or consequences were not desirable. They realised that others could trust someone who was consistent, and approach and interact with them if they were calm. They were also more prepared to be appropriately vulnerable, allowing others to give them constructive feedback, and as such, they wished to become role models for others to do the same. The participants' appropriate vulnerability also allowed for more honesty and relational transparency, as they displayed a willingness to go first, to show their weaknesses and to work on those, allowing trust to grow amongst participants.

Justin on appropriate vulnerability: *I think that was an example of appropriate vulnerability where it was appropriate to be vulnerable in terms of the feedback that was given to me. But in doing so, set an example for the team to say: if the leader of the team can take criticism, then I think everybody needs to be able to take criticism.*

Another state that especially the leader had to develop was moral courage. It was important that the leader stopped micromanaging, and started trusting that his team knew what they were doing. In terms of behaving ethically, participants needed to stay true to their core values and beliefs, and they found the moral courage to hold themselves and others accountable.

Liam on moral courage: *The new organisational intervention that we're trying in terms of the focused approach was probably the most demonstration of courage because it really, really goes into the heart of what we've always been as a company, how we operate, how we micromanage our people by measuring everything that moves in the brewery. It's just the nature of the business; we're over controlling in everything. To let go of that, has taken a helluva lot of courage.*

Finally, once they had increased their personal and interpersonal AL, leading to increased trust in self, they could build on this and develop further trust between themselves and others.

Effect of development of interpersonal AL on building trust

The enhancement of personal AL on building trust required only the third ALD process.

ALD3: **Reflection in behaviour:** When asked about their behavioural shifts, participants referred to the importance of interpersonal awareness, interpersonal trust, transparency and openness, an interpersonal feedback loop, relationship-building, a safe space to allow appropriate vulnerability toward building trust, and moving forward as a collective, as precursors to building trust. Justin had the following to say about relationship-building.

> *Justin on relationship-building: But a lot of it's got to do with relationship-building, and the trust and authenticity it's built on. It doesn't just happen. It happens over a period of getting to know one another, getting to know one another's realities, getting to know one another's truths.*

Where there was a lack of interpersonal trust before, some leaders made the effort to understand others better. They spent more time with those individuals and their interpersonal communication; trust and relationship-building improved to such an extent that safe spaces were being created to allow others to be appropriately vulnerable and let their guard down. Transparency and openness in general communication, and especially in terms of ethical considerations in decision-making, is also an antecedent of trust-building. This openness extends further, to allowing appropriate vulnerability in terms of receiving and considering reasonable interpersonal feedback, as this enables authentic change. Crucial conversations could start to take place between participants, allowing for further trust building, and this became an iterative process. There was a sense that the development of AL and inter-relational trust allowed the team to move forward as a collective.

> *Darren on investing time with others: A lot of the other team members who I never actually used to sit with, I made a point of going and sitting with them, just getting to know them, develop that bond and that trust; and it's worked well.*

> *Gugu on creating safe spaces that allow openness: I think the programme helped create a safe space for people to bring out themselves in a way that didn't feel threatening and I think that's the first big step in trusting each other a little bit more...*

Due to the previous lack of trust, some participants were still somewhat wary of their colleagues. Whilst realising that they themselves had to develop more leadership authenticity and self-trust before earning the trust of others, they also wished to see those developing in others. They therefore wanted to get to know others really well before they established a trust relationship. Trust in others does not automatically happen; it has to develop over time, and participants sought more consistency in the behaviour of their peers. This indicates that one could simultaneously be an authentic leader and an authentic follower.

Link between AL and inter-relational trust

When asked specifically about the link between leadership authenticity and inter-relational trust, leader participants responded that being able to bring a coaching underpinning into crucial conversations with others allowed them to be more effective as leaders.

> *Gugu on a coaching underpinning in interactions: I'm thinking about individual leadership effectiveness; the fact that I've taken on a coaching style and that I therefore am empowering others makes me more effective as a leader.*

Whilst trust was not specifically mentioned, this could not have happened without the development of inter-relational trust. A leader needs to create a safe space in which followers can learn. These coaching conversations are helpful in giving and receiving feedback, which was also the case for these leaders who, whilst experimenting with new behaviours, might have had to compromise their existing strengths, and as such, their team members helped them to regain balance.

Liam, the leader of the team, who previously micromanaged, illustrated more balanced processing in his behaviour, by allowing some freedom of thinking from his team, and was deliberate in giving more recognition where due, whilst also allowing his team members to make mistakes. Understanding that this was part of learning, he experimented with new behaviours while continuing his focus on the goals that needed to be achieved.

> *My question to Liam on allowing others to make mistakes: You said you're allowing people to go and try things out, understanding also that might mean that sometimes there might be mistakes.*

> *Liam's response: It's always something that's been in the back of my mind but I do it a little bit more deliberately now. Then coupled with that, I do a little bit more recognition as well, which boosts that effort that the guys are putting in. I'm allowing a lot more mistakes and it's a fine line. You've got to allow the freedom of thinking and let their own skills and competencies take over instead of you directing them all the time, but you've also got to keep in the back of your mind where you want to go and what you want to do with the business.*

However, not all leaders will always shift equally in terms of extent or speed, and this is linked to leader developmental readiness. One of the leaders, for instance, not buying into the need for self-change, initially did not truly engage in the individual self-development sessions. At best, he could be described as an authentic follower, as he eventually started to engage during the team sessions, after he had noticed the change in others. He was not trusted by many of his peers or his senior, and therefore described as *falsely authentic*, pretending to drive collective goals whilst he was still driving his own KPIs. His behaviour could be described as *impression management*.

However, the findings showed that AL enhances inter-relational trust; furthermore, that a symbiotic relationship exists between the two; that development of both occurs both iteratively and in parallel.

> *My question to Gugu on a symbiotic relationship between AL and trust: But what comes first because you're now putting trust first? Gugu's response: I wouldn't say necessary that trust comes first, but we first dealt with the self and being authentic, sorting the self out and then in terms of interacting with others, that trust had to be built. We all needed to know where we're at, what our gaps were, what we wanted out of this, and what was important to each of us. You almost needed to prepare each ingredient before you put it in the pot. You needed to fix yourself, be true to yourself, lead yourself before you could lead others.*

> *Vanya on the link between authenticity, and trust, and inauthenticity: You've got to trust the process, you've got to trust that this will come. And sometimes in being authentic you realise that inter-relational trust can be broken because people operate differently and that's something you need to understand. Sometimes being authentic allows you to see the wood for the trees. And if you're not authentic, if you sway either direction, you're never able to determine who're the true versus the false people.*

> *Liam on the link between authenticity and trust: I think to be authentic, to be true to yourself, to understand yourself and show other people who you are, and actually to be quite comfortable in doing that and to be quite clear on how you do that, it just breeds trust on its own.*

> *Andrea on the link between authenticity and trust: I think there's a very strong link between AL and trust simply because you need to be able to display who you are to other people because if they don't know you, if they don't know what you're about, they're very unlikely to trust you.*

These findings illustrate that leadership authenticity results in increased trust, and when people trust one another, it allows greater authenticity. However, change starts with self; one needs to work on self, be true to self, lead self, be willing to display appropriate vulnerability, and engage in relational transparency, as that allows the enhancement of interpersonal trust that allows one to lead others.

FURTHER PROGRAMME EFFECT ON INDIVIDUAL AUTHENTIC LEADERSHIP EFFECTIVENESS

In terms of the effect of developing AL on individual ALE, the findings indicate that this had increased considerably for the majority of participating leaders, mainly due to an increase in their personal, interpersonal, and organisational AL, and the symbiotic relationship between the enhancement of AL and inter-relational trust, as illustrated in the following figure.

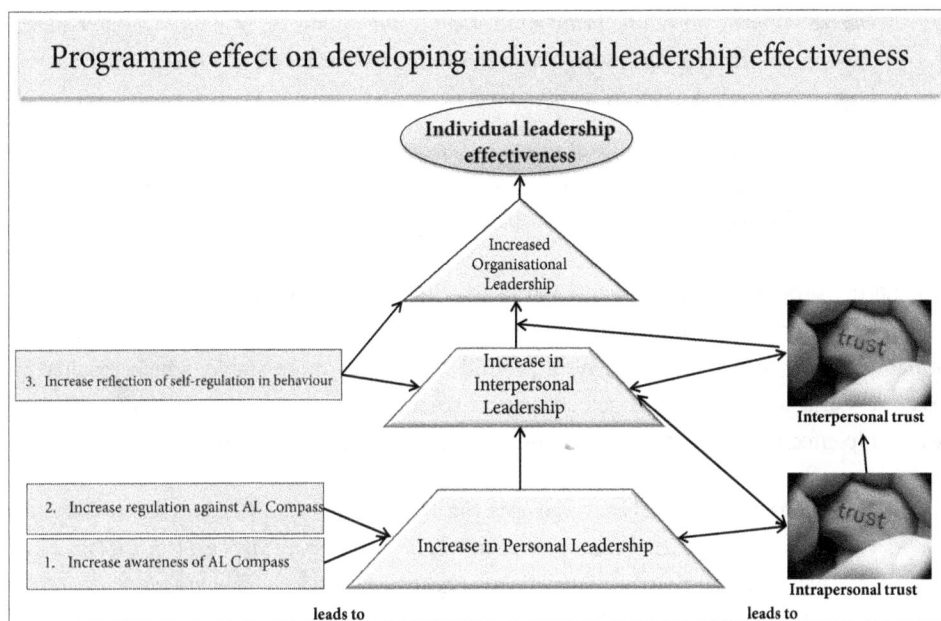

Figure 20. Programme effect on developing individual leadership effectiveness

Effect of enhancement of personal AL on individual leadership effectiveness

The effect of enhancing personal AL on individual leadership effectiveness requires the first two ALD processes, those being 1) increased awareness of internal AL Compass, and 2) increased self-regulation of internal AL Compass.

ALD1: **Self-awareness:** Participants referred to the positive effect of the increase in their self- and interpersonal awareness on their leadership effectiveness. Being aware of a previous limiting internal identity driving their behaviour, and of the more empowering internal identity that they were stepping into, allowed them to change the way they interacted with their teams.

> *Gugu on the effect of internal identity on leadership effectiveness: Before I was this **band aid** trying to fix everything and everybody; the to-be state that I wanted to end up at is **leader as coach**. For me that has moved or changed the way I do things; instead of instructing and telling, I now empower and give resources to people to make their own decisions.*

ALD2: **Self-regulation:** Previously, participants experienced a lack of psychological state management, such as a lack of consistency, rapport, and self-belief, and inappropriate trust.

Darren on being previously being inconsistent: I think before being inconsistent immediately made me ineffective in some ways. Not having the self-belief made me not challenge; it makes you ineffective because you don't really offer anything.

Hannah on previous emotional turmoil: ...at the start of the programme I was in a lot of emotional turmoil based on my circumstances. I wasn't playing the role of helping to facilitate the resolution of the drama; I was actually contributing to the drama.

During the programme, participants found that increased awareness resulted in increased psychological state management. They no longer allowed external circumstances to constantly impact on their states, and, as a result, found themselves more stable, which resulted in less stress and more open engagement in constructive communication. This affected their leadership effectiveness, as they were better able to contribute to the team delivery.

Hannah on psychological state management: How it improved my effectiveness is that if I'm going to allow external circumstances to constantly impact the space that I'm in, then it impacts on my ability to deliver. Now I'm at a point where I can play a facilitation role and positively contribute rather than being amidst all of it myself.

More specifically, participants committed to more empowering psychological states such as a positive regard for others, consistency, self-belief, transparency, and trust.

Andrea on positive regard for the potential of others: I think just letting them do what they need to do, relying on them, trusting them – as well as their potential – allowed them to grow; to see things from their view and know that there's no right or wrong answer, that if they put a logical case forward they can do whatever they want to do. I think it's helped them grow in their own self-belief.

Hannah on consistency: I can be more consistent, regardless of what's happening around me, so it improves my productivity.

Dobek on transparency: I think from that point of view, being more open, being able to discuss things more easily has obviously helped the team to move forward as well.

Hannah on trust: Well, I think the reality is that you cannot deliver anything on your own, you deliver through people. Improved trust results in improved delivery because you've got more commitment and buy-in from the people that need to deliver on it.

Gugu on trust: The first contribution is the fact that I'm still here. As you know, one of my biggest issues was around trust. There's more trust, the communication lines have opened up extensively.

In terms of trust, they had realised that they could not deliver anything on their own; they needed to deliver through others. Improved trust results in improved delivery because there is more buy-in from others when there is a relationship of trust.

Effect of development of interpersonal AL on individual leadership effectiveness

Feedback on the effect of enhancing interpersonal AL on individual leadership effectiveness required the ALD3 process to reflect AL self-regulation in behaviour.

ALD3: **Reflection in behaviour:** Participants found that whilst they had previously been following limiting role models, micromanaging, and engaging in selective relationship-building, during the programme their individual leadership effectiveness had increased. Whilst they demonstrated their trust in others by giving them space, they held them accountable and expected them to do their jobs well. This allowed them to attend to their own deliverables, and, in the case of the leader, this meant that he could focus on strategy and give thought to longer-term sustainability.

> *Liam on giving others space: By allowing people space, by demonstrating trust in doing that, I did put a lot of accountability on them. That helped me as a leader because it implies that they will do their jobs better. It also gave me a little more time for myself to be able to be more strategic, to sit down, to think about longer-term sustainability and those type of things.*

The leaders started focusing on relationship-building, allowing interactions to move beyond the transactional. This resulted in some leaders moving from an autocratic to a coaching style of interpersonal communication, an empowering leadership that involved listening to others and encouraging them to think creatively. Conversations moved from simply *what* needed to be done, to *how* to get things done effectively, and then allowing others to execute. This resulted not only in better vertical leadership, but also in improved lateral leadership, as participants started to contribute more towards the development of an effective leadership team.

> *Vanya on building better relationships: It's allowed me to build better relationships with individuals that are also on a journey towards improving themselves, and that definitely has resulted in effective teamwork. Particularly the one subordinate; before I didn't trust him in terms of delivering and I was very autocratic in my approach. I would tell him what to do; whereas now we've gone through a process where I ask and hear type of approach. I see him thinking outside the box now.*

Effect of development of organisational AL on individual leadership effectiveness

In terms of the effect of development of cognitive organisational AL on individual leadership effectiveness, participants focused more on the reflecting their AL Compass in their behaviour.

ALD3: **Reflection in behaviour:** Participants referred to the effect of an appropriate situational leadership style, and their ability to deliver. Because of their increased self-awareness, they realised that there was no one-fit-for-all leadership style, and that they needed to be cognisant of the individuality of others in terms of how best to lead. They realised that they always needed to focus on three guidelines. Following is how Justin explained it to me.

> ***Justin on the ability to deliver:*** *So 1) is certainly around delivery and delivering on the mandate that you've got to deliver for the business. 2) is becoming more effective in the contribution to the team and the development of the team and the brewery. 3) is becoming a better leader and becoming a better example so your people take your example and they run with it. It's not just about yourself and your delivery, it's what you can do for the team and develop the team as a whole.*

Their focus had to be what they could contribute to the systems of which they were a part. The initial and current self-ratings, shown in the following table and figure, were done subjectively, during the participant leaders' post-programme interview, based on what they understood at that time as their potential performance effectiveness, ranging from 0% (no effectiveness) to 100% (performing at full potential effectiveness). The P01 – P10 indicated the participant numbers. The darker bars highlight their initial performance ratings, and the lighter stacked bars their percentage shifts during the programme.

	P01	P02	P03	P04	P05	P06	P07	P08	P09	P10	Ave Team % Shift
Performance ratings											
Original performance %	40.00	40.00	60.00	50.00	70.00	30.00	40.00	45.00	50.00	65.00	49.99
Current performance %	77.50	70.00	77.50	70.00	75.00	60.00	77.50	70.00	80.00	82.50	74.00
% shift to current performance	37.50	30.00	17.50	20.00	5.00	30.00	37.50	25.00	30.00	17.50	25.00

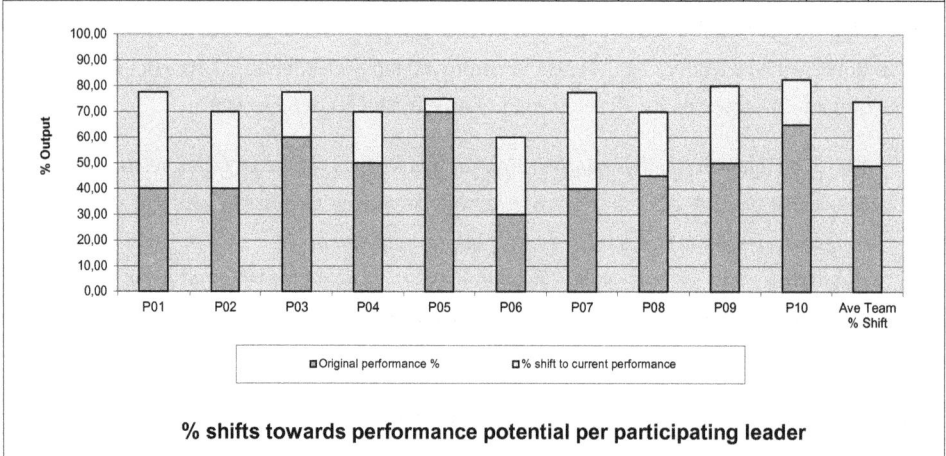

Figure 21. Percentage shifts towards potential performance effectiveness.

The table and graph above indicate that, in terms of their self-perceived potential performance effectiveness, the team had increased their individual performance effectiveness, on average by 25%, from just below 50% to almost 75%.

*Vanya on experiencing growth: I think I was about **40%** effective in terms of my ability. Right now, I'd say overall about **75 – 80%** and there's so much more. I see that potential and I see that ability. I see how time management is so important, how communication and being effective in terms of communication is so important. It's a process I need to go through and I really don't want to get lost. I need to constantly realise that it's a process and eventually I will get to 99.99% effective.*

Participant leaders understood that developing leadership authenticity was a journey, and expressed a desire to continue that journey of self-growth.

Link between AL, inter-relational trust, and individual leadership effectiveness

The majority of participants agreed that the enhancement of AL allowed for the enhancement of inter-relational trust, and together, these were antecedents in the enhancement of individual leadership effectiveness.

Peter on the effect of enhancing AL and inter-relational trust: It's much better for generating ideas. People are not reticent; they're open to put their stuff on the table. It also fosters a better wellbeing in people because they feel that they can share their problems – it might not even be work stuff – they can be nurtured by the team.

Gugu on the importance of trust: I think the basis for most interactions is trust. Be it a marriage, be it a relationship, be it a supplier and a customer type contract, the basis is trust.

Vanya on the importance of being true and inspirational on business results: Authentic leadership is about being true and being able to inspire people in your approach and your trueness to yourself. Inter-relational trust is about trusting one another and helping each other to deliver. If you have both you'll be able to help and support one another in driving the business KPIs.

Liam on the effect of being true and trustworthy, on leader effectiveness: When you're true to yourself, when people know who you are, when people know how you will behave, how you will respond, and therefore you create that trust, you do become a lot more effective as a leader.

Andrea on the effect of having trust, on leader effectiveness: I think if you have that trust, you're just more effective. You do things openly and just without hidden agendas, people are not second-guessing you, you're just so much more effective as a team, you're all focused on the same thing, you know why you're doing it, you know why you're driving it.

The afore-mentioned findings confirm the fact that an AL programme such as this one has the ability not only to enhance leadership authenticity, but also intrapersonal and interpersonal trust, and individual leadership effectiveness.

FURTHER PROGRAMME EFFECT ON TEAM AUTHENTIC LEADERSHIP EFFECTIVENESS

In terms of the positive effect of increasing AL on team ALE, the feedback pertains both to general team effectiveness and, more specifically, to the five levels of team effectiveness. Team ALE had increased in the team, and this was mainly due to an increase in their individual AL, and the symbiotic relationship between the enhancement of AL and inter-relational trust, and individual leadership effectiveness and team leadership effectiveness, as illustrated in the following figure.

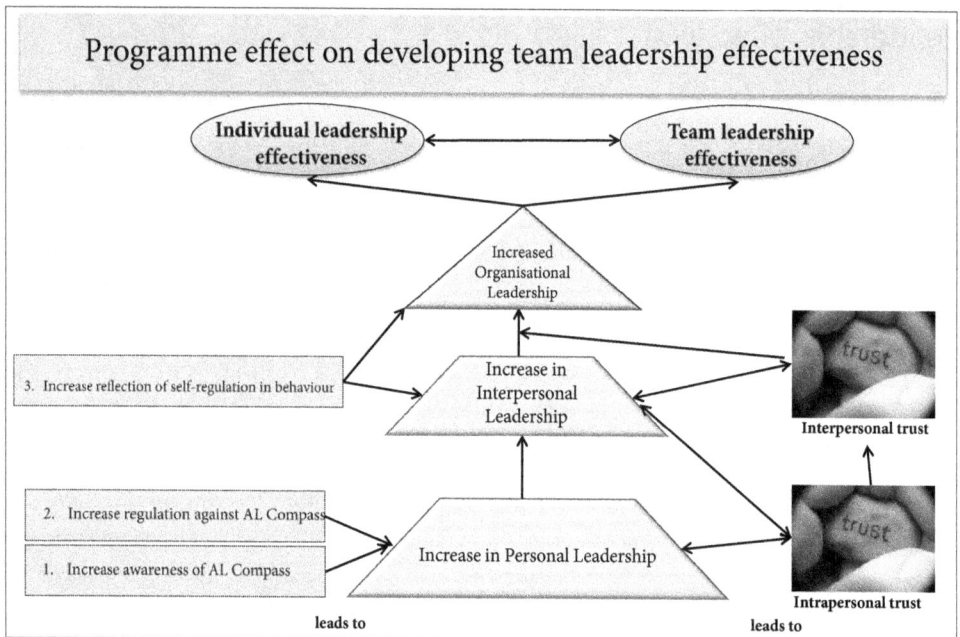

Figure 22. Programme effect on developing team leadership effectiveness

In terms of team ineffectiveness, leaders commented that previously, as in the case of the individuals themselves, there was a lack of awareness and self-regulation, especially in state management, which reflected in the team's behaviour. The team members were in a state of denial about their negative interpersonal dynamics, and issues were not being resolved. According to their leader, they were all bright and intelligent people who were operating on their own. They did not trust one another or ask one another for help, and they did not obtain input from others on difficult issues. They focused only on their own performance, rather than that of the team, which is often the root cause for ineffective teams.

Liam on lack of trust: I think we've said that a number of times during the course of the intervention that most of them are very bright, intelligent people but they operated on their own. They didn't trust each other to get into their areas, they didn't ask for help, they didn't put difficult issues on the table to get other people's reviews and opinions, and as long as their side was okay, they were okay. They weren't as worried about the total performance as a team, rather about their individual performance.

Effect in terms of general team effectiveness

In terms of general team effectiveness, the participants commented after the programme that continuous introspection allowed them to develop interpersonal awareness, which resulted in the building of camaraderie and the ability to confront issues together, as a team.

Justin on the effect of confronting issues together: By us all going through the programme and being forced to confront the issues together, both on a personal and a team level, it helped us to get closer. I think that builds team camaraderie and it develops a team together a lot quicker.

Increasing individual self-regulation, together with acquiring coaching skills, allowed them to increase state management, and embrace psychological states such as openness and sharing, and self-accountability. Specifically in terms of self-accountability in the case of emotional dynamics, they learnt to make a clear distinction between what was theirs to deal with and what was not, by not confusing their own issues with those of others. This reduced dynamics such as unnecessary personalisation, as they learnt to focus on facts during conversations.

In terms of reflecting self-regulation in their behaviour, there was a more open channel in terms of communication. For instance, participants were more willing to ask for help, and people with different strengths were more prepared to help others who did not necessarily have the same strengths. This allowed the team of smart individuals to transform to an effective team as a whole. They started to develop a team identity and a common vision, working towards a common goal.

Nikhil on openness and sharing: I think each team member acknowledges what their limitations are and by doing so, they actually solicit help. The dynamic I see is that where certain individuals are strong, and in the past they could help and they just stayed back while other team members struggled and trudged along, there's now that open channel in terms of communication, assistance, getting stuck in there, asking the guys to move up if they're actually slow, those sort of things.

Hannah on self-accountability: ...when you get to the point where you say "Okay, these are my issues and those are his issues" then you can have a conversation.

Nikhil on team identity and common vision: ...from a team perspective, it forced us to reduce that time span from forming, storming, norming and performing. Getting to know yourself, getting to know your colleagues, getting to your team, developing that team identity, that common vision so that we all are rowing in the same direction.

The majority of those close to the team responded that, with a few exceptions, the development of leadership authenticity had had a positive impact on leadership team effectiveness. Whilst little positive lateral or vertical impact had been noticed in leadership effectiveness on Peter, the programme had clearly had a positive important on Gugu's leadership effectiveness. Her subordinates had noticed that she was influencing the team more positively, making goals clearer, and driving accountability at all levels. As a result, her team was more positive as they believed in her as a leader. Her peers commented that she had brought a new standard to the team and that she challenged those peers who did not live up to that standard. Her senior commented that there was less conflict between her and her peers, and between the leader and her senior, as this had previously had a negative impact on the team. She was more aware and committed to the team and more prepared to be vulnerable and ask for help.

Effect in terms of five levels of team effectiveness

In terms of the five levels of team effectiveness, I focused on the shifts in the levels of trust, healthy conflict, commitment, accountability, and a focus on results in the team. I realised that the five levels of team ALE could be linked to psychological state management, which forms part of regulating one's internal AL Compass. Leaders commented on the positive effect of leadership authenticity on team leadership effectiveness, and were able to make further suggestions for enhancing leadership effectiveness within their team.

Team ALE Level 1: **Inter-relational trust within the team.** Participants felt that previously there was a lack of trust within the executive leadership team, not only laterally, but also vertically between the executive team members and their reporting teams, and as a result, no one would ever be completely honest with the executive leadership team.

> *Andrea on previous lack of trust: Due to the dynamics within the exec leadership team, trust was broken not only between our team members themselves, but also between those under the exec team, and the exec team itself. No one would ever be completely honest with the exec team.*

During the programme, leaders developed more self-trust and were more open with one another. This resulted in a further willingness to put issues on the table so that they could engage in healthy conflict in order to reach favourable solutions, allowing for the development of inter-relational trust. The team became more cohesive, trustworthy, and more open in their discussions.

> *Liam on the effect of increased openness: I think the fact that we're more open, that we've created this inter-relational trust and I suppose personal trust in our own abilities, the team feels a lot more comfortable as a unit. So you trust each other, and when you start trusting each other you're quite happy to put difficult issues on the table, you're quite happy to create that little bit of conflict and utilise the conflict to come to better solutions.*

Developing trust was the first step towards getting everyone co-operate effectively as a team. Suggestions for increasing inter-relational trust and team effectiveness indicated that participants now understood leadership authenticity. They wanted less corporate politics and rumour mongering, fewer unmet commitments, less avoidance of contentious issues, and more respect and tolerance for diverse opinions. In terms of increased lateral leadership, they also encouraged more openness and a willingness to engage in healthy and constructive feedback and disagreements; they wanted to develop more peer-to-peer accountability, and increase their focus on achieving results.

Team ALE Level 2: **Healthy conflict within the team.** Leaders felt that previously the team did engage in conflict, but that it was usually negative. Because of not trusting one another, they did not ask for help or discuss difficult issues in order to obtain others' views.

> **Liam on effect of previous lack of trust:** *They didn't trust each other to get into their areas, they didn't ask for help, they didn't put difficult issues on the table to get other people's views and opinions, and as long as their side was okay, they were okay.*

During the programme, they experienced the development of healthy conflict. This meant that they could say their say about issues, and have individual key performance indicators (KPIs) but in the end, they could agree on what needed to be achieved as a team.

> **Dobek on developing healthy conflict:** *Yes, you don't accept it and say "Okay, now I'm going to just go and do it because I was told to do it" type of thing. If you believe it's wrong you can have your say but at the end of the day then you must go and do what the collective says. We all agreed to that. Even if we don't agree, at the end of the day that's the decision, we go and we do it.*

> **Gugu on developing healthy conflict:** *...now for me conflict back then was a leader throwing hissy fits. Conflict now is about two members having opposing KPIs that have got to do with the business and we've got to chase both of them, so how do we do it.*

Suggestions for further development of embracing healthy conflict in order to increase team effectiveness also referred to increasing inter-relational trust; in addition, they mentioned more listening, more speaking up when necessary, and more courageous discussions with dignity and respect, backed up by facts that support it.

Team ALE Level 3: **Commitment within the team.** Leaders felt that previously, there was a lack of commitment in the team. For instance, there was an issue with follow-through as issues would be agreed upon in one meeting, to be completed before the next, but this would often not happen.

> **Liam on previous lack of commitment:** *What was not working in the team was lateral leadership: What needed to be discussed in the boardroom and what not? There was also a problem with follow-through, for instance, when things were committed to in one meeting, to be completed before the next, this did not happen.*

Although they were still on a journey, during the programme participants experienced increased team commitment as they started to feel part of their team.

> **Liam on developing commitment:** *I suppose it's still a journey for us, but we have created the environment where people feel comfortable. People feel they're part of the leadership team of the brewery and that they're actually contributing and not just puppets on a string; they're actually part of the team; they have an influence. There's no doubt in my mind that the team is a lot more effective than it was six months ago.*

Suggestions for further development towards increased team ALE included elements such as fewer individual egos and silo-mentalities, and less fear, frustration, and blaming one another for non-delivery; instead, to focus on increased trust-building, peer-to-peer accountability, and living the common vision.

Team ALE Level 4: **Accountability within the team.** Leaders felt that previously, there was a lack of self- and peer-to-peer accountability in the team. Accountability was inauthentic as it was forced on team members by the leader.

> **Nikhil on lack of authentic accountability:** *It's non-authentic accountability, if I can phrase it that way. It's forced on the individuals, not people taking the thing as "I own this thing and I've got to do something with it."*

During the programme, participants experienced increased accountability, and the team ALEC that they had developed, which included their team scorecard, underpinned by a belief structure and value system, had helped them to establish the individual accountability that they wished to have in place. Now, having peer-to-peer accountability discussions no longer needed to be personal, as they could have them against the charter that they had all helped to develop.

> **Justin on developing accountability:** *We collated a charter to say going forward this is how we're going to behave and this is how we believe the team needs to behave. When we now criticise somebody, we criticise them against the charter. It doesn't become something that becomes personal; it becomes something that you can use as a tool to drive accountability, to drive behaviour, to drive the way we want to lead and go forward. It's something that's very real.*

Suggestions for further development of accountability towards increased team effectiveness included less defensiveness and negativity and fewer individual agendas, and more of what had already been mentioned in prior discussions on team ALE.

Team ALE Level 5: **Focus on results.** Participants felt that previously, because of not resolving issues due to the negative state that the team was in, there was an inattention to results.

> *Gugu on previous inattention to results: Our team was in this negative state, It wasn't actually resolving issues. Sure, there were some high results but if you look, for example we had a hundred numbers in the air, some were doing okay, some not...*

In contrast, during the programme, participants experienced increased focus on results, and one of the biggest contributors to this was the change in the behaviour of Liam, their leader, who shifted his focus on what the team needed to do, rather than how ineffective the team was being.

> *Gugu on increased focus on results: With moving into the positive state, we're spending less time trying to resolve all these negative things. Now instead of Liam blowing his top for 30 minutes in a meeting about poor performance and how ineffective – you know, and all of that drama, it's now about "Okay, in terms of beer loss, what are we going to do, in terms of UFE what are we going to do." Now we're talking about actual business drivers versus emotional drama and tantrums.*

Participants stressed the importance of the leader going first, and even Peter, who often clashed with Liam, admitted that Liam tried hard to change his stance and become more authentic in his interactions with others. Liam became a role model for other team members like Vanya, who also started to trust their reporting teams and gave them more authority to make their own decisions.

> *Vanya on importance of leader going first: I've changed a lot in giving him [subordinate] more room, in giving him more advice and allowing him to make decisions rather than me making the decisions for him. That's changed my whole way of operating.*

This confirmed findings about the effect of developing AL on team ALE, and the importance of the leader as a positive role model in team leadership effectiveness. Suggestions for further development of an increased focus on achieving results included those highlighted in the prior discussion on team ALE levels. An additional suggestion was that team members needed to have less of a focus on their departmental outcomes and actions, and have a more focused approach on contributing to the whole team, and therefore the organisation's KPIs.

Link between AL, inter-relational trust, individual and team ALE

Leaders once again stressed the importance of AL as the foundation for team ALE as it allows one to understand one's own unique contribution to the team. Furthermore, when there is an issue, one can raise it as a concern and discuss it.

> *Justin on being real: I think authenticity is not political and you don't do things for a motive for getting your point across. You must be genuine and real and if you've got an issue, raise it as an issue, raise it as a concern and let's talk it through, let's have the discussion.*

When asked specifically about leadership authenticity and trust with reference to team ALE, leaders commented on the positive impact that these had had on enhancing team ALE. One of the most important considerations was the fact that most of the individual programme coaching sessions had been completed before the team sessions commenced, which meant that individual AL had been developed before commencing with further development of the team ALE. Leaders realised that no one had previously done continuous introspection; they did not know themselves well enough, and had the programme commenced with the team sessions, these would have been, in their words a, "bloodbath", "carnage", "fighting match", "blow out", or "a disaster".

> *Darren on individual development preceding team development: Phew. If you had done the team workshops first it would've been an absolute disaster – no one really knew themselves well enough. If they hadn't done that you would've had carnage. In fact the day wouldn't have happened, that I can guarantee you. Because there was no introspection of ourselves, of each other, of what we think, how this team is put together. Prepare the soil first, before sowing the seed.*

The development of leadership authenticity during the individual sessions had prepared participants for the team sessions. Fixing the team needs to start with working with the individuals. In addition, not everyone worked at the same speed, or had the same level of EQ, so the individual sessions had to allow for individual development before proceeding with team development.

> *Peter on individual development preceding team development: You had to do the individual sessions first. It was vitally important. I think we would've all been lost if you just dived into it in a group session, especially around emotional things, I'm not the sharpest chisel in the emotional toolbox (chuckles). You needed to draw that out with me. You needed individual approaches there.*

> *Hannah on individual development preceding team development: I think that's probably for me the most powerful thing in the process – Going through the individual first and then going into the team environment because you are an individual within a team and you can't fix a team without starting with the individual.*

> *Justin on individual development preceding team development: I think it would've turned out to be a fighting match around it. It would've been driven by emotions rather than the understanding of where we're from, there would've been a lot of egos and arrogance at play. I think there would've been a lot of finger pointing instead of reflection. It would've been "You are doing this", instead of "Well, you're doing that maybe because I did this" and I think that's important to understand.*

The development of AL therefore needed to precede the development of trust, individual and team leadership effectiveness, so that individuals would be more open, more self-aware, and better prepared to deal with feedback from others or with any potential conflict that could arise. Inter-relational trust, in turn, was the non-negotiable foundation of building a 'we' culture in the team.

Gugu on individual development preceding team development: We needed to prime each vessel before we loaded all of them onto the ship. And we needed to make sure that while they were primed, they were not primed with explosives because I think we were all vessels of torrid emotions, all of us. Now to try and take all of those people and put them into a room, that would've been a recipe for an explosion. We're trying to build a system and you needed to fix each component before you put the whole system together.

Liam on individual development preceding team development: It probably would've turned into a blow out. People wouldn't have been able to deal with the feedback, to absorb it and just handle the conflict that would have been in the room. I think they were just so much better prepared for it. Also at the same time, the process gave them some time to think about some of their ideas and views about people, and is that entirely true? Whereas if you just walked into it, all of that baggage would've just landed on the table, it would've been a disaster.

Andrea *on individual development preceding team development: I think you wouldn't have had the amount of openness, I think you would've got a lot more defensiveness, in terms of … I'm here, I'm great in the team – the rest of you are idiots.*

Peter on the importance of inter-relational trust: It fosters very much a 'we' culture which is quite powerful, "We can do this."

Once they had trust in the team, they could have open conversations, knowing that they were able to disagree if they had to. This allowed them to work towards a collective outcome, allowing the team to become more effective because they could reach better solutions. They could also identify better actions in order to achieve those solutions, as everyone was by now co-operating.

Andrea on the importance of trust and healthy disagreements: In terms of findings solutions, it's challenging. If that trust isn't there, you're not going to say you disagree with someone, you're just going to say nothing and do your own thing. Trust helps the team to be more effective because you get better solutions, and you ultimately get better actions, because everybody is pulling together.

Hannah on the importance of trust and healthy disagreements: …you have to have trust to have open conversations, or to be able to disagree, or to put a different perspective on the table. We are all individuals and to work as a collective it takes a give and take, so you have to have conversations to get to a point of give and take. You can't work as a team if you're not working towards a collective outcome. You can't work towards a collective outcome if you can't develop a collective outcome.

In terms of commitment within the team, the fact that individual team members could acknowledge their limitations, and that communication had improved, meant that they could solicit help, and others with the requisite strengths could assist them in achieving the team's objectives.

Nikhil on the importance of commitment: I think each team member acknowledges what their limitations are and by doing so, they actually solicit help. The dynamic I see is that where certain individuals are strong, and in the past they could help and they just stayed back while other team members struggled along and trudged along, there's that open channel in terms of communication, assistance, getting stuck in there, asking the guys to move up if they're actually slow, those sort of things. There's that open communication for me, so I think that dynamic has changed quite a bit whereas in the past like everybody was so in their own corner and they're protecting their turf...

In addition, by holding each other accountable when the expected actions have not been taken by those responsible for them, trust was maintained, and support offered where necessary.

My question to Hannah on team members holding one another accountable: ...how do you ensure that that outcome happens? Hannah: By holding each other accountable. The reality is that as a team – if I don't say "I've got a certain expectation and you don't deliver", I don't feel free to say to you "You have let me down" and hold you accountable for the fact that you haven't done it, then I suppose that ultimately breaks trust and it ultimately then again moves back to being individuals rather than a team. It is about peer-to-peer, not only accountability, but support as well.

Andrea on the importance of peer-to-peer accountability: That helps the team to be more effective because you get better solutions, and you get better actions at the end of it, because if people see that you're not pulling your weight they'll say that. That is peer accountability where I think people will be open from a solution point of view and from a, 'you're not doing your part', to actually talk about it; whether that's on a one-on-one basis or in a group.

This process helped the team to focus on the results that needed to be achieved, allowing for increased team ALE. Participants confirmed the importance of becoming a more cohesive team, whereas, before, they were simply a number of smart individuals, some of who were new to the team. Developing AL not only increased individual leadership effectiveness, but also team leadership effectiveness. The inverse had also occurred because as the executive leadership team had become more effective, the individual members had become more effective as leaders to their own reporting teams.

Dobek on the reciprocal link between team and individual leadership effectiveness: Whereas before we were almost – well, we were a lot of individuals – and in particular with the new people. I think that shift has translated into myself being more effective because of needing to work as a team rather than an individual. Definitely, now I feel more comfortable with sharing things, almost leading or directing things. The team effectiveness has led to more effectiveness in me. Because of that team, I think I'm more effective within my own team.

The aforementioned findings indicate that by participating in this AL programme, a previously toxic leadership team experienced a considerable effect on the development of their individual leadership authenticity. This further led to an enhancement of their trust in self, followed by the enhancement of inter-relational trust and individual and team leadership effectiveness. There is a definite link between the development of AL, inter-relational trust, and individual and team AL effectiveness, and this link is two-dimensional in a development process that is iterative.

CONCLUSION

This chapter focused on a real-life case study with an executive leadership team that had previously experienced toxic interpersonal dynamics, which had an adverse affect on their individual and team effectiveness. The findings indicated that during their participation in this individual and team ALE programme, most team members, both individually and collectively, enhanced their ALE.

A year after the leadership team had completed their individual and team ALE journey, I interviewed each leader again to establish how well they had sustained their ALE, and the feedback was encouraging. Since then, one leader, close to retirement at the time, had since retired. The two participants who had shown low leader developmental readiness had been moved out of their positions, into less strategic positions. One participant was still in his leadership position, and the remaining six participants had all been promoted into more senior and influential positions, either within their own organisations or in different organisations. Four years later, I still hear from time to time how they are guided by their internal AL Compasses.

In the following chapter, I discuss three further case studies, one of which refers more specifically to the return on investment in participating in this programme, and the positive effect of developing ALE on the business results of an organisation.

PERSONAL REFLECTIONS: AUTHENTIC LEADERSHIP CASE STUDY

What stands out for you in this case study regarding:

1. The requirements for developing individual AL,
2. The requirements for developing trust in self and interpersonal trust between self and others,
3. The requirements for developing individual ALE,
4. The requirements for developing team ALE?

Chapter 9

AUTHENTIC LEADERSHIP PROGRAMME EFFECT – HIGH-LEVEL CASE STUDIES

This chapter focuses on three high-level case studies. Each case study has a different focus on the effects of development of authentic leadership. These case studies took place in various different breweries that form part of an international beverage organisation.

The first case study focuses on the initial development of AL within only the leader of an executive team, followed by the collective authentic leadership development of his executive team as a whole, and the impact thereof on trust, individual and team leadership effectiveness, and very importantly, the business results of the brewery. The second case study focuses on an individual leader that participated in the individual and team AL programme, and her initial challenges with the notion that authentic leadership and political acumen are dialectically opposed. It explores how she eventually found a way of marrying the two constructs, and in doing so, enhanced her leadership effectiveness considerably.

Finally, the third case study explores ALE sustainability, and considers suggestions from the field for sustaining individual and team ALE, especially when the team undergoes changes. In the example offered, the team lost its leader who was promoted. Not only did the leader need to consider how to sustain his individual ALE in his new context, his original team collectively had to do the same, by incorporating their new leader into their ALE way of work.

CASE STUDY 1: EFFECT OF AUTHENTIC LEADERSHIP EFFECTIVENESS ON BUSINESS RESULTS

In 2014, this general manager, identified as John, embarked on my individual and team ALE programme. John personally contracted for individual ALE development as he was experiencing leadership challenges. Halfway through the programme he included his team, and we had a further three two-day team sessions to develop team ALE.

The following is the interview I had with John a little over two years later, which highlights the increase not only in his individual ALE, but also in that of his executive team as a whole. It further highlights the considerable return on investment that his organisation experienced because of the work that was done during this individual and collective ALE journey. When John initially approached me his organisation's balanced scorecard targets were mostly in the red, and a year later, almost all of their stretch targets were reflected in green. John was promoted within a year after that.

Question 1: What made you decide to embark on the individual and team ALE programme?

John: At a stage, I had a sense that specifically in my business unit, I was becoming harder and harder on the guys to achieve their numbers. For some reason we didn't really get momentum on the KPIs and the business performance. The team started to become more and more negative around numerous other peripheral issues. I didn't see it as critical but when my new director arrived from outside and he spent time with us, he said: there's something wrong here. The team's vibe is very negative. They don't react well to your leadership, John, and although you guys are really serious about doing better, your numbers are not getting better. They are all stagnant. I needed to do something. To first – from my own behaviour – take initiative and change things, and then get the whole organisation ultimately to follow. That is when I contacted you.

Question 2: In your opinion, how specifically did your participation in this leadership authenticity programme contribute to your development as an authentic leader?

John: I think initially it started off by me asking what were the current things in my leadership style that were not effective – not getting my team and the organisation to be at their full potential. As the journey progressed, I realised that there were things that I became aware of, which my team and other people didn't tell me. That specifically helped me to realise there's a next level of career growth and a next level of leadership involvement that I can step up to. Then even in terms of our career progression models – how we assess at what level of leadership one is – even when I then started to read through those models and descriptors of the career progression models I could suddenly start to spot – here are descriptors that I'm not living yet.

The key things that I have changed first is that I realised that at home, in my social life and in my sport life, I can actually be the full John. I can be authentic everywhere. I don't need to go to another type of persona to get results in a different part of my life. The full John is definitely one that stays competitive, stays results driven, but more specifically, that I needed to achieve that through other people by helping those people to first be recognised as whole persons, to live up to their full potential. I don't dictate and through negative pressure put guys on the spot; I actually help them to see their full potential. Through me caring for them and not harming them or just dictating to them, I get them to step up and see their full potential, both at home and at work. Realising that at the current level of leadership where I am, for me to still get the organisation to achieve good results, it's through getting people around me to move to their full potential and also become effective leaders. A lot of that is through removing limiting beliefs that I had of people; for instance, [I believed] that guys couldn't step up or they don't have the ability or they're not clever enough or they have the wrong values and those types of limiting beliefs.

Tineke: So you explored those limiting beliefs about others, and you reframed them and that helped you to empower your team members to work to the best of their ability. What did you realise about your internal identity?

*John: There was a time I would describe myself as **Thor** [metaphor], the guy that is really competitive, that really drives hard and gets what he wants but sometimes he can become destructive. Then I realised that my real authentic self is actually not that person. My real authentic self is actually a **Rhodesian Ridgeback dog** which is very tenacious and hard working, but also very loyal and wouldn't just, in a working group, become aggressive and become destructive. In those two pictures, I could describe most of my values that were actually sort of breached or not lived, before I made the transition to where I could actually live my values at work as well... This breed is very adaptive, and it is important to be adaptive. Things change in your environment – sometimes it is very warm and sometimes very cold, and sometimes you must work in a pack and sometimes you must work on your own. Then I can also be adaptive to that, so that I can respond to change.*

The other thing in my own way of dealing with people that I started to really change is that I realised that the way I would sometimes react to guys giving me untrue feedback, was not creating an environment of trust. One of my values is honesty so I wondered if I could work with this particular guy. I used my values of honesty to then just start to lock this guy out. Then I realised that if I created trust and I gave him the personal room to actually tell the truth then it was not an issue. An atmosphere of honesty whilst getting real relationships of trust going was also something I changed.

Question 3: In your opinion, how has this leadership authenticity programme contributed to your development of a) your trust in self, and b) your inter-relational trust with others? Starting with self?

John: Yes, first for me it is to have a healthy self-esteem again. The trust that I have the ability to be successful, that I have the ability to manage my responses and my emotions, that I have the ability to also balance what is happening at work and home, and that I also have the ability not to lose my temper. The moment when I started to trust myself with that and I felt good about myself, it was easier for me to feel good about others and to trust them. Then I could work on an atmosphere of honesty and I could have less negative discussions and thoughts and limiting beliefs about people.

Tineke: So what I'm hearing is that the fact that you became more authentic as a leader and you could have less limiting beliefs, allowed you to trust yourself and trust others. I'm just wondering if that had an impact again on you being able to be more authentic? The fact that you were able to trust others?

John: Because I could trust my team and they started to feel it and they could speak to me more openly, it was easier for me to be authentic in my leadership style with them. It was easier for them to start to develop, and when I gave them feedback on their development areas or blind spots, they really took it in a very positive manner. They didn't think – this is a way for John to humiliate me or just grind me ...they really got the feeling of – he's actually saying these things to me because he cares.

Question 4: In your opinion, a) how has this leadership authenticity programme, and the resultant development of trust, if any, contributed to your effectiveness as a leader? b) How does this compare to your effectiveness at the start of the programme in May 2014?

> *John: Yes, I think on the scales we would always use – from 0-10. I think in May after I became aware of the situation and my eyes opened to the realities I would probably give myself a 2 or a 3 out of 10. While when, sort of by March 2015, I would give myself a 7 or an 8, in that range. There are still things I would like to improve on. Even now in my new position and different challenges and new stress, there are again things I need to go back to and say – listen, let me not slip on this.*

Question 5: Since you've started the programme, explain how specific life or work events have helped you both to test and further develop yourself as an authentic leader, a) at work and b) elsewhere?

> *John: I think there was a specific time where our packaging hall also went through a dip and at that time, I could help my packaging manager to handle the change, to also reflect, to also travel a bit, and go see how other people do things. He became aware of his own shortcomings, and he suddenly started to step up as a leader. He started to realise that if he changed his style, if he changed the way he leads the pack that the results will actually come. I also gave him some space, that if it takes another one or two months before the numbers come, it's fine because he is doing the right things.*
>
> *There was a time when specifically the packaging results went through a dip and I could handle it in an authentic way, and from that, he became a stronger leader. I think the first part is that I kept a trust relationship between him and me. I didn't blame him, I didn't give him a feeling that if you don't get this right that this is all because of you. That trust relationship was created by me highlighting things to him but then giving him space and a bit of courage to try new ways of work. He responded very well and now he's one of the packaging managers that a couple of the other breweries are calling for and saying – can he come and work for them. The manufacturing director even asked at a stage: can he go to our biggest brewery and help those with their leadership styles there, as he also saw the changes in him.*
>
> *Tineke: What about outside work? Any event that you can think of, or situation where you really were tested in your leadership authenticity?*
>
> *John: At home, there were times where there was stress with the children, or there was stress with my wife also, struggling to adapt to a new city and not having many friends. In the past sometimes I would lock myself out of it and even become distant to those issues at home. Then I realised that if I become part of a solution, I help the family and I interact with them more. In the moment, I would give them emotional attention. For instance, I don't treat my phone as being more important than them by having it at the dining room table.*

Question 6: In your understanding now, what, if any, is the link between leadership authenticity, inter-relational trust, and individual and team leadership effectiveness?

> *John: I think the one thing that linked all of it for me in terms of the process, Tineke, was when I started to get the full view of my AL Compass. When I started to say – there is that personal leadership that I need to master first, then interpersonal leadership, the professional leadership that followed. How my values and beliefs need to be empowering, not limiting. That framework helped me to stay an authentic leader, and not only at work, but also at home and social and sport life. That's what gave me the frame or the link between all the other things – ensuring that my team still trusts me, ensuring that on the professional side there is growth, in the business results, and on the personal side. That, for me, was what linked everything.*

Question 7: In your opinion, how specifically did individual leadership authenticity development in this programme affect the effectiveness specifically of your leadership team?

> *John: The one thing that happened in the team, is that they started to see me interacting and working in a new way. They became very curious – John, how did you achieve this? How could you now handle some difficult situations in this nicer manner when in the past it would be one massive explosion? My team became curious, and approached me, asking me 'what are you doing? Who's this person you're working with? What are the concepts?' About half of the team became curious and developed a need for also doing something, because they also had a desire to grow as leaders. They said that here we can see something working and we want to do this too. When we started to involve the team in the authentic leadership work, because they saw my seriousness, they had full belief in it and they were fully committed. The one or two guys in the team who were moving a bit slower and weren't that committed quite quickly stood out in our team discussions of progress on individual work.*

> *Tineke: That's interesting. Because that is what happens – as the team becomes more cohesive, those that aren't actually really playing the game – they do stand out.*

> *John: I never had to say – you're not doing your work, you're behind, you're not with us. Over coffee or social talk, guys were saying, 'I finished this, it was difficult'; or all of us are finishing off our work for the next ALE session, those who weren't really on it would start to feel uncomfortable. The one thing that helped the team was that they could see that I was really on it and they could see me changing, and they really trusted the process.*
>
> *The other thing is when we started as a team doing it; we made it our whole way of working and operating, having meetings and interacting with the whole brewery. It wasn't a separate project on the side. This is authentic leadership, and caring for people while you're getting good results was the way we worked; the way we ran meetings; the way we ran projects; the way we would interact with the people in the brewery when we walked around or when we went to functions. There was a*

massive realisation in the brewery that the culture in the brewery was changing. People are caring about each other, stopping and greeting again. When we started to ask people how did this thing start that they cared about each other again and they worked together in a more positive manner? All teams called out that it started with our leaders; within a two-month period, they could see how our leaders started to change. That's when my director said: in my brewery, the fish was rotting from the head, but now the fish is swimming from the head.

One of the things that the team started to do; if they saw somebody was struggling, without being asked by the organisation or by me, they started to go help that person and just cover for them. One of the best examples is my QA manager was really struggling to interact with his guys in the right way. Then my HR manager stepped in and became his personal coach. She volunteered to go to his meetings, gave him constant feedback and helped him to get to a position where he was just much more effective and he didn't become a detractor or a negative influence in his team. He had the ability to say – John, I'm not there. My guys aren't happy and the more I'm trying to lead them in a positive manner the less it's working. My HR manager actually made a massive difference in the lab team and the quality team, which wasn't part of her responsibility.

Tineke: *I'm also thinking of times when your team members might have had challenges outside of work?*

John: *There were specific occasions when individuals had some issues at home with relationship or with health issues, and the team could say it was family and health first. Let's give you space to sort it out. As a team, we can cover for you. We can for two or three months make changes so that you don't feel that at work you are under full pressure and at home there are things that are quite difficult. Then, funnily enough, when they were given that freedom by the team to rather take the time to sort it out – in the end they didn't need that much time. They could quite quickly get the balance again and fix things at home as well as doing a full job at work.*

In the past, I wouldn't have reacted positively to it. I tried to ignore the family things. I would actually put more pressure on the guy at work to try and get him to focus at work, while I was fully aware that at home things weren't great and there were specific challenges.

Tineke: *What I find so interesting about this is that, think about yourself – you are very much a family man. Family is extremely important to you, so it is an espoused value but you're saying in the past it wouldn't have always been an enacted value.*

John: *Yes. It is still one of my core values, but I would for some funny reason ignore it at work. I would block it out; I would not live it.*

Tineke: *What was it in those team workshops that helped your team to become more authentic?*

John: *The workshops were structured in such a way that we could on a couple of themes and topics, quickly get the whole group to understand it in the same way. Then from there describe the actual behaviours and the things we will do on a continuous basis that will help us to stick with it when we leave the room. That part of being able as a team to say, 'but listen, what will be the physical things* *we do, how would we physically live this, what would be on the agenda, how would we interact with other people?' Saying that there would in the end be actual behaviour that we change, and the team being able to describe that and also document it for the team afterwards to call each other back to that type of behaviours.*

Tineke: *So that required your team ALEC?*

John: *The workshops – getting the full team understanding and buy in, and then the charter [team ALEC], that helped us to document it and then come back as a team in the next month or two to say: are we really doing it? That helped with it. I think the guys doing individual work between workshops also helped with keeping us together, keeping the guys true to the journey. Some guys even did the individual work after work time and did it at night or over weekends. That also made a big difference. It is not just team sessions and then we try it a bit. It's also: listen you need to do some more thinking on an individual basis. You need to submit some work on an individual basis. When the guys got stuck they would pop in HR's office or they would pop into my office and say: this thing is just too theoretical for me or it's a concept I don't understand. Just help me with this again. Then we could help the guys.*

Question 8: What do you believe about the importance of having preceded the team effectiveness workshops with the individual leadership authenticity coaching sessions?

John: *I think if you want to do some normal organisational effectiveness – how do you run meetings effectively, how do you set balanced scorecards – individuals or teams can do it without their leader and their team going through an authentic leadership journey. Everyone can learn how to coach and run meetings effectively. However, if you want a team to reinvent themselves or really move to a next level of leadership potential and really walk that authentic leadership journey, I think it would be very difficult for the whole team just to dive into it if they haven't seen some success and if the leader hasn't felt the success before they go. Because with my team – they saw it so a lot of them said: I also want to do it. Then when we were in it, because I know it works, that my belief in it and then my team's belief in it, was a definite success factor. I also think sometimes the whole team has a critical mass that is ready and they are mature and the whole team can start in one go.*

Question 9: In terms of the impact of developing individual and collective ALE, what effect did this have on your business results?

John: *I think apart from the results, the professional growth and becoming empowered for more senior positions, my whole team started to change. In our organisation we have a very structured system stating which guys are still growing in their current job and which guys are ready to move to bigger jobs, or more complex jobs even if it is on the same level but more complex. Initially, out of my team of nine people, none of them were actually covered for bigger jobs or other functions. About just over a year – eighteen months later, half of them were on cover lists for bigger jobs. Some* *of them also made the transition. Apart from the business results, my leaders also became guys that are sought after in the business and sought after even for higher level positions for bigger jobs.*

In terms of business results, I had a balanced scorecard in my business unit, with twelve key performance indicators in it where initially we struggled to get even three or four of the twelve performance indicators to green to meet the number. During the programme, we went through a period where eleven of the twelve were green. Then in the second half of the year, we set more stretch targets and then on year-end, eight of the twelve, even against the stretch targets, were green. It translated into the business unit doing very well, as well as my team and me getting very good performance feedback in our company's performance management system.

Question 10: In terms of ROI, how worthwhile was this ALE development investment?

*John: If you just look at financial results, the payback is within a month. Because some of the savings we started to generate on our financial KPI's are so big that the investment would just pay it back within one month. The return on investment in a pure financial sense is within a month. Although you do need to acknowledge that you need to put in three, four, five months of effort before a team starts to turn and the results start to follow. But no, the financial side of things, although corporate organisations are always scared to invest in it because there is a risk that it just may not work, that the financial side of it is something you need to ignore. **In just one of our usage variants KPI's, we saved 4 million Rand.** That's just one KPI. The return on investment is very quick. It's massive. It's much more than tenfold.*

The responses in this interview indicate the remarkable effect when a leadership team is willing to invest the financial and time resources to engage in an ALE programme such as this one. Not only does it allow leaders to develop individual and team ALE, but it also allows them to create an authentically effective organisational culture, where all are inspired by the perceived authenticity in the leadership team. Furthermore, an inspired and happy workforce leads to vastly improved business results, yielding a considerable return on the initial courageous decision made by the leader of the team, and on the financial, time and energy investment made by the leadership team. In fact, after the interview I realised that the afore-mentioned return on investment on that particular journey was much higher than tenfold.

CASE STUDY 2: DEVELOPMENT OF AUTHENTIC LEADERSHIP POLITICAL ACUMEN

In 2012, Vanya embarked on my individual and team ALE programme. She was moved from a specialist position to her current leadership position in 2014, where she inherited nine direct reports, and a team of about 70 members. In 2015, her team had the highest ratings out of six to seven teams in her brewery. One of her main challenges in her new position was organisational politics. In 2015, she contracted for additional individual ALE sessions. The following responses from Vanya during a conversational interview pertain to AL and political acumen, and it explores the difference between inauthentic and authentic leadership political acumen.

> *Tineke:* I would like to explore with you the relationship between authentic leadership and political acumen, also called political savvy. I'm specifically interested in that link. At face value anyone would think that these two constructs are diametrically opposed, meaning that they would never really sit side by side. In your case, endeavouring always to be very true to yourself with a strong moral underpinning in all that you do, you were initially very opposed to the idea of incorporating political acumen in your every day dealings. The closest you might have gotten to it in 2012 was to try put on, if you remember, a poker face during exec meetings while at times boiling inside.

Question 1: Please tell me more about your previous thoughts, as an authentic leader, on organisational politics, and on acquiring the skills of political acumen.

> *Vanya:* Yes, then I believed that you would move up in an organisation and you would be respected based on your performance and that one didn't have to brown-nose or have any political savvy – when I referred to political savvy at the time, I thought of it as political correctness.

> *Tineke:* What did that mean for you – political correctness?

> *Vanya:* Political correctness for me meant that you would not put the elephant on the table. That you would avoid the issues, avoid the conflict situations and rather keep quiet. I was absolutely against being politically correct because you did not highlight the real issues and move forward, and that was so not in my nature. I frowned upon political correctness, and I believed that performance was the only thing that mattered. The different levels in organisations do make you change the way you look at life and the way you look at political savvy. When you are at lower levels, you are protected from higher levels of management when they know you're a hard worker. They will not upset you and will let you perform, so you are allowed to behave a certain way or not have to be 'politically correct'.

Question 2: What are your thoughts now about the need even for authentic leaders to have some political acumen?

> *Tineke: Yes, I also want to add in that it seems that the higher the tree the more it catches the wind. You are in a more senior position now, so how possible is it to avoid organisational politics? What are your thoughts now about the need for authentic leaders to have political acumen?*

> *Vanya: Moving higher up in the organisation, there is less technical and less doing, and more strategy, and more interface with other people that are not always in critical jobs but have a lot to say. The time spent at strategic levels is more than the time spent with my team on the technical and the physical activities. It is quite energy sapping because it is something that I am not used to. I literally have to change the way I work with those people, compared to how I work with my own team.*

> *Firstly, for me to be able to survive the corporate world, for my team to be able to survive the corporate world and for us to be able to have more support than noise interference, I have to be the bigger person. I have to make sure that I choose the battles that are going to impact positively on my team. Even in choosing my battles, that I handle it in such a way that doesn't cause other people to resent my team or me. It's about being able to put things on the table in the right format, constructively for the right decisions to be made. It is very hard, so initially one has to really think about how it is going to be done. It is a journey that I am currently on, around developing that skill so that I get the outcome I want without any negative consequences. It is about fighting the battles that I want to fight, formulating a way of getting to the outcome without having unnecessary noise and negative impacts that are going to come back to my team or me.*

Question 3: In your opinion, what is the difference between non-authentic and authentic leadership political acumen? How can one have both authentic leadership and political acumen?

> *Vanya: So, non-authentic political acumen – I know of a particular individual senior to me that is exactly like that so I can actually speak about this person. This person is not authentic and I can see it because he changes his mind and his feelings and his opinions, and the way he does his work differently depending on the environment and the situation. I look at that and I frown upon the way that he has done that, because it is not authentic. If you had to compare to an authentic leader's political acumen, it is somebody whose **True North** is there and is able to manage a situation to the best of their ability by getting the effective results without affecting other people negatively.*

> *Tineke: Okay, so I define authentic leadership as being true to myself and being true to my leadership position, with a strong moral underpinning, for the greater good of all. If you use that definition and if you now look at political acumen of an authentic leader, how would that political acumen work?*

Vanya: That last part, 'for the greater good of all', that's when political acumen for me comes in. You might have the first three perfect, but for the greater good of all is where you actually now need to bring in the political acumen. It is being able to manage a situation that affects everybody positively. The **True North** leader is somebody who has the compass in the right direction, and is following that particular direction. But the compass has to be in the right direction so the underpinning beliefs, values and morals and ethics are in place. Having that in place, one is able to make decisions around how you manage a situation. That is the foundation. When I have to handle a situation that involves other people and conflicting views, thoughts or ideas, how do I ensure that I am still true to myself? I have to have the right values and ethics, the right beliefs whilst getting the output that I want to achieve.

Tineke: So you are really using that internal AL Compass – what I'm hearing therefore is that one can be an authentic leader and have political acumen – it's almost about being authentically strategic?

Vanya: One can be authentic in one's leadership and not move forward. Or one can be an authentic leader and move forward using political acumen.

Question 4: How has the adoption of political acumen helped you to increase your authentic leadership effectiveness? What work events have tested this?

Tineke: You have cottoned on to the fact that political acumen does not have to entail brown-nosing. How much has employing this political acumen increased your effectiveness?

Vanya: It is a fairly recent journey. I'm going to relate it to two separate examples of two individuals. The first example was this particular individual who was just creating unnecessary noise in my work space as well as in my team. It has changed now with the noise no longer there because I have changed my approach to him. Firstly, by having the courageous conversations with him, as that had to happen. It had to be put on the table between the two of us. The conversations were held where we each gave each other feedback around what we believed that the other person was doing. He gave me feedback, and I gave him feedback. We agreed that going forward that we would: 1) communicate better with each other and, 2) be able to call each other and ask for support. Yes, it was a bit rocky at the start after the agreement, but now I feel that we actually are doing what we have to do to work very well together. I don't think we will be friends, but it is about working together, and making sure that we achieve the outcomes that we want to achieve.

The second example around effectiveness is something that I am busy working on, and that is with the important senior I mentioned earlier. He feels that he can sway with the wind depending on situations and I need to be able to firstly give him feedback – tell him where I am from a space perspective, but in a nice way, and not in a condescending way! It's just to talk about my feelings and how his feedback impacts me. Then moving forward, the question would be: how do we move *forward and work things out? Again, it's going to require political savvy because previously I would have just said: this is the feedback and I don't believe in your feedback. Now it is about – this is how it makes me feel. And how do we work together going forward and make this work?*

Tineke: *How much of this political savvy that you're talking about, is actually really good and authentic strategic emotional and social intelligence? Emotional intelligence is awareness about self and also knowing how to manage one's emotions and behaviour, and social intelligence is awareness of others and the organisation, and managing those relationships. How much is political savvy just about knowing how to use your emotional intelligence and your social intelligence to be authentically effective as a leader?*

Vanya: *It is exactly that! It is combining those two. What I realised now versus the previous approach was that you are actually more respected when you have political savvy. More people want to hear what you have to say because before I was always the one putting the elephant on the table. It can become frustrating for other leaders where all they hear is the negative or the other side of the coin. Whereas now, when I do speak up, others now want to hear what I have to say. The less frequently you speak up, the more it becomes impactful and respected.*

Question 5: What remaining feedback or suggestions do you have?

Vanya: *I just think that working with leaders that are non-authentic makes one's life very difficult, and you have to be very strong to be able to deal with individuals like that. I've actually been put through a major challenge right now around dealing with people that are non-authentic, but they are in positional power and they impact me. It's a journey that I am on, and I have to continuously pull strength from my beliefs and what matters to me and what I want at the end of my journey, and using that to be able to manage situations. It is about being authentic to myself, and managing situations without damaging my relationships. How do you give somebody feedback when they are seen as favouring people? I know for a fact, that half the team feels the same way as me. Half my peers in the team feel exactly the same way!*

Wherever we find human beings, we will find politics, and it seems that the less authentic leaders are, the more they tend to use politics to further their own means. I found this interview very interesting, as it indicated that unless an organisation has a strong AL culture, the organisational dynamics could potentially be likened to a political minefield.

Therefore, whilst authentic leaders do not necessarily want to play politics, they do need to understand how to navigate through the political minefield in order to sustain individual ALE, for the benefit of their teams, and for those they serve as a whole. What this requires, is the employment of strategic emotional and social intelligence from the toolbox of an authentic leader.

CASE STUDY 3: HOW TO SUSTAIN INDIVIDUAL AND TEAM AUTHENTIC LEADERSHIP EFFECTIVENESS

Two years after John and his team commenced with the ALE journey, John was promoted to manage a larger brewery, and his original team received a new leader. The following responses from John pertain to the aspects of sustaining individual and collective ALE in times of change, with suggestions of how to ensure that ALE remains in place.

Question 1: How well have you managed to maintain your individual ALE since moving to your new and bigger brewery a few months ago?

> *John: I'm not happy. I think where on authentic leadership, I would give myself a 7 or an 8 out of 10 towards the end of my time at the previous brewery, I think I am at a 5 now. I definitely have work to do, and even as I talk today, I'm spotting things I need to become stronger on again. However, if I think of how I previously would enter a new business or go through change, I would typically arrive at the new business and be at a level of maximum 2, and in the first couple of months, really not be effective and be extremely stressed and anxious. I am at a 5 now, and I can within the next six to nine months progress to a 7 or 8 again. I'm just thinking how I can again involve more leaders, so it's not just a thing that I do and hope it rubs off, but how do I actually pass it on to other people again.*

> *Tineke: What I am hearing is that you have moved to a new environment. Everything is different. Your team is different. It is a bigger and more challenging brewery, and you have lost some of that effectiveness – for good reason. I'm also hearing that you have what you need in your ALE toolbox, to get yourself back on track again within the next six to nine months.*

> *John: Yes definitely! I can now spot where there are trust issues in the team. I can spot where there are negative dynamics, and I can actually write down what are the limiting beliefs I have about the people who are reporting to me, and start to change these to empowering beliefs. Those tools I still have. I still stretch my mind and I can apply them again.*

> *Tineke: So you have what you need in order for you to self-coach?*

> *John: Yes, and sometimes when I had a difficult session with the team, I do reflective journaling again. And asking someone for help, like my current HR lady – that still makes a difference. So self-coaching is better but I still enjoy, from time to time, talking to another person about it.*

Question 2: How well do you believe will your old team manage to retain their collective ALE?

> *John: I think it will go well. The team members believe in how they work, and they've started to pull the new general manager into that way of thinking and doing as well. When he realised how ready the team is to take up new challenges and do things differently, he started to help the team to be more focused on what's the new next level of high performance culture they want at the brewery;*

followed by describing the behaviours to support it – what they need to do to get to the next level. He was saying that he was very impressed at the maturity of the team and their ability to grasp the concepts quickly. That is currently rolling out as the next positive change in my previous brewery.

Question 3: What suggestions do you have to ensure that individual and collective authentic leadership effectiveness is sustained when all else changes? Starting with individual authentic leadership effectiveness?

John: *I think for an individual who has just moved to a different team, a different environment, is to go back to your individual AL Compass and ALEC. Read through it and share it with somebody that you trust, and use that person and the environment to keep you true to it. The concepts will come back and you will be able to use that. Get somebody that you can talk it through and say, this is what I want to do. These are the things that I have committed to. It will be good if you can be the mirror from time to time.*

John: *Then for teams, Tineke, I think it is more complex. Specifically in our organisation! Our corporate culture and our hierarchy in terms of how our leaders influence teams, is extremely strong. Leaders actually have immense power. If you get a very unhealthy and negative leader in a team, it can become very difficult for that team to sustain their authentic leadership behaviours under the leadership of that new leader because that leader really has a lot of power over that team in our organisation. The team can go through the team ALEC with the new leader and say: this is what we have committed to. Yes, we are going to update it because you are here, but we really believe it. If it is the right type of leader, I think he will be really influenced by that – like the new general manager is at my old brewery. But if the leader is on a total different page, there's still a very high risk that the team will derail again and go back to negative and old behaviours. I really think so.*

Tineke: *At what level should one ideally start? I'm just thinking now about the situation that we're talking about now. If you think about this, what would your advice be in terms of what level to pitch this kind of work so that one can create a sustainable authentic leadership culture?*

John: *You need to be able to spot at what level in an organisation are people still capable of changing culture and leadership style. When you get to that level, say: I shouldn't start below this because the guys above would just ruin it. Because of the different type of people that organisations recruit, you'll be able to see at what level do individuals have the capacity to filter what is coming from above. Then apply their own leadership style and culture on the organisation below them. So you can imagine, if a guy struggles to understand leadership concepts, he would also struggle to filter the culture coming from above and make it more positive in what he passes on to the people below him.*

Tineke: *I am just thinking now that authentic leadership is a leadership that goes beyond position in that it's a leadership by presence. I think because of whom you have become now, you've actually been able to have a positive relationship with your leader and, I'm sure, sometimes you can actually influence his way of thinking as well.*

John: Yes, there is some upward influencing. I think some leaders are more open to being influenced from below than others. I think in my case also, my director started to trust me. He started to lead me in a different way. Some of his autocratic and destructive behaviours and things that he would display when he came to the brewery really started to change. Because he realised that if the brewery is moving like that and he stuck to his old behaviours, then he may just get a very negative response from a bigger crowd of people.

Tineke: So, if you think about your organisation, at what level would you say is the right level to start?

John: I think GM level is the right level. I think in our organisation the brewery GMs do have the ability to filter the right amount of positive and negative things coming from above, and to still have a specific business unit culture. If your director is on it and he proposes it and he moves first, then it's obviously great. However, I do think individual GMs can also make a difference.

Question 4: Any remaining feedback or suggestions?

John: To know who is on the journey and who is not when you are a bigger group of people, is a very important factor, and we must perhaps get more structure in terms of that. For instance, with the previous leadership team – to quickly involve their reporting teams in their behaviours, and to involve them so that their teams are also more aware that this thing is happening, because I sort of halfway through January realised that half the previous leadership team told their teams about the journey, and the other half not. They never stood up in front of their team and said, this is what I am doing. It's not that their teams need to be with them on the journey, but their teams need to be aware.

Then I think the way you, Tineke, are doing it, by really being real with your feelings and to say you want to do this journey to help people to live their full potential – that thing is very different to some of the other programmes I have been on. I have, through one of our business schools, also had a coach and the coach was just so superficial and plastic that I said to the coordinator that I am not going to continue. Because it was just a coach doing it for the money and just saying that I have four sessions of 45 minutes – let me get through it. At stages when I had my sessions I realised that the real care and interest in the other person that is sitting on the other side of the table was just not there. Therefore, that care and real interest you have makes a huge difference.

In terms of what we can improve: I think we could do more coaching – getting more people to be excellent coaches. Even now when I think of the new brewery, I think it is one of the key things. It's having more leaders having the skill of real coaching. My boss calls it managing by agreement.

The journey of developing ALE is not a silver bullet, and it requires a considerable time and energy investment. It is extremely important to ensure that once the official programme has ended, that individuals and teams understand that they do have the tools to sustain this ALE. They need to make a concerted effort to ensure that they use these tools on a daily basis to sustain their ALE when all else changes. It is like staying fit; we stay fit by ensuring that we continue on a daily basis to do the exercises what we need to in order to stay fit. The interview with John indicated that this is possible. Good leadership can happen during business as usual, but extraordinary leadership is required during a storm, or when all else changes.

CONCLUSION

This chapter focused on three real-life case studies. Each case study had a slightly different focus on the positive effects of the development of ALE. The first case study focused on the initial development of ALE within only the leader of an executive team, followed by the collective ALE development of the team as a whole, and the positive effect thereof on trust, individual and leadership effectiveness, and very importantly, the business results of the brewery. The second case study focused on an individual leader who participated in the AL programme, and whose initial challenges were with the notion that authentic leadership and political acumen are dialectically opposed. It explored the way she eventually found a way of marrying the two constructs, and in doing so, enhanced her leadership effectiveness considerably. Finally, the third case study offered suggestions from the field regarding how individual and team authentic leadership effectiveness can be sustained during inevitable change.

GROUP DISCUSSION: AUTHENTIC LEADERSHIP CASE STUDIES

Consider the following:

1. How do organisational politics affect your organisational effectiveness?
2. What do you believe about the difference between inauthentic and authentic political acumen?
3. How could individual and team ALE benefit your organisation?
4. How willing would you be to invest in such an individual and collective ALD journey?
5. At what level would you start the development of an organisational ALE culture?
6. Once individual and collective ALE have been developed, how would you ensure sustainability when the only thing that is constant, is change?

PART III:
WELL-KNOWN LEADERS THROUGH THE LENS OF
AUTHENTIC LEADERSHIP

Chapter 10

WELL-KNOWN LEADERS THROUGH THE LENS OF AUTHENTIC LEADERSHIP

This chapter focuses on the South African context, as this is where I live. However, the intent of the following discussion is that it could be applied globally. I commence by examining the potential consequences when personal and professional authentic leadership is lacking. Through the lens of authentic leadership, I then focus on a study of two well-known highly effective and influential leaders in the history of South Africa, those being Helen Suzman, well-known political opposition leader who fought for equal human rights during the time of apartheid, and former President Nelson Mandela. What was it that these leaders did and did not do that made them so different from others, and that allowed them to be as effective and influential as they had been? This is followed by a comparison of the leadership authenticity of these two leaders.

WHAT HAPPENS WHEN INDIVIDUAL AND COLLECTIVE AUTHENTIC LEADERSHIP IS LACKING

I remember once facilitating a leadership workshop with a very diverse group of middle-management leaders, where I asked the following question to test their belief systems: "Is man basically good, or basically evil?" The majority of the members believed that man was good, except for two members, one White and one Black male. I state the race of these members because this is South Africa we are talking about, the country in which the concept of apartheid, meaning the legal separation of races, was instituted in 1948. I was curious to learn more, and asked both individuals the same two questions:

1. *How did you come to believe this?* The White male stated that whilst growing up, his religion informed him of such. The Black male stated that it was because of what he had experienced, growing up in the time of apartheid. Both men answered me very boldly. And then I asked:
2. *How does this belief still empower you today?* I noticed both men moving backwards in their seats, as far as possible from the question I had asked them. Pondering on my question, both then realised for the first time that they still held onto a belief that was no longer (if ever) empowering them.

Had I never asked them these questions, they would both have continued to hold onto self-limiting beliefs, and as illustrated in this book, beliefs do inform behaviour. It would be unusual to adopt any belief systems unless we have a positive intent for doing so at any moment in time. However, our circumstances often do change, and it does not always occur to us to re-examine these.

Following is an example of a leader who always put the needs of others before her own. At work this translated into her always helping others (even doing the work for them) when they asked for help, and she herself was continually under stress as she missed her own deadlines. In her coaching, we identified that she struggled with a sense of over-responsibility, resulting in taking inappropriate responsibility for others. We explored what might initially have informed a particular belief system that resulted in her behaviour. Upon reflection, she backtracked to when she lost her father when she was 10 years old. Her mother needed to become the breadwinner for the family, and as a result, at the age of 10, my client was told to take care of her two-year-old sibling whenever she arrived home from school. She was given a responsibility that could be considered age-inappropriate, and at that time, she had a positive intent in believing that she needed to put the needs of her two-year-old sister before her own. By doing so, she ensured that her sibling was taken care of, whilst managing to stay in favour with her mother. However, she never re-examined this belief system, and instead of it remaining helpful to her many years later, it now became limiting and stressful, as those who replaced her two-year-old sibling were adults who came to over-rely on her. Not only did she limit herself, she failed to empower them as well.

Years ago, a professor of mine told us that there is no such thing as objectivity; the closest we could get to that was through collective subjectivity. This can play out in interesting ways such as what we are experiencing, for instance, in South Africa today. Under the rule of apartheid, the four main groups of South Africans, comprising Blacks, Coloureds (mix race), Indians, and Whites, were separated in every way possible. We were not allowed to live, attend school, or travel on public transport together. We were also prohibited from loving or marrying across these divisions.

After many years of apartheid, in 1994 South Africa finally became a democratic country. We were extremely fortunate to have at least three exceptional leaders at the time who navigated our country through the transition from a divided and restricted country to a country that could be allowed to become democratic and free. To this end, Helen Suzman, Archbishop Desmond Tutu and President Nelson Mandela played a huge role. Helen Suzman, for many years on her own, fought for equal human rights against the apartheid government in Parliament. After she retired from her political career, she served on the Human Rights Commission from 1995 to 1998. After 1994, Archbishop Desmond Tutu oversaw the Truth and Reconciliation Commission whose purpose was to allow the perpetrators of injustice to come clean about their activities, and for those affected by those injustices to have the opportunity to understand, process, and if possible, to forgive. This process was intended to start the process of reconciliation so that we could move forward as a collective on a more democratic and free footing.

Simultaneously, Nelson Mandela, having been very instrumental in the process that allowed South Africa to become democratic, became the first Black president of democratic

South Africa. President Mandela chose to remain in power only for one term, during which he groomed his successor, Thabo Mbeki, to replace him once his term had ended. Mandela subsequently had an even bigger purpose to attend to, which was to start addressing the inequalities that remained in his country. This required strong leadership from him, and much of what he needed to, and had achieved, came not from his positional power, but rather from the influence that his inspirational presence generated. As a result, he influenced the private sector to get involved with developing much needed facilities such as schools and hospitals for the previously disadvantaged. Like Archbishop Tutu, he also did much work to build the metaphorical bridges required, for forgiveness and reconciliation to take place between people of different races.

Yet today, South Africa is not a happy country! Twenty-three years into our democracy, it appears that racial prejudice is more rife than ever. At the midst of the political atmosphere under the presidential leadership of Jacob Zuma, it seems to be manifesting especially in the post-1994 *born-free* generation, who have completed their secondary schooling, and who might now be at University to complete their tertiary education. This has played out especially in the tertiary education sector as frustrated young students embarked on the *Fees must Fall* protests, at times violent and continually disruptive to regular educational activities, in response to the government of the day's continually reduced financial support to education in South Africa. During these protests, Whites have been blamed for all the ills that are still present in this country. Therefore, the transition from the apartheid era to a well-run democratic South Africa has yet to be perfected.

Ferial Haffajee, Editor-in-Chief of the well-known South African newspaper publication *City Press*, in her recently published book[106] attempts to answer the question "What if there were no Whites in South Africa?"; an interesting question, the intent of which leaves the readers guessing until they start reading. Haffajee points out that in 2014 Whites constituted 8.4% whereas Blacks comprised over 80% of the total South African population and yet, even though South Africa is currently ruled and run by a Black government, there still appears to be White dominance in many respects, whether in culture, education, or the corporate world. She asks the question why, 22 years into our democracy, this is still so. She consulted Professor Melissa Steyn, the director of the Centre for Diversity Studies at the University of Witwatersrand in Johannesburg. Prof Melissa explained that "the two main ideological systems that have constructed the whole of the modern world [are] White supremacy and patriarchy"[107]. Haffajee then suggests that even if they were to drive the entire 8.4% of White people into the sea, you still would not dismantle White supremacy, as White supremacy has become a figment in the mind of those who think so. Bearing in mind that there is no such thing as absolute objectivity and that the closest to this is collective subjectivity, this could mean the following; that not only do these ideological systems construct the whole modern world; these ideological systems themselves are constructed as well. Where else could this happen, but in the minds of those who construct them!

One could argue that adhering to the belief of White supremacy has become a limiting part of a collective self-belief system of still too many people in South Africa and perhaps globally. It is limiting not only to those who believe it, whether they are Black or White, but it also limits the powerful interactions that can happen between people of diversity. For instance, many of my clients are different to me on the outside, but I am continually reminded that we all have so much in common, whilst each one of us is unique. Racism results from beliefs based on generalising and deleting information about others, and by seeing people externally different to ourselves as part of an amorphous mass. Until we underpin our interactions with a positive regard for others, our country has very little chance of blossoming into its full democratic potential.

Every one of us on this planet can become a leader by building that inner AL Compass that will allows us to stay grounded whilst growing towards our highest potential. For each of us, what is below the soil-line needs to be examined and aligned so that there is congruence between whom we are, and what we believe our leadership purpose, vision and values need to be. Furthermore, we need to examine how our belief systems and our emotional and mind states can empower us to become effective, for the greater good of all.

The criteria for team effectiveness can also be applied to national effectiveness. In any country, we cannot collectively focus on the outcomes we wish to achieve, until such time as we stop blaming others, and start holding not only others, but also ourselves accountable for what we collectively need to achieve towards getting our country back on track again. That requires us to commit from within our hearts to work together towards those outcomes, and that can happen only if we are able to engage in healthy conflict. Healthy conflict in turn can happen only if we as fellow human beings learn to trust one another. Trusting one another is very difficult if we do not trust ourselves first, and as I have already illustrated, this requires that each one of us needs to develop and sustain our personal ALE. Not all leadership positions are filled by leaders, and similarly, we do not have to wait to be in a leadership position for us to become leaders, firstly of self, and thereafter of others. Ideally, this should start with official leadership, whether in politics or in corporate organisations, but if this is absent, it can start from wherever individuals have sufficient leader developmental readiness to develop such leadership.

I believe that the best time in South Africa was the period after 1994, during the presidency of Nelson Mandela. Sadly, we lost our world-renowned and beloved Madiba on 5 December 2013, but we still have Archbishop Tutu with us today. Just imagine if Archbishop Desmond Tutu or the late President Nelson Mandela had adhered to such self-limiting belief systems that Blacks were inferior to Whites! If they had, they would never have achieved the extraordinary outcomes that they did during their lifetimes! As Mandela said, something is impossible until it is done!

TWO WELL-KNOWN EXAMPLES OF SOUTH AFRICAN POLITICAL LEADERS

Apartheid envisaged the creation of Bantustans, which were independent ethnic states, or homelands, in which Black South Africans would exercise 'separate freedoms'. Depending on the ethnic origin of Black South Africans, they were allocated as nationals to these homelands, resulting in their loss of citizenship of the country of their birth. Their presence in South Africa would be tolerated only to the extent that their labour resources were required. Whilst they worked in South Africa, their families often needed to stay behind in these homelands, restricting their mobility, opportunities to earn a livelihood, and their basic right to a family life. This disrupted family structures and resulted in children often being brought up by those other than their parents, who needed to be the breadwinners. In my opinion, this resulted in one of the biggest unpunished crimes committed by the governing party of the day during the apartheid years.

Two well-known examples of South African fighters for human rights for all of those who lived in this country, regardless of race, religion or gender, were Helen Suzman and Nelson Mandela. Whilst Nelson Mandela languished in jail for as long as it would take to see his purpose materialise, Helen Suzman, a privileged White South African of Jewish descent, fought tirelessly for the same cause, in and beyond Parliament. Helen Suzman allowed herself to be elected into the opposition party at the time, and for many years she represented on her own the opposition view to apartheid in Parliament.

Once Mandela was released from jail, he was strongly encouraged by South Africans to take up the position of the first president in 1994 in a democratic South Africa. He reluctantly agreed to take up one term as president, after which he wished to involve himself in even bigger global projects. The term of his presidency was most probably the happiest and healthiest of times for the population of South Africa. Two years into his presidency, Nelson Mandela started to groom his successor, Mr Thabo Mbeki in order to ensure that he left his beloved country in the hands of a capable leader. In 1998, President Nelson Mandela stepped down and Thabo Mbeki became the new President of South Africa.

I discuss both Helen Suzman and former president Nelson Mandela, affectionately known as Tata Madiba (or simply Madiba), by examining their impact on South Africa and the world, followed by a view of both as leaders through the lens of AL, and the processes they had followed to continue their development as authentic leaders. Viewing them through the lens of AL requires that we consider both the horizontal and vertical aspects of their ALD, as illustrated in Figure 14. In order to create context, and bearing in mind that as human beings our internal compasses are informed by our life experiences, we examine both leaders along a continuous horizontal time from their past to their current selves. Thereafter, we examine both leaders along a vertical dimension, with the understanding that the aspects below the soil-line, such as leadership internal identity, purpose and vision, values, beliefs, thoughts and feelings inform leadership behaviour, performance and effectiveness. Having said this, I do need to note that I managed to find less material on the private thoughts of Helen Suzman than on those of Nelson Mandela. I suppose Mandela had a lot more time at his disposal during his 27 years in prison for reflection and writing than Suzman did during her all-consuming activities in and beyond parliament to fight for equal human rights for all.

Helen Suzman – Leader of the Opposition during Apartheid in South Africa

Like Nelson Mandela, the diminutive Helen Suzman was an inspirational leader who was respected by friend and foe. Whilst Nelson Mandela fought for equal human rights whilst in hiding, followed by 27 years in prison, Helen used her privilege as an educated White woman to fight for the rights of those who were marginalised. As a White South African anti-apartheid activist and politician, she was a driving force for change. She was noted for her strong public criticism of the governing National Party's policies of apartheid at a time when this was atypical of fellow White South Africans, and found herself even more of an outsider because she was an English-speaking Jewish woman in a parliament dominated by Calvinist Afrikaner men. Following is evidence of her being regarded as inspirational by others. According to former prisoner Neville Alexander (imprisoned from July 1963 to April 1974) on Robben Island, the famous prison near Cape Town where Nelson Mandela was also incarcerated, Helen Suzman's visit to the Island in 1967 was one of the benchmarks of their time in imprisonment. Helen usually fought for what she believed in, and as such, she managed to get the authorities to allow her to visit the prison. Her perseverance demonstrated her commitment to human rights. After her visit, the prisoners were allowed more visits and letters, and it was easier to get permission to study[108]. The Press also had the following to say about Helen:

> Every so often, a parliament produces a personality to whom friend and foe alike can raise the hand in salute... Such a personality in our South African parliament is that remarkable woman, Mrs Helen Suzman... **Daily Dispatch 28/7/1964**
>
> Her performance, from the consistent high quality of her speeches, the thoroughness of her research and the remarkable range of subjects she handles, has set an altogether new parliamentary standard. **Rand Daily Mail 10/6/1965**
>
> It is not our job to tell the Whites whom to vote for. We make an exception in the case of Helen Suzman... this doughty fighter, this most respected component of the Government. The good wishes of millions of our people are with you, Helen. **The Post, a newspaper with mainly Black readership before the 1966 elections**

She was awarded 27 honorary doctorates, and twice nominated for the Nobel Peace Prize. She also received international awards for her contributions to human rights. So what was it that made Helen Suzman such an inspirational leader? Viewing Helen through the horizontal and vertical dimensions of ALD allowed me to understand just how authentic her story was, how well her puzzle pieces create an authentic picture. The following paints a picture of who Helen was throughout her life, above and below the soil-line, considering her life history (horizontal dimension), and her internal AL Compass (vertical dimension), during which I include some of her and others' quotes to corroborate all the AL elements.

AL horizontal dimension: Some historical context[109]

Whereas Madiba's roots were in rural South Africa, Helen Suzman's Jewish family roots were in Eastern Europe. Her mother and father met and married in South Africa around 1910, after the families of both had escaped the oppression and discrimination against the Jews in Lithuania in approximately 1902, prior to the outbreak of the First World War. They settled in Johannesburg, an area that attracted a large number of immigrants due to the discovery of gold.

Helen, the second of two daughters, was born in 1917, and she never knew her mother who had died shortly after her birth. Helen's father remarried when she was nine, and she was brought up in a traditional Jewish home. Helen believed that her understanding of the Jewish experience of discrimination and persecution heightened her awareness of the evils of the apartheid system that started to develop in South Africa in the late 1940s, when all races were segregated, and when all who were classified as 'Non-White' became lesser privileged.

Helen, whose father attached great importance to a good education for his children, sent her to an excellent private school where she learnt many lessons that she put to good use later on. This included her awareness that privilege and rights needed to be accompanied by responsibilities. She enjoyed her university years where she studied economics and economic history. She was an exceptional student and her economics professor said about her "...what distinguished all her work was the originality it displayed... She was very quick to see the main point of an argument, its strength and weakness and to state and examine it fearlessly..." These qualities stood her in good stead in her political career.

She married Moses Suzman at age 19 in 1937, and had two daughters, Frances and Patricia. In 1945, Helen started to lecture at the University of the Witwatersrand. It was her research into the migrant labour system that resulted in her entry into politics. This study developed awareness in Helen of the difficulties experienced by Black Africans when seeking work in urban areas. These difficulties included low wages, the denial of workers' mobility due a "pass" system, and the disruption of family life, because workers' rural families were not always allowed to live with them in urban areas. It was in 1948 when the National Party, in power at the time, legalised the system of apartheid, that Helen became actively involved in the United Party, the official opposition party at that time. She was elected in 1953 as a Member of Parliament (MP) where she conscientiously watched, listened and learnt at all times, in order to equip her to fight for equal human rights for all. She studied newly introduced Bills on specific subjects, mainly concerned with racial, gender, and labour affairs, as she started fighting for the human rights of the marginalised. During 1953 – 1959, approximately 30 new legislations were introduced that went against the grain of anyone who cared for democracy.

Helen was very purpose-driven, and fighting for the marginalised in a country that was run mainly by conservative males, left her working very long hours away from her family. This resulted in huge conflict between herself as a fighter for human rights, and as wife and mother of two young daughters. She needed to live in Cape Town for six months of the year, and she endeavoured to fly back home twice per month to spend time with her family. During her absence, she was supported by the presence of her husband, loving grandparents, as well as domestic staff members who took care of her children.

A polarisation within the United Party between the more conservative and more liberal elements eventually culminated in a split in 1959, when the Progressive Party was born with 12 initial members. The new party once again rejected racial discrimination, advocated equal opportunities and a common voters' role. During the general elections, with only Whites on the voters' roll, Helen was the only successful Progressive Party candidate, and she held this lonely position in Parliament from 1961 to 1974, in the face of unremitting hostility from the all-White all-male opposition members of Parliament.

Figure 23: Portrait of Helen Suzman
Courtesy of the South African Jewish Museum, Cape Town

During this time, her forthright critique and constant questioning during parliamentary sessions infuriated the Nationalists, as they were obliged to respond, and their responses were published by the Parliamentary Press. During these many years, she gained considerable respect from the English Press, both locally and overseas, who became her useful allies, by ensuring that all her speeches and questions in Parliament were extensively covered. At one point, one irate Cabinet Minister accused her of asking questions just to embarrass South

Africa overseas. Helen replied, "It is not my questions that embarrass South Africa – it is your answers."

Helen's work extended beyond Parliament. She had to attend to the affairs of the constituency that had elected her, which she did very diligently. She also maintained close links with the Black Sash, an anti-apartheid women's organisation, of which I was a member. The Black Sash did important work in helping the victims of apartheid, and often referred matters to her to take to Parliament.

She often went into the living areas of the marginalised, and did what she could to improve their living conditions. I remember meeting this remarkable woman once in the early 1980s, when she related incidents of planned forced removals of the homesteads of the poorer marginalised communities. They would be warned to remove their belongings from their humble homesteads before a specified date, after which these would be demolished by bulldozers. Helen would usually be warned beforehand, and on the days that the bulldozers arrived, this diminutive woman would stand in the way, blocking them, and warning them that they would need to bulldoze her down first. On such occasions, the bulldozers had to leave and the people retained their homes.

During the State of Emergency declared in 1960, she also started to visit prisons, schools and hospitals in marginalised areas. After these visits, she usually raised the issues with the relevant authorities, and managed to secure some improvements for these communities in and outside prison. One such prison was Robben Island where she met Nelson Mandela in 1967. She was immediately impressed with his dignity and unmistakable air of authority, and subsequently she continued to visit Mr Mandela in prison as often as she was allowed. In the meanwhile, believing that he was the only man who was capable of controlling an increasingly restless climate in South Africa, she frequently raised the issue of Nelson Mandela's release from prison, quoting his famous speech delivered in court after being sentenced to life imprisonment. She insisted that, "...this was the one man who would have the will and authority to persuade the ANC [then a freedom party] and the Government to suspend violence and who could create a climate for negotiations".

Helen was in Parliament for 36 years, and in those years she was extremely consistent in that she always "sang the same tune and for thirteen of those years it was a solo performance, ... always decrying the government's assault on civil liberties and the rule of law and exposing the dreadful human costs of its race policies". She never allowed the consistent abusive responses over the decades to still her voice, or alter, falter or fade her "tune".

After the 1961 elections, few would have given the Progressive Party much chance of survival. All those years until 1974, Helen had to fight the apartheid government on her own whilst enduring extensive hostility, gender, and anti-Semitic insults, especially from the ruling party. In 1975, the Progressive Party underwent another transformation, and the Progressive Federal Party was born, which in turn became the Democratic Party in 1989, and the Democratic Alliance (DA) in 2000. In 1989 and at age 71, Helen announced her retirement from politics, after having survived three apartheid presidents, those being HF Verwoerd, BJ Vorster and PW Botha. She received international accolades and tributes from heads of state all over the world, and from South Africans of all colours and walks of life. After her retirement from politics, she remained involved in public life. She served as president of the SA Institute of Race Relations from 1991 to 1993, and she was appointed to the Independent Electoral Commission that supervised South Africa's first democratic elections in 1994. She served as a member of the Human Rights Commission from 1995 to 1998. Helen passed away at age 91 in 2009. In 2017, Helen Suzman's legacy lives on in the Helen Suzman Foundation, a strong and active watchdog over ethical governance in South Africa.

AL vertical dimension: Suzman's internal AL Compass

The following considers Helen Suzman as a leader along an AL vertical dimension by examining aspects such as her leadership internal identity, purpose and vision, values, beliefs, thoughts and feelings, which informed her leadership behaviour, performance and effectiveness.

AL Level 1: **Internal/Self-identity:** Her internal identity was *Fighter for Human Rights.* Helen devoted her life from a young age to the fight for human rights and the rule of law in South Africa.

AL Level 2: **Leadership purpose, linked to vision/legacy:** Helen's purpose and vision were informed from an early age, as follows.

> *Leadership purpose:* Her purpose was to fight for equal human rights and dignity for all. To this end, she allowed herself to be voted into Parliament, so that she could fight for the human rights of all, inside and beyond Parliament.

> *Vision and legacy:* Helen's vision was to see a country that would be ruled by a free and fair government that respected the freedom and rights of all in South Africa. Her legacy lives on in the Helen Suzman Foundation.

AL Level 3: **Values, ethical and general:** Being fully aware of her leadership vision, purpose and values became an internal leadership compass that kept her *True North.* Following are examples of what she valued most.

> *Free and fair democracy, which included racial equality and gender equality:* Helen deeply valued living in a democratic system where all people were regarded as equal. She explained her values during a speech delivered on receiving an honorary doctorate from the University of Cape Town in 1986:

>> *I am proud to acknowledge that I am a liberal... who adheres to old-fashioned liberal values such as the rule of law, universal franchise, free elections, a free press, free association, guaranteed civil rights and an independent judiciary.*

> *Motherhood:* Helen had reservations about combining motherhood with a political career, but she realised the importance of her fight for human rights, and ensured that her family was well taken care of when she could not be home.

Education and learning: Apart from her formal education, which equipped her well for the career that she was to embark upon, she valued her continuous learning on-the-job, whilst in Parliament, so that she could continuously become more effective in serving her purpose.

AL Level 4: Beliefs about self, and others: Helen believed the following about herself, her purpose, and about democracy, equality, peace, harmony, self-determination, inferiority versus supremacy, freedom, her political colleagues, and policies of political opponents.

Self and purpose: During her address to her Houghton constituency during the 1966 election campaign, she stated the following:

> My main strength is the knowledge that I was voted into Parliament to represent a point of view that exists in South Africa – despite intimidation, despite the unfavourable climate, despite the bullying of the government and the toadying of the one-time anti-government forces.

Democracy, equality, self-determination, freedom, and inferiority versus supremacy: Helen's maiden speech in Parliament was on the 1953 Matrimonial Bill. Women's rights (and in particular those of Black women) became part of the larger fight for human rights, and this is what she had to say:

> Banning people does not mean that ideas disappear; it simply means that people go underground, that things are more difficult to control and you do not stop the rebellion that goes on in people's hearts against genuine grievances and genuine disabilities.

Political colleagues: After 13 years in Parliament where she had to hold the opposition fort on her own, she had the following to say:

> It is impossible to describe the pleasure – after all these solitary years – of having friends within the House to talk to, laugh with... even to argue with....

Political opponent policies: On 23 May 1969, Helen attacked the deputy minister of Bantu Administration for the government's so-called intention of "preserving the Bantu culture" in the Homelands. She pointed out the cynical contradiction of these policies that were in fact destroying the very basic unit of that culture, which was the family:

> You cannot bluff yourself forever that you are only dealing with Black hands and that, attached to those Black hands, there are no human beings with hearts, and aspirations, and normal desires. You cannot promise those people rights in areas where they are never going to live. They want their rights and their responsibilities where they live...

AL Level 5: Psychological states: Helen's behaviour was informed by positive psychological states such as moral courage, conscientiousness, intellectual curiosity, learning, consistency, empathy, resilience, interpersonal respect, and determined assistance. These positive psychological states allowed her to stay effective under challenging circumstances.

Moral courage: After being elected in 1953 to represent the opposition party in Parliament, she commented: "*So off I went to Cape Town in 1953...shaking in my boots*". About the governing National Party members (called the Nats) after the 1966 elections, when she was once again the only opposition member in Parliament, by now sitting in the front benches, she commented:

> *I am not only faced with Nats and flanked by Nats but I have them sitting behind me too – it is considerably unnerving to turn around and find myself confronted with several sets of beady eyes fixed on me with unblinking hostility.*

Conscientious curiosity, watching and learning: However, she had the following to say about herself, when she initially became a Member of Parliament (MP):

> *As a new MP, I sat there slogging away... a little backbench Member of Parliament, very conscientious, very interested, watching and listening and learning all the time.*

Consistency in her beliefs and messages: The following was meant to be an insult on 25 February 1964 from a National Party MP about Helen:

> *When she gets up in this House, she reminds me of a cricket in a thorn tree when it is very dry in the bushveld. His chirping makes you deaf but the tune remains the same year in and year out. In her fight for the Bantu, the honourable member... sings the same tune year after year.*

Empathy for the marginalised: In the following example, she commented on the lack of empathy in the governing party:

> *These honourable members sit here passing laws, but they never have the slightest contact with the individuals who suffer as result of these laws.*

Helen also used her parliamentary privilege to visit places normally inaccessible to normal White South Africans, and regularly visited squatter communities. In order to create global awareness, she took a group of US Congressmen to the site of destruction of the Nyanga squatter camps on the Cape Flats.

Resilience: For 13 years, Helen was the only member representing the opposition party in Parliament. Here is what she had to say, "My daughters have always said that I have the constitution of a Basutu pony". She described her immense workload as follows:

> *It was a frantic scramble to keep up with all the different subjects appearing on an order paper. I have a bunch of votes coming all together – Justice, Prisons, Police... and the miracle is that I manage to deliver the appropriate speech on each vote.*

Respect for others: About the Speaker of Parliament who was a member of the governing party and of the English local and international press, she had the following to say:

About the Speaker of Parliament... *throughout those years that I was the lone Progressive in Parliament, Speaker Klopper would send for me at the beginning of every session and make a little speech: 'Well I don't agree with a word of what you say, but it is my duty to see that minorities have their rights in this House. I am going to see that you get time to speak whenever you want to.' And he did.*

About the press ... *if I had been attacking these guys in parliament without anyone knowing about it, it would have had no effect. but it had such wide publicity in the press; they realised what I was saying was generally correct and agreed with the liberal view that I was expounding.*

Determined assistance: Helen's reputation for *determined assistance* meant that she was still asked to investigate pension issues as late as 1988.

I seem to have become the honorary ombudsman for all those people who have no vote and no MP – they write to me in their hundreds, asking for help over pass problems, house problems, jobs, bursaries, trading licences – I get requests for everything from a set of golf clubs to a bus...

AL Level 6: **Competencies:** Suzman obtained a Bachelor of Commerce degree in Economics and Economic history. One of her professors at the University of Witwatersrand, where she studied, described her as having the skill to understand the main point in arguments, the strengths and weaknesses, and to state and examine these fearlessly.

AL Level 7: **Behaviours:** These have been discussed in the impact that Helen's leadership has had in South Africa.

When one considers both the horizontal and vertical dimensions of Suzman's ALD, a strong golden thread is evident throughout. Viewing Helen through her internal AL Compass, it becomes clear why she was as highly regarded and impactful as a South African and global leader. She was very clear about her internal identity, her purpose and her values, and how she needed to support the people of South Africa. She knew what leadership vision she needed to work towards, and her beliefs and psychological states supported her towards staying true to her purpose and vision. Finally, her decisions and behaviour were aligned to values, purpose, and internal identity of *fighter for human rights*. If one considers what each AL level in her AL Compass contained, it becomes clear how authentic a leader Helen Suzman was throughout her courageous life.

Nelson Mandela – First President of Democratic South Africa

So what then was it that allowed Madiba's leadership to have such an extraordinary impact on us globally, and on South Africans in particular? As I started to research Madiba's history through the lens of AL, I realised that he was also a very inspirational leader. He was the change he wished to see in others, and he was a leader beyond position in that his authentic leadership emanated from his presence. I always think of him in terms of the three '*pr*'s that defined him. It did not matter whether he was the *president* of South Africa, or a *prisoner*, there was something in his *presence* that allowed others to trust his leadership. This further led to growing effectiveness in his individual leadership, and in the collective leadership of his political colleagues, and later others as well. The following illustrates some of the aspects that resulted in his extraordinary presence.

A leader beyond position by presence: Extraordinary leaders see no titles... human beings might have certain titles in order to perform the tasks entrusted to them... but they *are not* those titles. Madiba treated everyone the same, whether a taxi-driver or a political leader. Kalungu-Banda[110] points out that leaders with positional power would be more effective and powerful if they learn how *not* to use it. Therefore, what is it really that leadership needs to do? Mainly to empower, inspire and to influence others to be and do their best in whatever they need to achieve. This means that they firstly need the personal leadership skills to manage and lead self. They need to be the example of the change that they wish to see in others. Once the internal power is in place, they no longer need to lead others with positional power. What is then required are the good conversational skills that are present in a leader as coach. This requires good listening and questioning, which allows leaders to serve others whilst leading from the back; only a leader with gravitas in their presence can do this.

In the case of Madiba, he worked hard *not* to use his positional power, and instead he practised restraint when necessary, and worked in a consultative way with others, bringing others more willingly with him. He also made himself available as president for only one term, and immediately started grooming his then vice-president, Thabo Mbeki, to take over from him, as he admitted that Mbeki was a much more capable administrator than he was. He used his term in power to groom and empower Mbeki, so that he himself could become dispensable, with a smooth transition once his presidential term was over. As Madiba exited from the presidency, he continued to champion valuable causes for the benefit of his country.

Leaders such as Madiba often did not have to say anything, as was the case when he attended the funeral of a close colleague of his; just being at the funeral in silence to share the grief with others, allowed others to feel with him. Madiba lead beyond words with his actions. By sharing their authentic presence with others, "great leaders sow their energies in the air for other people to breathe and experience a personal renewal. Their energies and optimism are infectious. It is in this sense that great leaders share their life with everyone around them"[111].

When Madiba moved into his new, previously White suburb, he managed to escape his bodyguards one afternoon, to go for a walk down the road. He knocked on one of the neighbours' door to introduce himself as their new neighbour, and he was invited in for a cup of tea. Rather than insisting on being respected for his title as Mr President, he merely presented himself and expected to be treated as the new neighbour, remembering that the title referred to what his was tasked to do at the time rather than who he was as a human being.

Being the change he wished to see: Madiba responded as follows when asked why his speeches were no longer such rousing speeches[112]:

> *The masses like to see somebody who is responsible and who speaks in a responsible manner. They like that, and so I avoid rabble-rousing speech. I don't want to incite the crowd. I want the crowd to understand what we are doing and I want to infuse a spirit of reconciliation in them.*

An inspirational leader: Authentic leaders make their greatness contagious, they collaborate and celebrate with others, rather than winning at the cost of others and robbing others weaker than them of their self-esteem and self-confidence. Madiba stated that[113]:

> *A cardinal point that we must keep constantly in mind, the lodestar, which keeps us on course as we negotiate the uncharted twists and turns of the struggle for liberation, is that the breakthrough is never the result of individual effort. It is always a collective effort and triumph.*

Madiba treated everyone with awe, no matter what their position was, which resulted in them feeling like they were the most blessed people in the world. Madiba also made the time to show his care to other individuals, like in the case of Baby Jake, a SA boxer, after his victory over an American boxer on American soil. Instead of just writing and congratulating him, he went to his house to congratulate him in person, and spent an hour with him over a cup of tea. It was a simple thing that anyone could do, but he did these simple things sincerely, and Baby Jake felt invincible after that. It is about serving others... servant leadership. Self-love, self-belief, and self-confidence will increase as one chooses to be instrumental in the journey of developing self-confidence, self-belief, and self-love in others. In fact, this can become a very grounding experience for a leader as it creates a win-win outcome for all. Serving others is how a leader can *stoop to greatness.*

It is all about the lenses through which we look at everything and everyone, and even inspirational leaders need to find inspiration. Madiba found it easy to find inspiration in others as he looked at them through the lens of a positive regard for others. It is important to show this positive regard in one's behaviour, and he did so by going to the trouble to approach them, and to interact with them. Good examples are the interactions he had with Francois Pienaar who was the Captain of the South African Springbok Rugby team who won the Rugby World Cup in 1995, after being inspired by Madiba. As captured in the film entitled *Invictus,* this allowed the whole country of South Africa to be united, and it subsequently resulted in a similar experience of uniting the country during the 2010 Soccer World Cup, hosted in South Africa.

Many leaders, such as Bill Clinton and Barack Obama, were inspired by the sense of possibility that the life of Madiba demonstrated, and the sacrifices he had made to achieve his dream of justness and equality. It is such a life that informed his saying that something is impossible only until it is done. This saying always inspires me never to give up too soon. Madiba demonstrated that when change is hard and when one might wish to ignore one's calling and the road less travelled, one has to keep one's eye on one's purpose and vision, and one's values that support these. This then becomes that internal compass or lodestar that goes into the leadership toolbox to help keep one *True North*. Madiba chose hope over fear, future progress over the prisons of the past.

Because people bought into his vision, they would go the extra mile. Doctors would joke that over a weekend when they were not on call, they did not wish to be disturbed whilst watching an important rugby match "unless it was Madiba who was sick". Companies considering social investment would break the rules if it were a project inspired by Madiba, saying, "Who can say No to Madiba?" Kalungu-Banda explained it as follows[114]:

> *Inspirational leaders are like yeast that permeates ordinary flour and water, making them rise into a good dough. This illustrates what leadership is about: imperceptibly raising others to realising their own greatness and self-esteem. Considerable effect is gained simply by listening to people with respect.*

So what was it about Madiba that made him such an extraordinary leader? Viewing him through the horizontal and vertical dimensions of ALD allowed me to understand just how authentic his story is, how well the puzzle pieces create an authentic picture. The following paints the picture of who Tata Madiba was throughout his life, above and below the soil-line, as we consider his life history (horizontal dimension), and his internal AL Compass (vertical dimension), corroborated by his quotes that reflect the elements in his AL Compass.

AL horizontal dimension: Some historical context[115]

Rolihlahla Mandela was born on 18 July 1918 into the Madiba clan in the village of Mvezo, Transkei. His mother was Nonqaphi Nosekeni and his father was Nkosi Mphakanyiswa Gadla Mandela, principal counsellor to the regent of the Thembu people, Jongintaba Dalindyebo. In 1930, when he was 12 years old, his father died and the young Madiba became a ward of Jongintaba at the Great Place in Mqhekezweni. Madiba was profoundly influenced by observing the regent and his court[116]. He observed the tribal meetings in the regent's courtyard, and noticed that everyone was allowed to speak. He was astonished at the candour with which people were allowed to criticise the regent, and that the regent did not regard himself as above criticism. The regent simply listened, without defending himself, and the meetings continued until a consensus was reached. Democracy meant that all in the meeting were heard, and decisions were taken collaboratively. All the regent did was to sum up what had been said and to form some consensus among diverse opinions. No conclusions were forced on people who disagreed.

Hearing the elders' stories of his ancestors' valour during the wars of resistance, he dreamed also of making his own contribution to the freedom struggle of his people. He attended primary school in Qunu where his teacher, Miss Mdingane, gave him the name

Nelson, in accordance with the custom of giving all schoolchildren "Christian" names. He completed his Junior Certificate at Clarkebury Boarding Institute and went on to Healdtown, a Wesleyan secondary school of some repute, where he matriculated.

Mandela began his studies for a Bachelor of Arts degree at the University College of Fort Hare but did not complete the degree there as he was expelled for joining in a student protest. On his return to the Great Place at Mqhekezweni, the regent was furious and said that if he did not return to Fort Hare he would arrange wives for Nelson and his cousin Justice. They ran away to Johannesburg instead, arriving there in 1941. He worked as a mine security officer and after meeting Walter Sisulu, he was introduced to Lazer Sidelsky. He then did his articles through a firm of attorneys – Witkin, Eidelman and Sidelsky. He completed his BA through the University of South Africa. Meanwhile, he began studying for an LLB at the University of the Witwatersrand. By his own admission, he was a poor student and left the university in 1952 without graduating. He started studying again through the University of London only after his imprisonment in 1962 but also did not complete that degree. In 1989, while in the last months of his imprisonment, he obtained an LLB through the University of South Africa. He graduated in absentia at a ceremony in Cape Town.

In 1944, he married Walter Sisulu's cousin, Evelyn Mase, a nurse. They had two sons, Madiba Thembekile and Makgatho, and two daughters both called Makaziwe, the first of whom died in infancy. He and his wife divorced in 1958.

Mandela, while increasingly politically involved from 1942, joined the ANC in 1944 when he helped to form the ANC Youth League (ANCYL). Mandela rose through the ranks of the ANCYL, and through its efforts, the ANC adopted a more radical mass-based policy, the Programme of Action, in 1949. In 1952, he was chosen as the National Volunteer-in-Chief of the Defiance Campaign. This campaign of civil disobedience against six unjust laws was a joint programme between the ANC and the South African Indian Congress. He and 19 others were charged under the Suppression of Communism Act for their part in the campaign and sentenced to nine months of hard labour, suspended for two years.

Figure 24: Nelson Mandela on the roof of Kholvad House in 1953.
(Image courtesy of the Ahmed Kathrada Foundation)

A two-year diploma in law after his BA degree allowed Mandela to practise law, and in August 1952, he and Oliver Tambo established South Africa's first Black law firm, Mandela & Tambo. At the end of 1952, he was banned for the first time. As a restricted person, he had to watch in secret as the Freedom Charter was adopted in Kliptown on 26 June 1955. Mandela was arrested in a countrywide police swoop on 5 December 1955, which led to the 1956 Treason Trial. Men and women of all races found themselves in the dock in the marathon trial that ended only when the last 28 accused, including Mandela, were acquitted on 29 March 1961. On 21 March 1960, police killed 69 unarmed people in Sharpeville during a protest against the pass laws. This led to the country's first State of Emergency and the banning of the ANC and the Pan Africanist Congress (PAC). Mandela and his Treason Trial colleagues were among thousands detained during the State of Emergency. During the trial, Mandela married a social worker, Winnie Madikizela, on 14 June 1958. They had two daughters, Zenani and Zindziswa. The couple divorced in 1996.

Days before the end of the Treason Trial, Mandela travelled to Pietermaritzburg to speak at the All-in-Africa Conference, which resolved that he should write to Prime Minister Verwoerd requesting a national convention on a non-racial constitution, and to warn that should he not agree there would be a national strike against South Africa becoming a republic. After he and his colleagues were acquitted in the Treason Trial, Mandela went underground and began planning a national strike. In the face of massive mobilisation of state security, the strike was called off early. In June 1961 he was asked to lead the armed struggle and helped to establish the armed wing of the ANC, Umkhonto weSizwe (Spear of the Nation), which was launched on 16 December 1961.

On 11 January 1962, using the adopted name David Motsamayi, Mandela secretly left South Africa. He travelled around Africa and visited England to gain support for the armed struggle. He received military training in Morocco and Ethiopia and returned to South Africa in July 1962. He was arrested in a police roadblock outside Howick in August while returning from KwaZulu-Natal, where he had briefed ANC President Chief Albert Luthuli about his trip. He was charged with leaving the country without a permit and inciting workers to strike. He was convicted and sentenced to five years' imprisonment, which he began serving at the Pretoria Local Prison. On 27 May 1963, he was transferred to Robben Island and returned to Pretoria on 12 June. On 9 October 1963, Mandela joined 10 others on trial for sabotage in what became known as the Rivonia Trial. While facing the death penalty his words to the court at the end of his famous "Speech from the Dock" on 20 April 1964 became immortalised:

> I have fought against White domination, and I have fought against Black domination. I have cherished the ideal of a democratic and free society in which all persons live together in harmony and with equal opportunities. It is an ideal, which I hope to live for and to achieve. But if needs be, it is an ideal for which I am prepared to die"[17].

On 11 June 1964 Mandela and seven other accused, Walter Sisulu, Ahmed Kathrada, Govan Mbeki, Raymond Mhlaba, Denis Goldberg, Elias Motsoaledi and Andrew Mlangeni, were convicted and the next day were sentenced to life imprisonment. Goldberg was sent to Pretoria Prison because he was White, while the others went to Robben Island. Mandela's mother died in 1968 and his eldest son, Thembi, in 1969. He was not allowed to attend their funerals. On 31 March 1982, Mandela was transferred to Pollsmoor Prison in Cape Town with Sisulu, Mhlaba and Mlangeni. Kathrada joined them in October. When he returned to the prison in November 1985 after prostate surgery, Mandela was held alone. Justice Minister Kobie Coetsee visited him in hospital. Later Mandela initiated talks about an ultimate meeting between the apartheid government and the ANC.

On 12 August 1988, he was taken to hospital where he was diagnosed with tuberculosis. After more than three months in two hospitals, he was transferred on 7 December 1988 to a house at Victor Verster Prison near Paarl where he spent his last 14 months of imprisonment. He was released on Sunday 11 February 1990, nine days after the unbanning of the ANC and the PAC and nearly four months after the release of his remaining Rivonia comrades. Throughout his imprisonment, he had rejected at least three conditional offers of release. Mandela immersed himself in official talks to end White minority rule and in 1991 was elected ANC President to replace his ailing friend, Oliver Tambo. In 1993, he and President FW de Klerk jointly won the Nobel Peace Prize, and on 27 April 1994 at age 76, he voted for the first time in his life.

On 10 May 1994, he was inaugurated as the first democratically elected President of South Africa. On his 80th birthday in 1998, he married Graça Machel, his third wife. True to his promise, Mandela stepped down in 1999 after one term as President. He continued to work with the Nelson Mandela Children's Fund he set up in 1995, and established the Nelson Mandela Foundation and The Mandela Rhodes Foundation. Nelson Mandela never wavered in his devotion to democracy, equality and learning. Despite terrible provocation, he never answered racism with racism. His life is an inspiration to all who are oppressed and deprived; and to all who are opposed to oppression and deprivation. He died at his home in Johannesburg on 5 December 2013.

AL vertical dimension: Mandela's internal AL Compass

The following considers Nelson Mandela as a leader along an AL vertical dimension by examining aspects such as his leadership internal identity, purpose and vision, values, beliefs, thoughts and feelings, which would have informed his leadership behaviour, performance and effectiveness.

AL Level 1: **Internal/Self-identity:** His internal identity was *Freedom Fighter*. At the young age of 12, inspired by the elders' stories of his ancestors' valour during the wars of resistance, he dreamed of making his own contribution to the freedom struggle of his people. In his own words whilst in prison:

> *A story of one's life should deal frankly with political colleagues, their personalities, and their views. The reader would like to know what kind of person the writer is... But an autobiography of a* **freedom fighter** *must inevitably be influenced by the question whether the revelation of certain facts, however true they may be, will help advance the struggle, or not*[118].

AL Level 2: **Leadership purpose, linked to vision/legacy:** Madiba knew what his vision, and highest value, or leadership purpose was. Living in a country of inequality, he visualised a country where no one race would dominate another.

Vision and legacy: Here is what he had to say about his vision and legacy:

> *The ideals we cherish, our fondest dreams and fervent hopes may not be realised in our lifetime. But that is besides the point. The knowledge that in your day you did your duty, and lived up to the expectations of your fellow men is in itself a rewarding experience and magnificent achievement*[119].

Leadership purpose: During his own defence in his (Rivonia) court trial in 1964, he stated:

> *During my lifetime, I have dedicated myself to this struggle of the African people. I have fought against White domination, and I have fought against Black domination. I have cherished the ideal of a democratic and free society in which all persons live together in harmony and with equal opportunities. It is an ideal I hope to live for and to achieve. But if needs be, it is an ideal for which I am prepared to die*[120].

His leadership purpose was to realise his vision, and for this he was prepared to stay in prison as long as it would take to materialise. It took 27 years of prison life, with multiple attempts from the authorities to tempt him with earlier releases, but he was not to be bought. Only once an acceptable agreement had been arranged between the then apartheid authorities and himself, in consultation with his companions, did he agree to be released from prison.

AL Level 3: **Values, ethical and general:** Being fully aware of his leadership vision, purpose and values, became an internal leadership compass that kept him *True North*. Following are examples of what he valued most.

Family: Staying true to his leadership purpose seperated Madiba from his family for long periods. This was not an easy task, as he valued his family immensely. He loved his mother dearly, and wanted to take good care of her, which was not possible whilst he was in prison. He continually struggled between his personal obligations to his family and his larger obligations to society, asking *"Is politics in such case not a mere excuse to shirk one's responsibilities?"* and *"...whether a person is justified in neglecting his own family to fight for the opportunities for others"*[121]. However, he found solace in knowing that millions were suffering in his country due to the injustices, and he had taken the correct decision. During his time in prison, he also dearly missed his wife and children whom he loved very much, and he experienced great torment in the knowledge that he was not there for them when they needed him. At times, his family were also adversely affected by the authorities, as a way of getting back at Madiba, and that must have hurt him immensely. However, he had to acknowledge that his whole-hearted commitment to the liberation of his people gave meaning and yielded in him a sense of pride and joy. Ultimately, this was his leadership purpose, whilst trying to support his respective and collective family members as best as he could whilst in prison.

Forgiveness and reconciliation: Madiba and his comrades' initial collective leadership purpose was to fight for a free and fair South Africa, and thereafter he committed the remainder of his life to serving his nation and the world through the power of forgiveness and reconciliation[122]. By observing Madiba's words and actions, it was easily evident that he *walked his talk*, the sign of an extraordinary authentic leader.

Relational transparency: Madiba said the following about his manuscript of his book[123].

> *An essential part of that caution and fair play would be to have the widest possible measure of consultation with your colleagues about what you intend to say about them, to circulate your manuscript and give them the opportunity of stating their own views on any controversial issue discussed, so that the facts themselves may accurately reflect the standpoints of all concerned.*

Democracy and freedom, self-determination, peace and harmony: Madiba valued and was prepared to fight for *"...a democratic South Africa, free from the evils of Colour oppression, and where all South Africans, regardless of race or belief, would live together in peace and harmony on a basis of equality"*[124].

He valued self-determination as follows: *"self-determination, acknowledged throughout the civilized world as the inalienable birthright of all human beings"*[125], and linked it to his leadership identity as follows: *"The purpose of freedom is to create it for others"*[126].

Respect in general and for law and order: Mandela believed in exploiting *"every opportunity to promote the respect for the law and the judiciary ... in the new South Africa there is nobody, not even the President, [who] is above the law ... the rule of law generally and in particular the judiciary should be respected"*[127].

AL Level 4: **Beliefs about self, and others:** Madiba believed the following about himself, his family and home, his political colleagues and opponents, leadership in South Africa, and people in general.

Self: Madiba believed about himself that *"I have neither the achievements of which I could boast nor the skills to do it... I sometimes believe that through me Creation intended to give the world the example of a mediocre man in the proper sense of the term"*[128]. He also stated:

> *When a man commits himself to the type of life he has lived for 45 years, even though he may well have been aware from the outset of all the hazards, the actual course of events, and the precise manner in which they would influence his life... If I had been able to foresee all that has since happened, I would certainly have made the same decision; so I believe at least*[129].

Family and home: Madiba's family and home were very important to him, and he reminisced in prison about how he loved playing and chatting with the children, giving them a bath, feeding, and putting them to bed with a little story; and being away from the family has troubled him throughout his political life. He loved relaxing at the house, reading quietly, taking in the sweet smell that comes from the pots, sitting around the table with the family[130].

Political colleagues: Mandela viewed his comrades in prison as *"men of honesty and principle"*[131], and he had the following to say about them:

> *The spotlight has focussed on a few well-known figures amongst us such as... This is but natural because they are amongst our leading men in the country, admired by hundreds of thousands of people here and abroad for their courage and dedication. All of them have been cheerful and optimistic and have been a source of inspiration to all my fellow prisoners*[132].

Political opponents: When Madiba was asked about his prison warders, he responded, *"I don't want us to create the impression that all warders were just animals, rogues, No. Right* *from the beginning, there were warders who felt we should be treated correctly*"[133]. About working closely with a political opponent, Mr Gatsha Buthelezi, he responded:

> *Is it not that, although he is in the opposition, Mr Buthelezi is one of the most capable leaders we have in this country? The fact that Mr Buthelezi and I disagree on a number of issues cannot blind me from seeing, and appreciating many of his great qualities*[134].

Leadership in South Africa and good leadership in general: "We in South Africa and the world out there must know that this country has many more capable leaders besides my African National Congress colleagues and myself. And this is good for the country"[135]. Mandela's experiences as a young boy, observing the regent's behaviour during meetings held in his court, influenced his beliefs about what he needed to strive for in his own leadership:

> *As a leader, I have always followed the principles I first saw demonstrated by the regent... I have always endeavoured to listen to what each and every person in a discussion had to say before venturing my own opinion. Oftentimes, my own opinion will simply represent a consensus of what I heard in the discussion. I always remember the regent's axiom: "A leader is like a shepherd. He stays behind the flock, letting the most nimble go on ahead, whereupon the others follow, not realizing that all along they are being directed from behind*[136].

This description aligns with servant leadership, and again, only great leaders can lead in such a manner. Mandela believed that leadership fell into two categories, of which the second category constituted AL:

> *a) Those who are inconsistent, who[se] actions cannot be predicted, who agree today on a [matter] and repudiated it the following day, and b) Those who are consistent, who have a sense of honour, and who have a vision*[137].

He continued that leadership is there for the greater good of society as a whole:

> *Good leaders fully appreciate that the removal of tensions in society, of whatever pressure, puts creative thinkers on centre stage by creating an ideal environment for men and women of vision to influence society. Extremists, on the other hand, thrive on tension and mutual suspicion. Clear thinking and good planning was never their weapon*[138].

Madiba believed that the tasks of a good leader are:

> *Firstly, to create a vision and secondly, to create a following to help him implement the vision and to manage the process through effective teams. The people being led know where they are going because the leader has communicated the vision and the followers have bought into the goal he had set as well as the process of getting there*[139].

About people in general: Mandela stated that "*I shall stick to our vow: never, never under any circumstances, to say anything unbecoming of the other...*"[140]. As I read about what he had to say about others, it was almost impossible to find something negative. He also said that:

> *It is a good thing to assume, to act on the basis that...others are men of integrity and honour... because you tend to attract integrity and honour if that is how you regard those with whom you work. ...one has made a great deal of progress in developing personal relationships because you [make] the basic assumption...that those you deal with are men of integrity. I believe in that*[141].

Mandela also believed the best about others:

> *During my political career, I have discovered that in all communities, African, Coloured, Indian and Whites, and in all political organisations, without exception, there are good men and women who fervently wish to go on with their lives who yearn for peace and stability, who want a decent income, good houses and to send their children to the best schools, who respect and want to maintain the social fabric of society*[142].

AL Level 5: **Psychological states:** Madiba's behaviour was informed by psychological states such as hope and optimism, a sense of humour, a sense of freedom, humility, resilience, strength-based vulnerability, and moral courage. He aimed to live in the present moment, celebrated life despite the challenging past, had a positive regard, utmost respect, and a desire to understand others. He embraced forgiveness, and being able to apologise.

> ***Hope and optimism:*** From prison Madiba wrote to his wife that "*To a freedom fighter hope is what a life belt is to a swimmer – a guarantee that one will keep afloat and free from danger*"[143]. He stated that something is impossible until the deed is done, proving it possible, and stayed optimistic that South Africa would become a democratic country. He proved this with his leadership vision and purpose, to which he stayed true. He wrote the following[144]:

> *I am highly optimistic, even behind prison walls I can see heavy clouds and the blue sky over the horizon,... whatever difficulties we must still face, that in my lifetime I shall step out into the sunshine, walk with firm feet because that event will be brought about by the strength of my organisation and the sheer determination of our people.*

In one of Madiba's paintings whilst on Robben Island, through prison bars he painted a beautiful South Africa, with Table Mountain and the Atlantic Ocean, and a beautiful rainbow that would eventually represent the rainbow nation. He used the ability to reframe his reality at the time, into the beautiful vision that he held onto. This frame allowed him to retain the hope and optimism that he required, to hold onto his vision during his 27 years in prison.

A sense of humour: Madiba could joke about his painful past and his time in prison. He was able to allow others to make fun of his time there. For instance when he was asked how he still managed to be so active at the age of 83, he blamed his secretary, Zelda la Grange, who used to tell him that he had been loafing for 27 years, and now it was time for some work[145].

A sense of freedom: Madiba wrote that[146]:

> .... it is only my flesh and blood that are shut up behind these tight walls.... in my thoughts I am as free as a falcon. The anchor of my dreams is the collective wisdom of mankind as a whole. I am influenced more than ever before by the conviction that social equality is the only basis of human happiness...

Humility: Even though Madiba was an extraordinary leader, he was never prepared to take the credit for any of his achievements, always re-iterating that *"the reality of the struggle is that no individual among us can claim to have played a greater role than the rest"*[147]. On a particular occasion when a CD with all of his speeches was launched, he responded during an interview *"I would have been happier if my speeches were simply some among great speeches that were made by our country's eminent personalities such as Oliver Tambo, Chris Hani, Walter Sisulu, among many others"*[148].

Resilience and strength-based vulnerability: Resilience could be linked to strength-based vulnerability. When Madiba lost his beloved son to HIV/AIDS, he chose to share this news with the entire world, stressing that HIV/AIDS did not differentiate between status, gender, race, or age. He did this so that the world could take this pandemic seriously, and unite in order to beat this disease. This strength-based vulnerability demonstrated a strong leader that cared for a greater purpose, in this case, being able to get rid of the stigma of HIV/AIDS, whilst encouraging collaboration towards finding a solution to beat this disease.

In another example, especially during the first few years on Robben Island when conditions were very harsh, Madiba displayed resilience. The food was poor, the work hard, the summers hot, the winters very cold, and the warders brutal. Physical and psychological suffering and pain was significant, and the authorities' petty-mindedness relentless. However, he accommodated the circumstances, and ultimately became the victor rather than the victim[149].

Moral courage: When everyone was afraid of disagreeing with President George Bush's foreign policy towards Iraq, Mandela referred to the leader of the world's most powerful nation as *"someone who did not want to belong to the modern age."* When nations in general chose to disagree quietly with the US policy at the time, he chose to speak up, and understanding the ethical weight that his voice carried, millions took heed of his message[150].

Living in the present moment: To keep their morale high in prison, Mandela and his compatriots learnt to live in the moment. To keep their spirits up, they often sang, and they studied. They kept their cells clean, and they attended to and cared for one another when any of them became sick or frustrated. They also shared learnings with one another, considering each day yet another gift, realising that all they had, was now. Whilst they kept their eye on their goals, they invested all into every present moment they had, in order to optimise their investment into their future. This strategy allowed them to retain their positive psychological states under challenging circumstances.

Celebrating life despite the challenging past: Throughout his years in prison and thereafter, Madiba always danced to express his feelings and to celebrate life. Kalungu-Banda stated that he heard it said that *"when Madiba engages in that dance, he is totally consumed by being alive. Life glows in his eyes. His face beams with incredible joy. There must be something fundamental he celebrates"*[151].

A positive regard for and celebration of others: Authentic leaders recognise and honour other human beings, no matter who they are what they do, and they enable and empower others to realise their potential, knowing that there is more to everyone than the eye can currently see or the ear can hear. A leader grows own goodness by recognising the goodness in others. Madiba was interested in whomever he met. He asked them igniting questions and listened to their responses with utmost interest, and he then thanked them for the time that they had given him. People seek out those who make them feel listened to.

Madiba also did not show prejudice against the staff of the previous apartheid regime, and decided to retain them as his staff, saying that he had found them very supportive and competent in their roles since he had started working with them. He felt that each person was unique and special, and he refrained from dividing them up into categories such as race, gender, religion, and political affiliations. As Kalungu-Banda reflects, the paradox is that the more we acknowledge and celebrate the capacities and contributions of those around us, the more we deepen the strength of our own character[152]. We become poised to do greater things because others feel confident enough to win with us.

Madiba publicly acknowledged the capabilities of political opponents, and recognised the fact that these resided in parties different to his own as a benefit for the greater good of South Africa. He moved beyond ego, and understood that he and others in his position were privileged to serve their nation, and in so doing, he was able to see the good side of those whom he could have regarded as his party's enemies. This allows leaders to make the right decision for the greater good rather than considering only their own narrow personal or party political interests, which surely must be very fulfilling in the knowledge that they are working in the best interests of all those they serve.

Forgiveness: Rather than preaching, Madiba reflected his values, one of them being forgiveness, through his actions. For instance, during his inauguration ceremony, he invited as his guest the warder that had guarded him in prison on Robben Island. Through actions such as these, Madiba illustrated that practising forgiveness releases more pain, freedom, and peace, than would revenge. Through shining his light in this manner, after having spent 27 years in prison, he unwittingly gave others permission to explore the extraordinary power of forgiveness. By releasing anger and allowing forgiveness to enter, one also nurtures physical health and wellness, as anger and emotional *dis-eases*, can quite often result in physical diseases. This is not to be confused with holding others accountable for unethical behaviour, in which case those need to be held accountable for their behaviour, which might include punishment. Forgiveness is an interpersonal dynamic that allows especially the forgiver to be liberated from unnecessary debilitating emotional baggage, whilst giving the one who is forgiven permission to learn from this and to grow as well.

Humility and ability to apologise: No leader, no matter how great, is perfect and we all make mistakes! As Mandela himself said, "I am not a saint, unless you think of a saint as a sinner who keeps on trying." Madiba made mistakes as well, but always reflected and introspected, and when appropriate, he was prepared to publicly admit his mistakes and apologise to those to whom he did wrong[153]. This also illustrated the quality of humility within Madiba. As leaders, we should all strive to do what is right, but inevitably, we are bound to make mistakes from time to time, as we are only human. This has the potential to break trust, so it is at times like these that a leader needs to be able to show strength-based vulnerability, admit that he or she had misjudged, and be able to offer an apology, whilst considering what further needs to be done to correct the situation. Finally, they need to be able to learn from it. Strength-based vulnerability allows others to feel that the leader is as human as they are, and it creates trust.

A desire to understand and respect others: Madiba had the capacity to be filled with wonder and curiosity at the richness of others as he listened and sought to understand them. Great leaders do indeed listen, as Madiba did many times when in the company of seemingly ordinary and extra-ordinary people. To listen truly, one has to step into the states of *know-nothing*, meaning that one suspends assumptions about another's reality, and one combines this with a state of deep interest and authentic curiosity about the reality of another. This also means that one needs to suspend one's own internal and competing conversations, not an easy task for most of us. This requires that one must be truly silent, and as was pointed out to me, the words *listen* and *silent* actually contain the same letters. It is about listening in a way that makes others feel heard and understood, and in so doing, experiencing the empathy of the leader. Attentive silence such as this is therefore a way of respecting others, as it allows others to tell their story uninterrupted whilst the leader stays silent and allows the silence to speak for them. Instead of simply assuming what communities needed, it is through the inspirational way he listened and questioned that Madiba learnt about the needs of the community he served, followed by dedicating his time and resources to meet those needs. This evoked commitment from others that he leaned upon to help him address the needs of the communities.

AL Level 6: **Competencies:** Madiba earned a BA LLB degree in law, and he practised as a lawyer in Johannesburg, South Africa. In 1952, he founded his own law firm together with Oliver Tambo. It was the first and only all Black African law firm in the country at that time.

AL Level 7: **Behaviours:** These have been discussed in the impact that Madiba's leadership has had on the world.

When one looks closely at Madiba's internal AL Compass, it is not hard to see the strong golden thread that runs through his AL levels. This begs the question whether he had just always been as congruent and authentic as his AL Compass reflects, or whether it was a work-in-progress. I considered his development processes and found the following. Madiba did continuous learning, and continuous introspection and reflection. He was aware that he was a culmination of all of his experiences, and he embraced honest feedback from others he trusted, as follows.

Continuous learning: Madiba was always interested in, and curious about others, wanting to know more about them and about how they think about the things that they are interested in. This involves a process of continuous learning that is very rejuvenating, invigorating and inspirational. He self-studied and read extensively literature in English, Afrikaans, Sesotho and isiZulu. He also completed a BA in Law and an LLB.

Continuous introspection and reflection: Madiba had great powers of reflection and especially whilst in prison, and adopted a daily practice of introspection and reflection. He acknowledged easily that we are all human, and he expressed it as follows:

> *In real life we deal, not with gods, but with ordinary humans like ourselves; men and women who are full of contradictions, who are stable and fickle, strong and weak, famous and infamous, people in whose bloodstream the muckworm battles daily with potent pesticides. On which aspect one concentrates in judging others will depend on the character of the particular judge. As we judge others so we are judged by others*[154].

Aware that he was a culmination of all his experiences: Mandela stated that although he was introduced to, and absorbed the Western culture at the age of 23 when he moved to Johannesburg, by that time his opinions were already formed from the rural countryside and indigenous culture from which he hailed. He had an enormous respect for his own culture, a culture that contained considerable outside freedom, and many stories, legends, myths and fables that were passed on verbally from one generation to the next. It was during those years that he learned to value education, and of working collaboratively with others. He also stated that:

> *Western civilisation has not entirely rubbed off my African background and I have not forgotten the days of my childhood when we used to gather round community elders to listen to their wealth of wisdom and experience*[155].

Embraced honest feedback from those he trusted: Mandela shared the following about his colleagues:

> Walter [Sisulu] and Kathy [Kathrada] share one common feature, which forms an essential part of our friendship and which I value very much – they never hesitate to criticise me for my mistakes and throughout my political career have served as a mirror through which I can see myself[156].
>
> It is a grave error for any leader to be oversensitive in the face of criticism ...A leader should encourage and welcome [a] free and unfettered exchange of views. But no one should ever question the honesty of another comrade, whether he or she is a leader or ordinary member[157].

Viewing Madiba through his AL Compass, it becomes clear why he was as highly regarded and impactful as a global leader. Madiba was very clear about who he was (his internal identity), and what he needed to bring to the world and especially the people of South Africa (his leadership purpose). He knew what leadership vision he was working towards, even if it meant that he might lose his life in the process. His leadership purpose was his highest value, a value even higher than his love for his family or his own freedom. His beliefs and psychological states supported him in staying true to his purpose and vision. Finally, his decisions and behaviour were aligned to his values, purpose, and internal identity of *freedom fighter*. If one considers what each level in his AL Compass contained, it becomes clear how authentic a leader Madiba was throughout his life.

COMPARING TWO WELL-KNOWN AUTHENTIC LEADERS

Mandela was a great reflector and writer, and we are therefore very fortunate to be privy to many of his private thoughts, whilst Suzman was a much more private, and an extremely busy person. As a result, far fewer of her private thoughts are available for our reflection. Even so, the following illustrates how viewing two highly impactful leaders through the lens of AL, and more specifically the AL Compass, assists in understanding how, based on universal principles, two leaders from very different backgrounds can be very closely aligned as authentic leaders.

AL horizontal dimension: When one compares the backgrounds of Mandela and Suzman, what both had in common was that they came from marginalised yet privileged backgrounds and were aware from an early age that they wished to make a difference in the lives of others. Both were also supported by those that came before them to grow themselves into the authentic leaders that they had become. Although Suzman lost her mother soon after she was born, she was brought up in a stable home that valued education. Similarly, when Mandela lost his father at a young age, the paternal and maternal caring continued, as did his education. As a young boy, Mandela was in the privileged position to attend the regent's meetings as an observer, and in his adult life, the memories of these meetings informed him of the notion of effective servant leadership. Both therefore were fortunate to receive a good education that allowed them to enhance their worldviews. During their early adult lives, they became more aware of the injustices that were experienced by those who were less fortunate at the hands of an oppressive government.

The fact that both Suzman and Mandela were well educated and widely read, was reflected in their worldviews, which allowed for the inclusion of all people of South Africa as *their people*. Whilst Mandela never lost his rural and cultural roots, and deeply respected those, he also managed to embrace the Western culture, allowing him to build relationships with diverse leaders across the world.

Where their backgrounds differed, was that whilst Suzman might have at times been marginalised for being Jewish, she was a member of the White community, whilst Mandela grew up as a member of the Black disenfranchised community. Whilst they both fought for similar causes, Suzman could fight for these as an unwelcome member from within the political system, whilst Mandela had to fight it from the outside, initially from the underground movements, and thereafter in a peaceful way from within the prison system.

AL vertical dimension: In the case of both Suzman and Madiba, one could see that they were authentic leaders who stayed true to their purpose and vision, despite immense sacrifices. As they became the change they wished to see in their country, demonstrating extraordinary commitment to the cause and betterment of others, they inspired many others to go the extra mile, to do the same in any cause that they led. What is interesting is that the qualities that Madiba held dear, as outlined in his letter to his wife on 1 Feb 1975[158], are also qualities that others noticed in him; qualities such as kindness, generosity, wisdom, love of family and friends, honesty, courage, strength-based vulnerability, and serving others.

Inspiration is a reciprocal process that requires a positive regard for others. Once this happens, in one's interactions with others, one becomes both inspired and inspirational. Once we become truly inspired by both Suzman and Madiba's life and choices, we have no choice but to do our own introspection, ask the questions that especially Madiba regularly asked of himself, and to become more purposeful and courageous in life. This is what allows us to become more of an authentic leader, whether in a leadership position or merely in presence. This also increases our ability to be grounded, to see goodness in self and others, and to grow intra- and inter-relational trust between self and others, further resulting in increased leadership effectiveness.

I believe that the three most important qualities that need to be present in authentic leaders are the abilities to reflect strength-based vulnerability, relational transparency, and values-based balanced processing in their behaviour. Both leaders were able to show their vulnerability from a position of strength, showing that although they were strong, they were still human. Both Suzman and Mandela were able to incorporate transparency in their relationships with others. As a result, their followers trusted them, and whilst their opponents might not always have liked them, they were forced to respect them.

Finally, balanced processing requires that one consider the outcomes that one wishes to achieve, all the available facts, and all the stakeholders involved, whilst being guided by one's internal values-based AL Compass. Both of these leaders consistently reflected balanced processing in all that they did, and once again, this allowed them to be trusted and at least respected by others, allowing them to develop authentic leadership effectiveness.

CONCLUSION

AL is a leadership by presence that leads beyond position. When one considers that an authentic leader is a leader who is true to self, true to the appointed leadership position, with a strong moral underpinning, for the greater good of all that one serves, then viewing both Suzman and Mandela through the lens of AL reflects that they both fitted this definition comfortably. Not only did they show up strongly as authentic leaders, they both also validated the internal AL Compass model outlined in this book.

GROUP DISCUSSION: LEADERS THROUGH THE LENS OF AUTHENTIC LEADERSHIP

> **Consider the following:**
>
> 1. View through the lens of AL a political leader you admire most. What are you realising about that leader?
> 2. View through the lens of AL an organisational leader you admire most. What are you realising about that leader?
> 3. View yourselves through the lens of AL. What are you realising about yourselves as leaders?

Chapter 11

A FINAL WORD

At the outset of this book, I stated that not all leadership positions are filled by true leaders, and similarly, one does not have to be in a leadership position to be regarded as a true leader. In leadership positions, leaders usually have solid reporting lines where, in theory, those reporting to them need to do as they instruct. However, in most organisations, leaders also have dotted reporting lines, where they need to deliver through others who do not necessarily report to them, and in such scenarios, positional power is not necessarily as effective as influential power. In both situations leaders become more effective when they lead beyond position and by an AL presence.

The difference between general leadership effectiveness and ALE is that it is not only about *what* needs to be achieved, but also about *how* the *what* needs to be achieved. In this final chapter, I consider the lessons learnt from our authentic leaders, and I conclude by sharing some of my personal reflections.

LEADERSHIP LESSONS

More than ever, we live in a world that is volatile, uncertain, complex and ambiguous, and more than ever the quality of leaders affects the well-being of the system and the members that form part of the system in which they lead. Viewing both Suzman and Madiba through their internal AL Compasses demonstrates why they were regarded as highly effective and impactful global leaders. I realised during my work that there is a hierarchy for each of us in our set of values, where I define the word *values* as that which we value. At the top of our hierarchy of values is our *purpose*; that value that we value more than any other value. In the context of leadership, this refers to our leadership purpose, which is accompanied by a leadership vision; that which the leader, true to his or her purpose, is working towards. One does not have to occupy the most powerful leadership position to be experienced as a leader. It is more about aligning our enacted with our espoused values. This means that we need to know what these are, and reflect them in our behaviour, so that others also know what our values are, simply by observing our behaviour.

There is an African saying that it takes a whole village to bring up one child. The other side of the coin is that a great leader acknowledges that he or she cannot deliver on their own; that they need to deliver with and through others. Their main function becomes to influence, empower, and inspire others to deliver to the best of their abilities for the greater good of all.

In the case of AL, as in spiritual or servant leadership, we realise that our leadership purpose is divinely inspired, and that all that appears to come from us actually comes through us; that we become the vessel through which the energy and work flows. It therefore transcends ego, and becomes a blessing to realise that we are part of a bigger picture. This can be very grounding, especially in times of stormy weather, it becomes the internal compass to guide leaders to stay on track.

Celebration, especially with others, therefore becomes a life skill as it allows us to count blessings, and those blessings usually involve others and their contributions to the outcomes that we collectively aim to achieve. The act of celebration allows us to reinforce individual and collective positive behaviours, especially in times of challenge, whilst holding on to the empowering beliefs that we are all supported by forces much larger and more powerful than our own power.

Moral courage, one of the underpinnings of AL, is about standing up for what one holds to be true, even if one might feel fearful, and it is one of the distinguishing characteristics of great leaders. It is about being prepared to say or do things for the right reasons even if it might not find the acceptance of the majority. It is about being able to do so even when the potential impact on the self might not be favourable. Moral courage is not about a lack of fear; rather, it is about realising that the purpose one is working towards and that requires courage is bigger and more important than one's fear. This was true about the leadership of both Suzman and Mandela!

Principles of systems thinking imply that if one does not grow, entropy sets in. There is no such thing as remaining stagnant. Therefore, growing can be linked to joy and vitality, whilst entropy is linked to aging and dying. I once had a coaching leadership client who was the CEO of an international financial institution. This client always arrived late for our sessions, and continually had not done the self-work upon which we had previously agreed. I was forced to stop the process and asked my client to unpack this behaviour. The response I received was that this client would not have been the CEO if there were still personal development required. I then enquired about the rationale for embarking on an AL leadership programme, and the motivation offered was to be a good example to the rest of the organisational leader coachees. At this point, I chose to withdraw from the journey with this leader, as the leader developmental readiness was not sufficient to allow for openness to learning in response to the question "What is it that I do not yet know that I do not yet know?" As suggested during the interview with Prof Nicola earlier in this book, knowledge and growth are generated by remaining curious, and through having the skill to ask good questions, of oneself and others.

PERSONAL REFLECTIONS

"Your children are not your children. They are the sons and daughters of life's longing for itself. They come through you but not from you, and though they are with you, they belong not to you. You may give them your love but not your thoughts, for they have their own thoughts."[159] These words by Gibran left a profound impression on me, not only when my daughter was born, but also when this programme came into being, as I realised that this work came through me, rather than from me. It felt to me that this was bigger than me, which was liberating, but left me with a huge responsibility to ensure that the impact goes beyond me. Most of all it gave me permission always to be deeply authentic, even if it meant that I would make mistakes along the way.

The world that our children are inheriting is in crisis in many respects! I believe that the wellness of any system, be it a country, a political party, a corporate, academic or even a religious institution, is dependent on the quality of its leadership. Poor and unethical leadership affects the very fibre of society, as I am witnessing in my own country, where headlines are currently dominated by unethical leadership by our current national president. There is an outcry for more ethical and leadership effectiveness, both in South Africa, and abroad. There is a sense that leadership authenticity could be the answer to this crisis. For me, leadership authenticity, simply stated, is to be true to thy self and thy leadership position, for the greater good of all whom one serves. It starts with the self and, as it pertains to leadership, it needs to include others. It is a leadership beyond position, and a leadership that emanates from the presence of the leader. In response to the call for more ethical leadership, it appropriately includes a strong moral component.

Including the moral component does not detract from leadership authenticity, as the following story will illustrate. Years ago, when I had my telephone lines installed in my new office, I mentioned to the technician of the telecommunication organisation that I needed to buy some telephone handsets and I asked him where I could buy these. He invited me to his vehicle parked outside my office, showed me some handsets that belonged to his organisation, and offered them to me at half price as part of a private deal between him and me. I invited him to reflect back on himself as a little boy, dreaming about himself one day as a big hero, as we tend to do as little children. I then asked him whether this incident formed part of that dream. He hung his head in shame and left quietly. This episode illustrated to me that we may well start as ethical human beings, and, somewhere along the way, life events can *squeeze the best of self out of the self*. It is for this reason that I choose to include the moral component in reconnecting us with our authentic best selves.

What my AL research and practice have confirmed for me is that defining leadership authenticity, unlike so many other styles of leadership, cannot become too prescriptive. Whilst we do want to have a sense of what AL is, we need to allow it to be as unique as each human being is within their various contexts. The focus of my book is not so much on what AL is as there are ample publications that focus on that aspect. Rather, it provides more of a developmental lens on how we journey, with the support of an AL programme, towards increasing leadership authenticity.

I have therefore outlined how we take our authenticity to the next level by means of an ALD programme. I have illustrated how our history assists in informing us who we currently are (horizontal congruency). This then allows us to start building our internal compass of our current selves, after which we need to determine the level of congruency that exists within that compass (vertical congruency, above and below the soil-line). Once we have determined that, we are able to establish which further aspects we need to tweak so that we develop an internal AL Compass that empowers rather than limits us in remaining true to self and our leadership position, with a moral underpinning, for the greater good of all whom we serve.

The reason why a programme such as this one is so suitable for the development of AL is that it is process- rather than content-driven. It is a structured process, facilitated in a coaching style, which allows leaders as human beings to explore and refine their own, authentic context-specific content within their internal AL Compass.

Developing and sustaining leadership authenticity needs to be ongoing; it could be likened to AL fitness. It is a muscle that continually has to be exercised, and is continually tested in leadership and life challenges. In particular, I think of the importance of continuous introspection and the daily regulation of positive psychological states. Although it can be challenging, it becomes easier when we know who we are, why we are here, what we wish to achieve, what legacy we wish to leave, and to which values we wish to remain true. These become our inner resources to keep us facing *True North*, so that we can be who we were created to be.

The saying goes: "The fish rots from the head." Just as authentic leaders develop authentic followers, the same can be said for inauthentic and unethical leadership. In my own country, and around the world, we need to see fewer headlines about unethical leadership, and more of those influenced by leaders such as Helen Suzman and Nelson Mandela. Although both have physically left us, their legacies, underpinned by leadership authenticity, will far outlive them so that these can continue to guide us towards increased moral and influential leadership.

We, on the other hand, individually and collectively need to allow ourselves to be guided by the legacies of such leaders. Whilst each one of us is unique and we can therefore not be them, increasing our AL can help to make us more effective and influential as leaders in the way that they were. We need to balance 'problem thinking' with 'possibility thinking'. We need avoid psychological states such as apathy, and embrace the value of democracy, relational transparency, balanced processing, resilience, and moral courage, both in our thoughts and behaviours, in order to stand up against what we know to be wrong and unethical in the behaviour of especially those in powerful leadership positions. That is our responsibility! Unless we do that, it is possible for the immoral and inauthentic leadership behaviour of a few to dominate in corporate and political organisations, resulting in an adverse impact on the destinies of the majority whom they were appointed to serve.

CONCLUSION

For some in leadership positions, it can take years, even a lifetime, if at all, to discover the true self at a very deep and meaningful level. It can take even longer to master the regulation of the various processes below the soil-line that allow us as leaders to become more authentic and congruent, not only within, but in the leadership role and purpose to which we need to be true.

Leaders need to create environments that allow others to flourish and deliver to the best of their abilities, for the greater good of those they have been appointed to serve. This is what is required to allow inter-relational trust to develop between self and others in such a way that, both individually and collectively, effective and much-needed moral authentic leadership effectiveness can be experienced in our world.

APPENDICES

APPENDIX 1: LEADER PARTICIPANT PROFILES

The first ten leaders participated in my doctoral study completed in 2014 on evaluating the individual and team authentic leadership effectiveness programme. The participants comprised six males and four females. The racial spread comprised six Whites, two Indians and two Blacks. Their ages ranged between 34 and 58 years old, and most were married with children. These participants had been employed in the organisation between 5 and 33 years, and had gradually been promoted into their current positions. Other than the brewmaster, all participants had reporting teams, with between four and sixteen direct reports, and reporting teams of up to 270 people.

Pseudonym		Detailed profile
Darren	Gender and age:	Male, 46 years old
	Family status:	Married, with one teenage son
	Duration in job:	Fifteen years
	Reporting team:	74 people in his department, with 4 direct reports
Hannah	Gender and age:	Female, 37 years old
	Family status:	Married, with two young sons
	Duration in job:	Four years.
	Reporting team:	Small HR team
Dobek	Gender and age:	Male, 56 years old
	Family status:	Married, with three adult children
	Duration in job:	20 years
	Reporting team:	24 people, and 5 direct reports
Justin	Gender and age:	Male, 40 years old
	Family status:	Married, with three young children
	Duration in job:	Five years
	Reporting team:	8 people, all direct reports
Peter	Gender and age:	Male, 58 years old.
	Family status:	Married, with three adult children
	Duration in job:	11 years.
	Reporting team:	25 people, with four direct reports
Gugu	Gender and age:	Female, 34 years old
	Family status:	Single, with one young child
	Duration in job:	One year
	Reporting team:	100 people, with 10 direct reports

Pseudonym		Detailed profile
Vanya	Gender and age:	Female, 34 years old
	Family status:	Married, with two young children
	Duration in job:	One year
	Reporting team:	Her department was small, with one direct report
Liam	Gender and age:	Male, 51 years old
	Family status:	Married, with two teenage children
	Duration in job:	Five years
	Reporting team:	The whole of the brewery, with nine direct reports
Nikhil	Gender and age:	Male, 39 years old
	Family status:	Married, with two small children
	Duration in job:	One year
	Reporting team:	270 people, and he had 16 direct reports
Andrea	Gender and age:	Female, 39 years old
	Family status:	Single, with partner
	Duration in job:	Three years
	Reporting team:	25 people, and she had 4 direct reports

APPENDIX 2: TEMPLATE FOR TESTING LEADERSHIP DEVELOPMENTAL READINESS

How coachable are you?

Coachability has to do with the ability to receive coaching and to use coaching for discovery, awareness, change, improvement, etc. In order to establish how ready you are for coaching, please answer the following questions:

Coachable factors:	Yes/No	To what degree?
Openness: Am I open to change, learning, and personal development?		
Feedback openness: Am I open for receiving feedback?		
Ego strength: Do I have sufficient ego strength to face reality as it is?		
Committed to growth: Am I committed to my own development?		
Relationship readiness: Am I ready and able to enter into a coaching relationship?		
Vulnerable: Am I ready and able to make myself vulnerable to another?		
Hungry for transformation: Am I really hungry for making a meaningful change or transformation?		
Dreams and goals: Do I have goals, hopes, and dreams?		
Patience: Do I have the patience to stay with the coaching process?		

APPENDIX 3: PROGRAMME CONTRACTING – COMMITMENT DOCUMENT

The AL facilitator's commitment to the client:

- I will be open, frank, and honest with you at all times.
- I will remain unbiased, unprejudiced, and non-judgmental.
- I will ensure confidentiality.
- I will do what I say I will do.
- I will use language you can understand rather than jargon.
- I will maintain regular contact with you during the programme.
- I will respond promptly to your phone calls and correspondence.
- I won't keep you waiting for appointments nor take phone calls when you're with me.
- I will provide you with timely and accurate information, materials, and resources.
- I will design an individual coaching plan for you, and work with you on its implementation.
- I will recommend other service providers where appropriate.
- Your well-being is my top priority.
- I will guarantee our effort and dedication will be of the highest standard.

The ALE programme participant's commitment to the AL facilitator:

- You will be open, frank, and honest at all times.
- You will be on time for your appointments with me.
- You will cancel or reschedule an appointment at least 48 workday hours before or sacrifice this session.
- You will let me know immediately of any concerns you have about our work together.
- You will give me all the information I need to do the work.
- You will make time available to work on the things you've agreed to work on.
- You will be willing and committed to doing the work and to completing assignments in sufficient time for me to process them, if necessary, before our next meeting.
- You will listen to my advice or ideas, but retain the absolute right to accept or reject them.
- You will give feedback about my performance when asked, and provide helpful feedback on how you experienced the coaching at the end of the ALD programme.
- You will pay forward to those around you the benefits gained from your ALD programme.

Leader: _____

AL facilitator: _____

Date: _____

APPENDIX 4: PROGRAMME COMPONENT – ADULT EXPERIENTIAL LEARNING

Kolb's experiential learning theory draws on the work of prominent 20th-century scholars who gave experience a central role in the theories of human learning and development, notably John Dewey, Kurt Lewin, Jean Piaget, William James, Carl Jung, Paulo Freire, Carl Rogers, and others – to develop a holistic model of the experiential learning process for human beings. This theory[160] is built on six propositions based on the work done by the aforementioned scholars.

1. Learning is best thought of in terms of a process, rather than outcomes; the focus should be on engaging students in a process that best enhances their learning as various individuals have different styles of learning. This process should include feedback on the effectiveness of the learning efforts.
2. All learning is about relearning. It is therefore a continuous process, which allows them to refine their ideas.
3. Learning requires the resolution of conflicts between dialectically opposed modes of adaptation to the world. In the process of learning, one is called upon to move back and forth between opposing modes of reflecting and acting, and thinking and feeling.
4. Learning is also a holistic process of adapting to the world. It is not just the result of cognition, but also involves integrating the functioning of the total person, which includes thinking, feeling, perceiving, and behaving.
5. Learning results from the interaction between the person and the environment. Learning occurs by assimilating new experiences into existing concepts, and accommodating existing contents into new experiences.
6. Learning is the process of creating knowledge. Experiential learning theory proposes a constructivist theory of learning, whereby social knowledge is created and re-created in the personal knowledge of the learner.

Reflective journaling template for the use of adult experiential learning

What? (concrete experience)	So what? (reflective observation)	Now what? (new learnings)
Behavioural description of what happened (in coaching or elsewhere) – 1st experience	My thoughts about it My feelings about it	Notice connections, trends, patterns or themes. Include new thoughts, awareness, and insights.
Behavioural description of what happened after it happened – 2nd experience	My thoughts about it My feelings about it	
Behavioural description – 3rd experience	My thoughts about it My feelings about it	

APPENDIX 5: PROGRAMME COMPONENT – LIFE CHAPTERS

Chapter 1:   *Title:*

Dates: From: _____ To: _____

Memorable Events (detailed writing in narrative style): _____

_____

_____

_____

Significant Places: _____

_____

_____

_____

Significant People: _____

_____

_____

_____

Main Challenges: _____

_____

_____

_____

Themes from this chapter that impacted on who you are today (values, beliefs, emotional and mind states): _____

_____

_____

_____

Features of the ending and transition to Chapter 2: _____

_____

_____

_____

© Life Chapters – MCC Wulffers 2009 – Adapted from template by Elaine Cox, 2006, p. 207.

APPENDIX 6: PROGRAMME COMPONENT – INDIVIDUAL AL COMPASS

	Current	Possible Self
Behaviour/ performance At work: Outside work / with others:		
My skills		
My Thoughts (internal conversations): About work: Outside work:		
My Emotional States / Feelings: Work: Outside work:		
Beliefs: About Self: About NB Others: At Work: For instance My senior (s): My peers: My reports / team: My Organisation: Outside work: Family: My friends: Friend 1 Etc:		
Values		
Leader Purpose		
Leadership Legacy		
Leadership Vision		
Leadership Internal Identity		

© 2009 – 2016 – MCC Wulffers – Internal AL Compass

APPENDIX 7: PROGRAMME COMPONENT – INDIVIDUAL ALEC

My Authentic Leadership Effectiveness Charter

Name: _____ Date: _____

OUTPUT – Quality of My Authentic Leadership

I wish to achieve performance excellence in the following Leadership outcomes:
You can take your coaching outcomes, for instance, and their accompanying key behavioural indicators (KBIs), and divide those into the following categories:

(Intra)-Personal/Self-Leadership: Leading from the inside out
•

Interpersonal/People Leadership:
•

Professional Leadership
•

Societal Leadership: (at home and in community, where applicable)
•

INPUT – Meaningful drivers that underpin and inform me

Themes from my Life and Work History
Themes that have emerged from Life Chapters exercise that still limit or empower me!
- LIMITING
- EMPOWERING

My Training and Development
Aspects of my training and development that still play a big role and help fill my toolbox
-

Theoretical Perspectives
Theories from others that stand out and inform me. Be specific.
-

My Internal Identity
A two- or three-word metaphor that describes the internal identity that drives me, e.g. 'victim' or 'people-pleaser'
-

My Leadership Purpose
My belief about why I am here
-

My Leadership Vision (and Legacy)
That which is very compelling for me to work towards so that I can leave a worthy legacy behind…
-

My Values and Ethics
The principles and guidelines that classify what beliefs and behaviours are important in my life.
-

My Beliefs about Self and Others
The limiting or empowering opinions I have that I believe to be true in terms of:
- Self
  -
- Others (divide these others into groups that are meaningful to you, such as: boss, peers, team, organisation, life-partner, children, friends, etc)
  -

My Emotional States and States of Mind
The limiting or empowering states of mind and emotions that drive my thoughts and behaviour.
-

THRU'PUT – Usage of My Toolbox

My toolbox, based on my underpinnings, in terms of leadership skills/processes/models (be specific) in terms of the following:

(Intra)-Personal/Self-Leadership

-

Interpersonal/People Leadership.

-

Professional Leadership. These are your technical skills, such as financial, strategy, legal acumen.

-

Societal Leadership (at home and in community, where applicable)

-

© Authentic Leadership Effectiveness Charter – MCC Wulffers – 2008 – 2016

APPENDIX 8: PROGRAMME COMPONENT – TEAM ALEC

TEAM SCORECARD – Key Performance Indicators (KPIs)

OUR TEAM SKILLS

TECHNICAL	PEOPLE

TEAM INTERNAL IDENTITY

TEAM PURPOSE

TEAM VISION AND LEGACY

VISION	LEGACY

TEAM VALUES

OUR TEAM

BELIEFS	BEHAVIOURS

OUR ORGANISATION

BELIEFS	BEHAVIOURS

FIVE TEAM ALE LEVELS

LATERAL TRUST

BELIEFS	BEHAVIOURS

ENCOURAGING HEALTHY DISAGREEMENT

BELIEFS	BEHAVIOURS

COMMITTING TO ACTION

BELIEFS	BEHAVIOURS

EMBRACING ACCOUNTABILITY

BELIEFS	BEHAVIOURS

FOCUSING ON RESULTS

BELIEFS	BEHAVIOURS

REFERENCES

Abbot, P., & Bennett, K. (2011). *A guide to coachees.* Randburg: Knowres Publishing.

Akrivou, K., Bourantas, D., Mo, S., & Papalois, E. (2011). The sound of silence - A Space for Morality? The role of solitude for ethical decision making. *Journal of Business Ethics, 102,* 119-133. doi:10.1007/s10551-011-0803-3.

Archer, M. A. (2009). Authentic teaming: Undiscussables, leadership and the role of the consultant. *Organization Development Journal, 27*(4), 83-92.

Archer, S. (2012). Barclays – a lesson in leadership. Retrieved from http://www.growthbusiness.co.uk/growing-a-business/leadership-and-mentors/2113093/barclays-a-lesson-in-leadership.thtml

Avolio, B. J. (2010). Pursuing Authentic Leadership Development. In N. Nohria & R. Khurana (Eds.), *Handbook of Leadership Theory and Practice* (pp. 721-750). Boston: Harvard Business Press Books.

Avolio, B. J., & Gardner, W. L. (2005). Authentic Leadership Development: Getting to the root of positive forms of leadership. *The Leadership Quarterly, 16*(3), 315-337.

Avolio, B. J., Gardner, W. L., & Walumbwa, F. O. (2005). Preface. In W. L. Gardner, B. J. Avolio, & F. O. Walumbwa (Eds.), *Monographs in leadership and management volume 3: Authentic leadership theory and practice: Origins, effects and development* (pp. xxi-xxix). Amsterdam: Elsevier.

Avolio, B. J., Gardner, W. L., & Walumbwa, F. O. (2007). Authentic leadership questionnaire (ALQ). Retrieved from http://www.mlq.com.au/Network/Secure/vJ8vtcrc396d/docs/ALQSampleReport.pdf

Avolio, B. J., Gardner, W. L., Walumbwa, F. O., Luthans, F., & May, D. R. (2004). Unlocking the mask: A look at the process by which authentic leaders impact follower attitudes and behaviors. *The Leadership Quarterly, 15*(15), 801-823. doi:10.1016/j.leaqua.2004.09.003

Barr, R. (2012, July 7). Bob Diamond, Barclays Chief Executive, Quits Amid Mounting Pressure Over Rate-Fixing Scandal.

Barrett, R. (2010). *The new leadership paradigm.* Waynesville, US: Richard Barrett.

Cascio, W., & Luthans, F. (2014). Reflections on the Metamorphosis Institutional Work and Positive Psychological Capital. *Journal of Management Inquiry, 23*(1), 51-67. doi:10.1177/1056492612474348

Cashman, K. (2008). *Leadership from the Inside Out. Becoming a Leader for Life.* San Francisco: Berrett-Koehler Publishers, Inc.

Chan, A. (2005). Authentic leadership measurement and development: challenges and suggestions. In W. L. Gardner, B. J. Avolio, & F. O. Walumbwa (Eds.), *Monographs in leadership and management volume 3: Authentic leadership theory and practice: Origins, effects and development* (pp. 227-250). Amsterdam: Elsevier.

Chan, A., Hannah, S. T., & Gardner, W. L. (2005). Veritable authentic leadership: Emergence, functioning and impacts. In W. L. Gardner, B. J. Avolio, & F. O. Walumbwa (Eds.), *Monographs in leadership and management volume 3: Authentic leadership theory and practice: Origins, effects and development* (pp. 3 - 41). Amsterdam: Elsevier.

Clapp-Smith, R., Vogelgesang, G. R., & Avey, J. B. (2009). Authentic leadership and positive psychological capital: the mediating role of trust at the group level of analysis. *Journal of Leadership & Organizational Studies, 15*(3), 227-240.

Clutterbuck, D., & Megginson, D. (2005). *Making coaching work: Creating a coaching culture.* London, UK: The Chartered Institute of Personnel and Development (CIPD).

Cooper, C., Scandura, T., & Schriesheim, C. (2005). Looking forward but learning from our past: Potential challenges to developing authentic leadership theory and authentic leaders. *The Leadership Quarterly, 16*(3), 475-494. doi:10.1016/j.leaqua.2005.03.008

Covey, S. R. (1989). *The 7 habits of highly effective people.* London, UK: Simon & Schuster UK Ltd.

Cox, E. (2006). An adult learning approach to coaching. In D. R. Stober & A. Grant (Eds.), *Evidence based coaching handbook* (pp. 193-218). New Jersey: John Wiley & Sons, Inc.

Cox , E. (2013). *Coaching understood: A pragmatic inquiry into the coaching process*. London: Sage Publications.

Cummings, E. E. (1958). A Poet's Advice. Retrieved from http://www.thepositivemind.com/poetry/APoet%27sAdvicepoem.html

Dasborough, M. T., & Ashkanasy, N. M. (2005). Follower emotional reactions to authentic and inauthentic leadership influence. In W. L. Gardner, B. J. Avolio, & F. O. Walumbwa (Eds.), *Monographs in leadership and management volume 3: Authentic leadership theory and practice: Origins, effects and development* (pp. 281-302). Amsterdam: Elsevier.

Demartini, J. (2013). *The values factor*. New York: Penguin Group.

Diddams, M., & Chang, G. C. (2012). Only human. Exploring the nature of weakness in authentic leadership. *The Leadership Quarterly, 23*, 593-603. doi:10.1016/j.leaqua.2011.12.010

Dilts, R. (2003). Neurological levels. Retrieved from www.brefigroup.co.uk/acrobat/neurolog.pdf

Dolny, H. (2009). *Team coaching: Artists at work*. Rosebank: Penguin Books.

Douglas, C., Ferris, G. R., & Perrewe, P. L. (2005). Leader political skill and authentic leadership. In W. L. Gardner, B. J. Avolio, & F. O. Walumba (Eds.), *Monographs in leadership and management volume 3: Authentic leadership theory and practice: Origins, effects and development* (Vol. 3, pp. 139-154). Amsterdam: Elsevier.

Dweck, C. S. (2008). *Mindset: The new psychology of success*. New York: Ballantyne Books.

Editorial. (2013, 29th November). Nkandla report: Zuma in the deep end. *Mail & Guardian*.

Eigel, K. M., & Kuhnert, K. W. (2005). Authentic development: Leadership development level and executive effectiveness. In W. L. Gardner, B. J. Avolio, & F. O. Walumbwa (Eds.), *Monographs in leadership and management volume 3: Authentic leadership theory and practice: Origins, effects and development* (pp. 357-386). Amsterdam: Elsevier.

Fisher Turesky, E., & Gallagher, D. (2011). Coaching for leadership using Kolb's experiential learning theory. *The Coaching Psychologist, 7*(1), 5-14.

Frankl, V. E. (2004). *Man's search for meaning*. London: Rider.

Franzese, A. T. (2007). *To Thine Own Self Be True? An exploration in authenticity*. (Doctorate of of Philosophy in the department of Sociology), Graduate School of Duke University, New York.

Freeman, R., & Auster, E. R. (2011). Values, authenticity, and responsible leadership. *Journal of Business Ethics, 98*, 15-23. doi:10.1007/s10551-011-1022-7

Friedman, S. D. (2006). Learning to lead in all domains of life. *American Behavioral Scientist, 49*(9), 1270-1297. doi:10.1177/0002764206286389

Fry, L. W., & Whittington, J. L. (2005). In search of authenticity: Spiritual leadership theory as a source for future theory, research, and practice on authentic leadership. In W. L. Gardner, B. J. Avolio, & F. O. Walumbwa (Eds.), *Monographs in leadership and management volume 3: Authentic leadership theory and practice: Origins, effects and development* (pp. 183-202). Amsterdam: Elsevier.

Gallagher, C. (2015). VW's emissions scandal: a test of authentic leadership? Retrieved from http://www.insidechr.com.au/volkswagen-emissions-debacle/

Gandhi, M. (2012). Mahatma Gandhi quotes. Retrieved from http://thinkexist.com/quotes/mahatma_gandhi/

Gardner, W. L., Avolio, B. J., Luthans, F., May, D. R., & Walumbwa, F. O. (2005). "Can you see the real me?" A self-based model of authentic leader and follower development. *The Leadership Quarterly, 16*(16), 343-372. doi:10.1016/j.leaqua.2005.03.003

Gardner, W. L., Avolio, B. J., & Walumbwa, F. O. (2005). Authentic leadership development: Emergent themes and future directions. In W. L. Gardner, B. J. Avolio, & F. O. Walumbwa (Eds.), *Monographs in leadership and management volume 3: Authentic leadership theory and practice: Origins, effects and development* (pp. 357-386). Amsterdam: Elsevier.

George, B. (2003). *Authentic leadership: Rediscover the secrets to creating lasting value*. San Francisco: Jossey-Bass, USA.

George, B. (2004). The journey to authenticity. Retrieved from http://www.hbs.edu/faculty/Pages/item.aspx?num=16233

George, B., & Sims, P. (2007). *True north: Discover your authentic leadership*. San Francisco: Jossey-Bass, USA.

Gibran, K. (1926). *The Prophet*. Oxford: Macmillan Publishers.

Gosling, M., & Huang, H. J. (2010). The fit between integrity and integrative social contracts theory. *Journal of Business Ethics, 90*, 407-417. doi:10.1007/s10551-010-0425-1

Haffajee, F. (2015). *What if there were no Whites in South Africa?* Johannesburg: Picador Africa.

Haines, S. G., Aller-Stead, G., & McKinlay, J. (2005). *Enterprise-wide change: Superior results through systems thinking*. San Francisco: John Wiley & Sons Inc.

Hall, L. M., & Bodenhamer, B. G. (2004). *Figuring out people*. Carmarthen, Wales: Crown House Publishing Ltd.

Hall, L. M., & Duval, M. (2002). Meta-Coach training system and certification. Clifton: NSP – Neuro-Semantic Publications.

Hall, L. M., & Duval, M. (2005). Axes of change: A new way for coaching. Retrieved from http://www.neurosemantics. com

Hannah, S. T., & Avolio, B. J. (2010). Ready or not: How do we accelerate the developmental readiness of leaders? *Organizational Behavior, 31*, 1181-1187. doi:10.1002/job.675

Hannah, S. T., Avolio, B. J., & Walumbwa, F. O. (2011). Relationships between authentic leadership, moral courage, and ethical and pro-social behaviors. *Business Ethics Quarterly, 21*(4), 555-578.

Hannah, S. T., Lester, P. B., & Vogelgesang, G. R. (2005). Moral leadership: Explicating the moral component of authentic leadership. In W. L. Gardner, B. J. Avolio, & F. O. Walumbwa (Eds.), *Monographs in leadership and management volume 3: Authentic leadership theory and Practice: Origins, effects and development* (pp. 43-82). Amsterdam: Elsevier.

Hannah, S. T., Walumbwa, F. O., & Fry, L. W. (2011). Leadership in action teams: Team leader and members' authenticity, authenticity strength, and team outcomes. *Personnel Psychology, 64*(1), 771-802.

Hassan, A., & Ahmed, F. (2011). Authentic leadership, trust and work engagement. *World Academy of Science, Engineering and Technology, 80*(1), 750-756.

Hawkins, P. (2014). *Leadership team coaching: Developing collective transformational leadership*. London: Kogan Page Ltd.

Hedman, A. (2001). The person-centered approach. In B. Peltier (Ed.), *The psychology of executive coaching: Theory and application* (pp. 66-80). New York: Routledge: Taylor and Francis Group, LLC.

Heineman, B. W. (2009). High performance with high integrity: The foundation of global capitalism. Retrieved from http://ethisphere.com/high-performance-with-integrity-the-foundation-of-global-capitalism/

Hernez-Broome, G., & Hughes, R. L. (2004). Leadership Development: Past, present and future. *Human Resource Planning, 27*(1), 24-32.

Hotten, R. (2015). Volkswagen: The scandal explained. *BBC News*. Retrieved from http://www.bbc.com/news/business-34324772

Hudson, F. M., & McLean, P. D. (1995). *Lifelaunch: A passionate guide to the rest of your life*. California: The Hudson Institute Press.

Hughes, L. W. (2005). Developing transparent relationships through humor in the authentic leader-follower relationship. In W. L. Gardner, B. J. Avolio, & F. O. Walumbwa (Eds.), *Monographs in leadership and management volume 3: Authentic leadership theory and practice: Origins, effects and development.* (pp. 83-106). Amsterdam: Elsevier.

Ilies, R., Morgeson, F. P., & Nahrgang, J. D. (2005). Authentic leadership and eudaemonic well-being: Understanding leader–follower outcomes. *The Leadership Quarterly, 16*, 373-394. doi:10.1016/j.leaqua.2005.03.002

Kalungu-Banda, M. (2006). *Leading like Madiba: Leadership lessons from Nelson Mandela*. Cape Town: Double Storey Books.

Katzenbach, J. R., & Smith, D. K. (1993a). The discipline of teams. *Harvard Business Review*, 111-120.

Katzenbach, J. R., & Smith, D. K. (1993b). *The wisdom of teams: Creating a high-performance organisation*. London: The McGraw-Hill Companies.

Kauffman, C. (2006). Positive psychology: The science at the heart of coaching. In D. R. Stober & A. M. Grant (Eds.), *Evidence based coaching handbook* (pp. 219-254). Hoboken, New Jersey: John Wiley & Sons, Inc.

Kets de Vries, M. F. R. (2005). The dangers of feeling like a fake. *Harvard Business Review*.

Khan, S. N. (2010). Impact of authentic leaders on organization performance. *International Journal of Business and Management, 5*(12), 167-172.

Klenke, K. (2005). The internal theater of the authentic leader: integrating cognitive, affective, cognative and spiritual facets of authentic leadership. In W. L. Gardner, B. J. Avolio, & F. O. Walumbwa (Eds.), *Monographs in leadership and management volume 3: Authentic leadership theory and practice: Origins, effects and development* (pp. 155-182). Amsterdam: Elsevier.

Kline, N. (1999). *Time to think: listening to ignite the mind*. London: Cassel Illustrated.

Kolb, A. Y., & Kolb, D. A. (2005). *The Kolb learning style inventory – Version 3.1 2005 Technical Specifications*: Cape Western Reserve University: Hay Group.

Kolditz, T. A., & Brazil, D. M. (2005). Authentic leadership in extremis settings: A concept for extraordinary leaders in exceptional situations. In W. L. Gardner, B. J. Avolio, & F. O. Walumbwa (Eds.), *Monographs in leadership and management volume 3: Authentic leadership theory and practice: Origins, effects and development* (pp. 345-356). Amsterdam: Elsevier.

Kretzschmar, I. (2010). Exploring client's readiness for coaching. *International Journal of Evidence based Coaching and Mentoring* (Special issue no. 4), 1-19.

Ladkin, D., & Taylor, S. S. (2010). Enacting the 'true self': Towards a theory of embodied authentic leadership. *Leadership Quarterly, 21*(1), 64-74. doi:10.1016/j.leaqua.2009.10.005

Lencioni, P. (2002). *The five dysfunctions of a team: a leadership fable*. San Francisco: Jossey-Bass.

Lencioni, P. (2005). *Overcoming the five dysfunctions of a team: A field guide*. San Francisco: Jossey-Bass.

Leroy, H., Palanski, M. E., & Simons, T. (2012). Authentic leadership and behavioral integrity as drivers of follower commitment and performance. *Journal of Business Ethics, 107*, 255-264. doi:10.1007/s10551-011-1036-1

Leroy, H., & Sels, L. (2008). Authentic functioning: Being true to the Self in the organisation. Retrieved from https://lirias.kuleuven.be/handle/123456789/198466

Luthans, F., & Avolio, B. J. (2009). The "point" of positive organizational behavior. *Journal of Organizational Behaviour, 30*(1), 291-307. doi:10.1002/job.589

Luthans, F., & Youssef, C. M. (2004). Human, social, and now positive psychological capital management: Investing in people for competitive advantage. *Organizational dynamics, 33*(2), 143-160. doi:10.1016/j.orgdyn.2004.01.003

Mandela, N. (1994). *Long walk to freedom: The autobiography of Nelson Mandela*. Randburg: Macdonald Purnell.

Mandela, N. (2010). *Conversations with myself*. London: Macmillan.

Masarech, M. A. (2001). Authentic leadership: A challenge and a process. *Employment relations today, 28*(3), 79-84.

Maus, H. A. (2011). *Forget about motivation: Focus on productive engagement*. Charlotte, North Carolina: Kona Publishing & Media Group.

Mawson, N. (2012, 15th May 2012). Absa backs down on retrenchments ITWeb_php.

May, D. R., Chan, A., Hodges, T. D., & Avolio, B. J. (2003). Developing the moral component of authentic leadership. *Organizational Dynamics, 32*(3), 247-260.

Meyer, T. (2007). The nature of leadership: Perspectives. In T. Meyer & I. Boninelli (Eds.), *Conversations in leadership: South African perspectives* (pp. 3-17). Randburg, South Africa: Knowledge Resources.

Michie, S., & Gooty, J. (2005). Values, emotions, and authenticity: Will the real leader please stand up? *The Leadership Quarterly, 16*, 441-457. doi:10.1016/j.leaqua.2005.03.006

Mintz, S. (2015). Is Donald Trump an Authentic Leader? *Ethics Sage*. Retrieved from http://www.ethicssage.com/2015/09/is-donald-trump-an-authentic-leader-.html

Mkokeli, S., Paton, C., Ndzamela, P., & Ensor, L. (2015, 10th December 2015). Rand crashes after Zuma fires Nene. *Business Day*. Retrieved from http://www.bdlive.co.za/markets/2015/12/10/rand-crashes-after-zuma-fires-nene

Nelson Mandela Foundation. (2014). Biography of Nelson Mandela. Retrieved from https://www.nelsonmandela.org/content/page/biography/

O'Neill, M. B. (2000). *Executive coaching with backbone and heart: A systems approach to engaging leaders with their challenges.* San Francisco: Jossey-Bass.

Peltier, B. (2001). *The psychology of executive coaching: Theory and application.* New York: Routledge.

Peterson, S. J., Walumbwa, F. O., Avolio, B. J., & Hannah, S. T. (2012). The relationship between authentic leadership and follower job performance: The mediating role of follower positivity in extreme contexts. *The Leadership Quarterly, 23,* 502-516. doi:10.1016/j.leaqua.2011.12.004

Peus, C., Wesche, J. S., Streicher, B., Braun, S., & Frey, D. (2012). Authentic leadership: An empirical test of its antecedents, consequences, and mediating mechanisms. *Journal of Business Ethics, 107*(3), 331-348. doi:10.1007/s10551-011-1042-3

Pimstone, M., & Suzman, H. (2005). Helen Suzman, fighter for human rights:[exhibition catalogue]. Cape Town: Kaplan Centre.

Prince, R. (2012). MPs admit they let Diamond slip away ahead of inquiry vote http://www.telegraph.co.uk/news/politics/9377922/MPs-admit-they-let-Diamond-slip-away-ahead-of-inquiry-vote.html

Rego, A., Sousa, F., Marques, C., & Pina e Cunha, M. (2012). Hope and positive affect mediating the authentic leadership and creativity relationship. *Journal of Business Research, In press,* 1-11. doi:10.1016/j.jbusres.2012.10.003

Rego, A., Vitoria, A., Magalhaes, A., Ribiero, N., & Pina e Cunha, M. (2013). Are authentic leaders associated with more virtuous, committed and potent teams? *The Leadership Quarterly, 24,* 61-79. doi:10.1016/j.leaqua.2012.08.002

Reichard, R. J., & Avolio, B. J. (2005). Where are we? The status of leadership intervention research: a meta-analytic summary. In W. L. Gardner, B. J. Avolio, & F. O. Walumbwa (Eds.), *Monographs in leadership and management volume 3: Authentic leadership theory and practice: Origins, effects and development.* (pp. 203-226). Amsterdam: Elsevier.

Roberts, L. M., Dutton, J. E., Spreitzer, G. M., Heaphy, E. D., & Quinn, R. E. (2005). Composing the reflected best-self portrait: Building pathways for becoming extraordinary in work organizations. *Academy of Management Review, 30*(4), 712-736.

Rock, D. (2006). *Quiet leadership: Six steps to transforming performance at work.* New York: HarperCollins Publishers.

Rock, D., & Cox, C. (2012). SCARF in 2012: updating the social neuroscience of collaborating with others. *Neuroleadership Journal, 2012*(4).

Rock, D., & Page, L. (2009). *Coaching with the brain in mind.* Hoboken, New Jersey: John Wiley and Sons.

SAPA, R. a. B. D. (2012). Absa feels Barclays' pain.

Scharmer, O. (2007). *Theory U.* Cambridge: Society for Organisational Learning.

Scheepers, C. (2012). *Coaching leaders – 7 'P' Tools to propel change.* Randburg: Knowres Publishing (Pty) Ltd.

Seligman, M. E. P., & Csikszentmihalyi, M. (2000). Positive psychology: An introduction. *The American psychologist, 55*(1), 5-14.

Shamir, B., & Eilam, G. (2005). 'What's your story?' A life stories approach to authentic leadership development. *The Leadership Quarterly, 16*(3), 395-417.

Sieler, A. (1999). The art of listening.

Sieler, A. (2005). *Coaching to the Human Soul: Ontological coaching and deep change* (Vol. 1). Blackburn, Victoria, Australia: Newfield, Australia.

Sparrowe, R. T. (2005). Authentic leadership and the narrative self. *The Leadership Quarterly, 16*(16), 419-439. doi:10.1016/j.leaqua.2005.03.004

Spinelli, E. (2007). *Practising existential psychotherapy: The relational world.* London: Sage.

Stamp, G. (2016). The Tripod of Work. Retrieved from http://bioss.com/gillian-stamp/the-tripod-of-work/

Stapleton, J. (2015). What is the Barclays Libor Rigging Scandal. Retrieved from http://www.lbc.co.uk/the-barclays-libor-rigging-scandal-explained-56812

Stop-Absa-Solidarity. (2012). Today, tomorrow, goodbye Retrieved from https://www.youtube.com/watch?v=TwJcaNqumZE

Stout Rostron, S. (2009). *Business coaching wisdom and practice: Unleashing the secrets of business coaching*. Randburg, South Africa: Knowledge Resources.

Terry, R. W. (1993). *Authentic Leadership: Courage in Action*. San Francisco: Jossey-Bass Publishers.

Ting, S. (2006). Our view of coaching for leadership development. In S. Ting & P. Scisco (Eds.), *The CCL handbook of coaching: A guide for the leader coach* (pp. 15-33). San Francisco, US: Jossey-Bass business & management series and the Centre for Creative Leadership.

Tobias, R. M., & Taylor, D. (2012). Tough economic times call for authentic leaders. *The public manager, 41*(1), 48-52.

Tutu, D. (2015). Desmond Tutu. Retrieved from http://www.biography.com/people/desmond-tutu-9512516

Van Coller-Peter, S. (2015). *Coaching leadership teams*. Randburg, South Africa: Knowledge Resources.

Van Onselen, G. (2014). *Clever Blacks, Jesus and Nkandla: The real Jacob Zuma in his own words*. Johannesburg: Jonathan Ball Publishers (Pty) Ltd.

Van Velsor, E., & McCauley, C. D. (2004). Introduction: Our view of leadership development. In C. D. McCauley & E. Van Velsor (Eds.), *The centre for creative leadership handbook of leadership development* (pp. 1-22). San Francisco: Jossey-Bass.

Varella, P., Javidan, M., & Waldman, D. (2005). The differential effects of socialised and personalized leadership on group social capital. In W. L. Gardner, B. J. Avolio, & F. O. Walumbwa (Eds.), *Monographs in leadership and management volume 3: Authentic leadership theory and practice: Origins, effects and development.* (pp. 107-138). Amsterdam: Elsevier.

Walumbwa, F. O., Avolio, B. J., Gardner, W. L., & Peterson, S. J. (2008). Authentic leadership: Development and validation of a theory-based measure. *Journal of Management, 34*(1), 89-126. doi:10.1177/0149206307308913

Walumbwa, F. O., Luthans, F., Avey, J. B., & Oke, A. (2011). Authentically leading groups: The mediating role of collective psychological capital and trust. *Journal of Organisational Behaviour, 32*(1), 4-24. doi:10.1002/job

Walumbwa, F. O., Wang, P., Schaubroeck, J., & Avolio, B. J. (2010). Psychological processes linking authentic leadership to follower behaviors. *The Leadership Quarterly, 21*, 901-914. doi:10.1016/leaqua.2010.07.015

Weischer, A. E., Weibler, J., & Peterson, M. (2013). "To thine own self be true":The effects of enactment and life storytelling on perceived leader authenticity. *The Leadership Quarterly, 24*(4), 477-495. doi:10.1016/j.leaqua.2013.03.003

Wulffers, M. C. C. (2009). Exploring the perceived benefits of the self-development of authentic leadership in organisations through one-to-one coaching.

Wulffers, M. C. C. (2014). *Evaluating a leadership authenticity programme.* (PhD), University of Johannesburg, Johannesburg.

Yammarino, F. J., Dionne, S. D., Schriesheim, C. A., & Dansereau, F. (2008). Authentic leadership and positive organizational behavior: A meso, multilevel perspective. *The Leadership Quarterly, 19*(6), 693-707. doi:10.1016/j.leaqua.2008.09.004

Youssef, C. M., & Luthans, F. (2005). Resiliency development of organizations, leaders and employees: Multi level theory building for sustained performance. In W. L. Gardner, B. J. Avolio, & F. O. Walumbwa (Eds.), *Monographs in leadership and management volume 3: Authentic leadership theory and practice: Origins, effects and development* (pp. 303-344). Amsterdam: Elsevier.

Zhu, W., Avolio, B. J., Riggio, R. E., & Sosik, J. J. (2011). The effect of authentic transformational leadership on follower and group ethics. *The Leadership Quarterly, 22*, 801-817. doi:10.1016/j.leaqua.2011.07.004

ENDNOTES

1. Mandela, 2010, pp. 211-212
2. Kalungu-Banda, 2006, p. 9
3. Hotten, 2015
4. George, 2007
5. Barr, 2012, July 7
6. Prince, 2012
7. SAPA, 2012
8. Mawson, 2012
9. Stop-Absa-Solidarity, 2012
10. Stapleton, 2015
11. Lencioni, 2002, p. vii
12. Heineman, p. 2009
13. Mintz, Stephen, 2015
14. Cummings, 1958, p.1
15. Cited in Chan, Hannah & Gardner, 2005, p.3
16. Frankl, 2004
17. Chan, Hannah & Gardner, 2005
18. Avolio, Gardner, & Walumba, 2005, p. xxiii
19. Roberts, Dutton, Spreitzer, Heaphy & Quinn, 2005, p. 713
20. Lencioni, 2002
21. Chan, Hannah & Gardner, 2005
22. Eigel & Kuhnert, 2005
23. Eigel & Kuhnert, 2005
24. Chan, Hannah & Gardner, 2005
25. Avolio & Gardner, 2005, p. 322
26. Tutu, 2015
27. Kalungu-Banda, 2006, p. 10
28. Meyer, 2007, p. 4
29. Editorial, *Mail & Guardian*, 29th November 2013
30. Terry, 1993
31. Avolio et al., 2005
32. Frankl, 2004, p. 124
33. Chan, Hannah & Gardner, 2005, p. 12
34. Kernis, 2003
35. Seligman & Csikszentmihalyi, 2000
36. Avolio & Gardner, 2005
37. Avolio, Gardner, & Walumbwa, 2005
38. Chan, Hannah & Gardner, 2005
39. Meyer, 2007, p. 4
40. Spinelli, 2007
41. Chan, Hannah & Gardner, 2005, p. 14
42. Frankl, 2004
43. Covey, 1989
44. Douglas, Ferris, and Perrewe, 2005, p. 141
45. Gardner, Avolio, & Walumbwa, 2005
46. Klenke, 2005
47. Shamir & Eilam, 2005
48. Sparrowe, 2005
49. Archer, Stephen, 2012
50. Gallagher, Claire, 2015
51. Hassan & Ahmed, 2011, p. 750
52. Katzenbach & Smith, 1993a
53. Lencioni, 2002
54. Archer, 2009
55. Eigel & Kuhnert 2005
56. Eigel & Kuhner, 2005
57. Eigel & Kuhnert 2005
58. Eigel & Kuhnert, 2005
59. Dweck, 2008
60. Scheepers, 2012, p. 199
61. Scheepers, 2012
62. Chan, 2005
63. Cooper & Scandura, 2005
64. Chan, 2005
65. Sieler, 2005
66. Hawkins, 2014, p. 77
67. Stout Rostron
68. Kline, 1999
69. (www.neurosemantics.com)
70. (www.kenwilber.com)
71. (www.performanceconsultants.com)
72. Hawkins, 2014
73. Rock & Page, 2009
74. Rock & Cox, 2012
75. Dolny, 2009
76. Hawkins, 2014, p. 78
77. Hawkins, 2014, p. 80
78. Hedman, 2001, p. 69
79. O' Neill, 2000
80. Van Coller-Peter, 2015
81. Wulffers, 2014
82. Kretzschmar, 2010
83. Wulffers, 2014
84. Kolb & Kolb, 2005
85. Chan, Hannah & Gardner, 2005
86. Lencioni, 2002
87. Lencioni, 2002
88. Lencioni, 2012, p. 2
89. Hall & Bodenhamer, 2004

90. Maus, 2011, p. 336
91. Kolb & Kolb, 2005, p. 2
92. Abbot & Bennett, 2011
93. Cox, 2006
94. Frankl, 2004
95. Dilts, 2003
96. Barrett, 2010, p. 111
97. Demartini, 2013, p. 2
98. Avolio, Gardner, & Walumbwa, 2007
99. Lencioni, 2005, p. 61
100. Stamp, Gillian, 2016
101. Ting, 2006
102. Covey, 1989, p. 235
103. Clutterbuck & Megginson, 2005
104. Hall & Duval, 2002
105. Kline 1999, p. 102
106. Haffajee, 2015
107. Haffajee, 2015, p. 35
108. Cascio & Luthans, 2014
109. Pimstone & Suzman, 2005
110. Kalungu-Banda, 2006
111. Kalungu-Banda, 2006, p. 51
112. Mandela, 2010, pp. 325-326
113. Mandela, 2010, pp. 329-330
114. Kalungu-Banda, 2006, p. 78
115. Nelson Mandela Foundation, 2016
116. Mandela, 1994, pp. 19-20
117. Mandela, 1994, p. 354
118. Mandela, 2010, p. 209
119. Mandela, 2010, p. 243
120. Mandela, 1994, p. 354
121. Mandela 2010, p. 62
122. Kalungu-Banda, 2006
123. Mandela, 2010, pp. 209-210
124. Mandela, 2010, p. 145
125. Mandela, 2010, p. 145
126. Mandela, 2010, p. 270
127. Mandela, 2010, p. 357
128. Mandela, 2010, p. 7
129. Mandela, 2010, p. 8
130. Mandela, 2010
131. Mandela, 2010, p. 248
132. Mandela, 2010, p. 210
133. Mandela, 2010, p. 214
134. Kalungu-Banda, 2006
135. Kalungu-Banda, 2006, p. 97
136. Mandela 1994, pp. 20-21

137. Mandela, 2010, p. 344
138. Mandela, 2010, p. 357
139. Mandela, 2010, pp. 344-345
140. Mandela, 2010, p. 7
141. Mandela, 2010, p. 263
142. Mandela, 2010, p. 330
143. Mandela, 2010, p. 184
144. Mandela, 2010, p. 244
145. Kalungu-Banda, 2006, p. 105
146. Mandela, 2010, p. 182
147. Kalungu-Banda, 2006, p. 36
148. Kalungu-Banda, 2006, p. 36
149. Mandela, 2010, p. 128
150. Kalungu-Banda, 2006, p. 40
151. Kalungu-Banda, 2006, p. 106
152. Kalungu-Banda, 2006, p. 37
153. Kalungu-Banda, 2006
154. Mandela, 2010, p. 234
155. Mandela, 2010, p. 22
156. Mandela, 2010, p. 211
157. Mandela, 2010, p. 326
158. Mandela, 2010, pp. 211-212
159. Gibran, 1926
160. Kolb & Kolb, 2005

INDEX